Higher Education and the Student

As one of the pioneers and leading advocates of neoliberalism, Britain, and in particular England, has radically transformed its higher education system over the last decades. Universities have increasingly been required to act like businesses, and students are frequently referred to as customers nowadays. *Higher Education and the Student* investigates precisely this relation between the changing function of higher education and what we consider the term 'student' to stand for.

Based on a detailed analysis of government papers, reports, and speeches as well as publications by academics and students, the book explores how the student has been conceptualised within the debate on higher education from the birth of the British welfare state in the 1940s until today. It thus offers a novel assessment of the history of higher education and shows how closely the concept of the student and the way we comprehend higher education are intertwined. *Higher Education and the Student* opens up a new perspective that can critically inform public debate and future policy – in Britain and beyond.

The book should be of great interest to scholars, researchers, and postgraduate students in the fields of higher education; educational policy and politics; and the philosophy, sociology, and history of higher education.

Robert Troschitz currently works at Dresden University of Technology.

Routledge Research in Higher Education

For a full list of titles in this series, please visit www.routledge.com

Graduate Education at Historically Black Colleges and Universities (HBCUs)
A Student Perspective
Edited by Robert T. Palmer, Larry J. Walker, Ramon B. Goings, Charmaine Troy, Chaz T. Gipson, and Felecia Commodore

Transnational Education Crossing 'Asia' and 'the West
Adjusted Desire, Transformative Mediocrity, Neo-colonial Disguise
Phan Le-Ha

Experiencing Master's Supervision
Perspectives of International Students and their Supervisors
Nigel Harwood and Bojana Petrić

The Design of the University
German, American, and "World Class"
Heinz-Dieter Meyer

The Politics of Widening Participation and University Access for Young People
Making Educational Futures
Valerie Harwood, Anna Hickey-Moody, Samantha McMahon and Sarah O'Shea

Narrative, Identity, and Academic Community in Higher Education
Edited by Brian Attebery, John Gribas, Mark K. McBeth, Paul Sivitz, Kandi Turley-Ames

Higher Education and the Student
From Welfare State to Neoliberalism
Robert Troschitz

Higher Education and the Student

From welfare state to neoliberalism

Robert Troschitz

Routledge
Taylor & Francis Group
LONDON AND NEW YORK

First published 2017 by Routledge

2 Park Square, Milton Park, Abingdon, Oxfordshire OX14 4RN
52 Vanderbilt Avenue, New York, NY 10017

Routledge is an imprint of the Taylor & Francis Group, an informa business

First issued in paperback 2018

British Library Cataloguing-in-Publication Data
A catalogue record for this book is available from the British Library

Library of Congress Cataloging-in-Publication Data
A catalog record for this book has been requested

ISBN: 978-1-138-21350-0 (hbk)
ISBN: 978-0-367-13349-8 (pbk)

Typeset in Bembo
by Apex CoVantage, LLC

Contents

Acknowledgements

Over the course of writing this book, I have benefitted from the support of a great many people, and I would like to take this opportunity to express my gratitude to some of them. First and foremost, I want to thank Thomas Kühn. He not only sparked my interest in higher education as a research topic and provided unceasing encouragement and advice, but he also supervised my PhD thesis, which was accepted by Dresden University of Technology in 2015 and of which this book is a revised and updated version. I am very grateful to Stefan Horlacher for all his support and constructive feedback over the years as well as Jürgen Kamm, who also read and critically commented on the manuscript. Moreover, I owe a lot to my (former) colleagues, in particular Sophie Spieler, who took the time to go through the complete manuscript and whose remarks and suggestions greatly improved it, Celina Wald, who proofread most of the manuscript, and Mirjam Frotscher.

At Routledge, I want to thank all those who made this publication possible, in particular Heidi Lowther and Thomas Storr. Many thanks also go to Routledge's anonymous reviewers for their kind remarks and constructive criticism.

Last but not least, I am indebted to my family and friends, who were there for me over the years and who ensured that I never forgot that there is a wonderful world outside of academia. But above all, I thank Elisabeth for the countless and often endless discussions we had and for her unwavering support.

Abbreviations

BIS	Department for Business, Innovation and Skills (since 2009)
CAT	College of Advanced Technology
CVCP	Committee of Vice-Chancellors and Principals
DES	Department of Education and Science (1964–1992)
DfE	Department for Education (1992–1995)
DfEE	Department for Education and Employment (1995–2001)
DfES	Department for Education and Skills (2001–2007)
EMA	Education Maintenance Allowance
HEFC	Higher Education Funding Council
HEFCE	Higher Education Funding Council for England
KIS	Key Information Set
LEA	Local Education Authority
NAB	National Advisory Board for Local Authority Higher Education
NCAFC	National Campaign Against Fees and Cuts
NCIHE	National Committee of Inquiry into Higher Education (Dearing Committee)
NSS	National Student Survey
NUS	National Union of Students
OFFA	Office for Fair Access
PCFC	Polytechnics and Colleges Funding Council
RAE	Research Assessment Exercise
REF	Research Excellence Framework
RSA	Radical Student Alliance
RSSF	Revolutionary Socialist Students' Federation
TEF	Teaching Excellence Framework
UCU	University and College Union
UFC	Universities Funding Council
UGC	University Grants Committee
WEA	Workers' Educational Association

Chapter 1

Introduction

Students are at the centre of higher education. Without students, lecture halls and seminar rooms would be empty, most academics would have no job, and higher education would have lost its *raison d'être*. But apart from their sheer physical presence, students are also central to higher education in a different sense. For whenever the question is raised what higher education is and what it is good for, this inevitably entails the question of what a student is. In other words, how we comprehend higher education is inextricably linked to the question of what we consider a student to be.

When we speak of students, we do not necessarily have specific human beings in mind, but we refer to a social category to which we attach various meanings. These meanings, however, are everything but stable. Thus, in order to grasp the history and the present of higher education, it is vital to investigate how the concept of the student – what the term 'student' stands for – has shifted over time.

Of course, the word 'student' – apart from its extension into secondary education – is still used to refer to those enrolled in higher education, but otherwise its meaning has altered rather radically. Whereas for centuries being a student had meant to belong to the privileged few, British higher education has become a mass system providing for nearly half of the age group.[1] This massive expansion has been accompanied by a diversification of the student body. What was once the reserve of young, white, male, British, middle and upper-class students has been opened significantly in terms of class, gender, ethnicity, age, and nationality.[2] Besides this transformation of the student body, the position of the student in terms of power has shifted as well. For centuries, students had been under the authority of the university or college with strict rules governing their conduct and social life. In the 1960s, this situation was heavily attacked as students increasingly demanded to be treated as adults and to be given a say in the government of their university or college. Over the last decades, the position of the student has shifted once again. Not only has there been a 'decline of donnish dominion' (Halsey 1992), but power has increasingly moved towards the students – at least this is what the White Paper *Higher Education: Students at the Heart of the System* (2011) claims. Students are now expected to act as customers who are entitled to a high quality student experience and whose choices are not only supposed to drive up quality but also to determine whether a university or department will survive or not. Clearly, the whole concept of the student – who is considered eligible for higher education, the student's role within the system of higher education, as well as the kind of graduates higher education is supposed to produce – has changed fundamentally.

This book does, however, not merely explore how the concept of the student has altered over time. The focus is rather on how these changes are linked to the shifting function and position of higher education in society. What this function of higher education might be is by no means clear. Indeed, the history of higher education has been a continuous fight over questions such as whether universities and colleges should disseminate existing wisdom or search for new knowledge, whether they ought to produce and spread knowledge for its own sake or be a means of social change or act as handmaidens to business and industry, whether they form separate communities with their own values and traditions or function as service providers that fulfil the wants of their customers. It is this debate over the 'idea of higher education' that this book investigates from the birth of the British welfare state to the rise of neoliberalism and the end of publicly financed higher education.

The overall aim of this investigation is twofold. First, by analysing how the student has been conceptualised, written about, and positioned within the struggle over 'the idea of higher education', this book offers a new perspective on the history of British higher education; and second, by doing so, it seeks to show how vital it is to comprehend higher education as a continuous struggle over meanings, in which the question what the term 'student' actually stands for is of central importance.

Britain in a global perspective

Over the last couple of years, students around the world have repeatedly made it into the news as they took to the streets to express their anger. In the US, the number of graduates who are unable to repay their loans has so dramatically risen that students have protested throughout the country and thus turned the student debt crisis into a major political issue. In 2010, thousands of British students stood up against education cuts and rising tuition fees. The increase of tuition of fees also caused mass protests in Québec, where students organised demonstrations and strikes that involved hundreds of thousands of people. Students in Austria and Germany took to the streets in order to prevent the introduction of student fees and to bring a halt to the further economisation and 'schoolification' of higher education. In Chile, students have repeatedly staged mass protests calling for a repeal of neoliberal education reforms of privatisation. In South Africa, student action has not only resulted in the pulling down of the Rhodes statue but in more widespread protests attacking white supremacy. And in Hong Kong, students have been at the forefront of the

Umbrella Movement of 2014 and the fight for democratic reforms. Of course, the contexts of all these protests differ, and it would thus be unwise to draw any easy parallels between the situations in say Chile, South Africa, and Austria. Nevertheless, what is sure is that around the world students have not only been involved in political struggles, but education has been recognised as an issue of such importance that it ignited mass protests. Seen from such a global perspective, a question that necessarily arises is why British higher education is worth special attention and hence a worthwhile object of study.

With universities such as Cambridge, Oxford, or the London School of Economics, Britain has some of the most internationally acclaimed institutions of higher education. Though this is even more true for the US, whose universities dominate world rankings, Britain holds an unchallenged second place within these rankings. The *Times Higher Education* World University Ranking for 2015/16, for instance, lists 17 US institutions amongst the world's best 25, followed by the UK with six institutions of higher education in the top 25 (THE 2016: n.p.). In addition to the high position that some universities occupy within such rankings, British higher education in general is also of major international relevance in terms of student mobility. For students from all over the world, the UK has proven to be one of the most attractive destinations, second, again, only to the US. With more than 400,000 foreign students enrolled, one-tenth of all internationally mobile students chose to study in the UK in 2014 (UIS 2016: n.p.). Hence, from a global perspective, Britain, and even more so the US, are without doubt of special importance.

But what makes British higher education particularly interesting is that, in contrast to the US system, it experienced a rather radical transformation within only a short period of time. While the US already embarked on the expansion of higher education in the nineteenth century, higher education was still the privilege of a minority in mid-twentieth century Britain.[3] And in contrast to the US, which has had a significant private higher education sector for centuries and where student fees have been an important part of university income for a long time (Marcucci 2013: 18), the UK has only more recently switched from a system in which the state took over both tuition and living costs for students to a market system in which students pay fees of up to £9,000 per year. It is this radical transformation and the struggles that evolved around it that make the study of Britain particularly worthwhile as countries around the globe not only expand their higher education systems but also embark on a neoliberal course and introduce market mechanisms.

Britain, England, the UK

So far the talk has been of 'British' higher education, though this is in fact rather problematic. The higher education systems of England, Wales, Scotland, and Northern Ireland are all but the same. Each of the four nations has its own distinct funding mechanism, and in particular policies regarding student finance have differed tremendously in recent years. Thus, the maximum fees that universities can charge vary and so do loan and grant schemes. Not only are students charged dissimilar fees depending on where in the UK they study, but students on the same course in the same university might pay different fees and be eligible for different grants and loans depending on where they come from.[4] Apart from these more recent distinctions that result from devolution, the various parts of the UK and in particular Scotland also have rather different traditions of higher education.

While recent government papers clearly reflect these differences in particular with regard to funding, differentiations between the various traditions have otherwise been wanting in the debate on higher education. Though major documents like the Robbins Report (1963) and the Dearing Report (1997) discussed the provision of higher education for each part of Britain individually, the aims and principles they formulated referred to Britain as a whole. Writers from within academia such as Walter Moberly, Eric Ashby, F.R. Leavis, Kenneth Minogue, or Ronald Barnett always focused on Britain in general or even abandoned the national focus and put forth arguments that concerned the role of the university in Western societies in general.

As this book is concerned not with the actual experience of students or systems of higher education but with the debate on higher education, it follows, as far as terminology is concerned, the material it analyses. Hence, reference is primarily to Britain until the late 1990s, and, as far as the policy discourse is concerned, from then onwards the focus is chiefly on England, where the marketisation of higher education has been strongest and which has therefore been at the centre of the debate.

Research into higher education and the student

Research into higher education is by no means a small or underdeveloped field. There are numerous journals on higher education as well as conferences, and many of the major publishers have books on their lists that are specifically concerned with higher education. But higher education is not only a field that is widely written about, it also attracts a wide range of disciplines such as economics, education, history, sociology, philosophy, psychology, or political sciences – each of which brings its own questions and approaches to the field.[5]

Apart from studies that are concerned with pedagogy and hence investigate learning and teaching processes, the student has been particularly central for studies into what is commonly referred to as 'the student experience'. This comprises research into issues such as "accessing higher education, the on-course experience, success and non-completion, the postgraduate experience, the experience of different student groups, [and] the transition from higher education to work" (Tight 2012: 83). In these studies, which often built on statistical data or interviews, the focus is primarily on the experience of 'real' people and less on the concept of the student or how the function of higher education and its position in society have changed over time.

The shifting function of higher education in society, however, has been of concern in historical studies such as Robert D. Anderson's *British Universities: Past and Present* (2006), which charts the history of the British universities since the foundation of Oxford, or studies that focus explicitly on the post-war era such as Malcolm Tight's *The Development of Higher Education in the United Kingdom since 1945* (2009). A rather different approach has been taken by Harold Silver, whose *Higher Education and Opinion Making in Twentieth-Century England* (2003) is less concerned with the actual development of the system of higher education but concentrates on major voices in the debate on higher education. Apart from these rather wide-ranging accounts of the history of British higher education, numerous studies have focused on individual universities or particular types of institutions such as the polytechnics or the Redbricks.[6] While many of these studies feature some accounts of student life, the student is hardly ever the central object of analysis. But of course, there are also exceptions such as Harold and Pamela Silver's *Students: Changing Roles, Changing Lives* (1997), which explores how students' life and their role in the institutions of higher education changed from the 1960s to the 1990s, or Carol Dyhouse's *Students: A Gendered History* (2006). Though these studies also discuss how the concept of the student has shifted over time, they are primarily interested in actual student life and less on how the student has been conceptualised and positioned in the debate on higher education.

A historical perspective has also featured in numerous studies of higher education policy and governance. Indeed, there are so many that these cannot be listed here.[7] However, apart from the occasional chapter, these studies have hardly made the student their prime concern. It is only in response to marketisation that the concept of the student has become a topic.[8] But though there are dozens of critical studies on the notion of the student as customer, these studies often lack the broader historical dimension – a dimension that is, however vital, not just for a better understanding of the past but also to gain a critical perspective on the present (McCulloch and Richardson 2000: 5). Precisely for this reason, this book takes a wider historical perspective and examines how the student has been conceptualised within the debate on higher education from the birth of the British welfare state in the 1940s until today.

Analysing the idea of higher education and the student

This book is neither a study of student life or students' actual experience of higher education nor is its aim to provide a chronological account of the history of British higher education. Instead, it investigates how the idea of higher education and the concept of the student have shifted over time with a particular focus on questions such as who is considered eligible for higher education, the characteristics of the ideal student, the understanding of higher education that students ought to have, and the position of the student within higher education in terms of power.

Such an analysis of the changing concept of the student could be based on various types of material, ranging from interviews, novels and films, newspapers and blogs, architecture, webpages and prospectuses, to government papers and reports. All these materials offer a different perspective on higher education and the student, and their analysis would without doubt produce valuable insights. As the focus of this book is the debate about 'the idea of higher education', it draws primarily on texts that explicitly put forth arguments concerning the purpose, structure, and function of higher education in society and its future development. This includes a wide range of material such as White Papers and government reports; articles and books written by academics like Walter Moberly's *The Crisis in the University* (1949), the Black Papers (1969–77), or the Alternative White Paper *In Defence of Public Higher Education* (2011); reports and statements from bodies such as the University Grants Committee or the Committee of Vice-Chancellors and Principals; as well as publications of the National Union of Students and other student organisations or even individual students whenever these entered the debate, for instance in the context of the student protests of the late 1960s or 2010.

Though these texts only provide limited access to the 'reality' of higher education in the sense that they reveal what higher education and actual student life were like at a specific time, what they do show is how thinking about higher education has altered, which issues were considered important or were questioned at a certain time, and how the meaning of terms such as 'higher education' and 'student' has shifted.

Chapter overview

Before the debate on higher education is analysed, Chapter 2 establishes the theoretical framework for the analysis. After examining the various perspectives that institutional theory offers for the study of higher education, this chapter develops a discourse theoretical framework. It is argued that higher education can best be understood as a relatively stable discursive system and that the history of higher education is primarily a struggle for discursive hegemony and thus a fight over the meaning of terms like 'higher education' and 'student'. The actual analysis of the debate on higher education is then divided into four parts.

Part I focuses on the 1940s and 1950s. In order to set the debates of this time in context, Chapter 3 provides a short overview of the development of British higher education from the foundation of Oxford until the early decades of the twentieth century. Thereafter, Chapter 4 takes issue with the economic view of higher education as advanced in particular by the governments of the post-war period. As the debate on higher education was still dominated by the universities in the 1940s and 1950s, Chapter 5 investigates the most important voices from within academia and shows that, despite much disagreement, there were a number of issues that were shared by writers such as Bruce Truscot and Walter Moberly as well as the UGC. These included not only their opposition to a purely utilitarian approach to education but also how they saw the student. Finally, Chapter 6 discusses the student voice. Though students were still hardly recognised within the debate on higher education at that time, it is not the case that they had nothing to say. After a brief outline of the rise of student activism, this chapter therefore turns in more detail to the Charter of Student Rights and Responsibilities of 1940 as well as Brian Simon's *A Student View of the Universities* (1943).

Part II comprises the more turbulent 1960s and early 1970s. Chapter 7 concentrates on the two central government papers of the early 1960s: the Anderson Report (1960), which recommended the introduction of maintenance grants, and the Robbins Report (1963), which argued for a further expansion of higher education. These two reports not only marked the increasing inclusion of higher education into the welfare state, but they also reconfigured the position of the student within the system of higher education. As the post-war expansion of higher education and the Robbins Report's recommendation to further increase the number of students were not applauded by everyone, Chapter 8 deals with voices that were critical of expansion and analyses in particular the debate about the so-called 'new students', that is students from a socio-cultural background with no tradition of higher education. As the analysis shows, it is precisely through this figure of the 'new student' that one can see how fundamental the concept of the student actually is for the legitimacy of higher education and its power structures. The 1960s were, however, not only marked by expansion but also by a widening of the institutional landscape. Therefore, Chapter 9 focuses on the newly founded campus universities of the early 1960s, the Open University, as well as the polytechnics and explores to what extent these foundations stood for new ideas of higher education as well as for a new concept of the student. Last but not least, Chapter 10 examines the student protests of the late 1960s. Even though the British protests never reached the intensity of the protests in Paris, Berlin, Prague, or Berkley, they are nevertheless important as they questioned higher education in its established form, put forth different ideals of education, and attacked the traditional role of the student.

Part III concentrates on the policy discourse since the 1980s and the reconfiguration of higher education in terms of the market. Chapter 11 analyses the rise of New Public Management under the governments of Margaret Thatcher and John Major. Chapter 12 covers the Dearing Report (1997) – the second major investigation into British higher education after the Robbins Report of 1963 – and investigates how the student was positioned in the report's vision of a learning society as well as its arguments for the introduction of student fees. New Labour's Third Way and its view concerning the aims of higher education, widening participation, as well as the introduction of variable fees are at the centre of Chapter 13. Thereafter, Chapter 14 turns towards the most recent policy developments, in particular the rise of student fees in 2010 and the proposals for the Teaching Excellence Framework in 2015. Chapter 15 brings the findings of the preceding four chapters together and argues that at the heart of the neoliberal reforms that started with Thatcher and have been driven further ever since has been a new governmentality which explicitly tries to influence the students' self-understanding.

Part IV examines in detail various criticisms of marketisation as well as attempts to formulate new ideas of higher education that go beyond the market. Chapter 16 reviews a selection of writings from within academia that have tried to defend higher education against the growing dominance of the market discourse and analyses how the concept of the student has changed within such writings over time. Chapter 17 concentrates on the numerous criticisms that have been levelled against the notion of the student as customer and also critically surveys several other metaphors that have been proposed as an alternative to the notion of the customer. Apart from these primarily defensive voices, a number of academics such as Ronald Barnett, Nicholas Maxwell, or Jon Nixon have also formulated new visions of higher education. These are discussed in Chapter 18, which also critically analyses the notion of higher education as a 'public good' – a notion that has become rather widespread in recent debates. The ongoing marketisation of higher education was, however, not only attacked by academics but also by students. Thus, Chapter 19 examines the student protests of 2010 and investigates to what extent these actually challenged marketisation and the concept of the student as customer.

The concluding Chapter 20 pulls together the central findings of the study. But instead of merely summarising the preceding chapters, it identifies common themes, lines of argument, and dominant ideas that have shaped the debate on higher education. By doing so, it not only shows how the concept of the student has shifted in the struggle over higher education but also how central the question of what the term 'student' stands for is to the way higher education is understood.

Notes

1 In 1938, 2 percent of the 19-year-olds were in full-time education (Committee on Higher Education 1963: §42). Today, the initial participation rate on full-time courses of those aged between 17 and 30 is above 40 percent (BIS 2015b: 5).

2 Although the percentage of working-class students has remained low, their absolute number has still increased massively, and with regard to gender, higher education is no longer a male domain as women have by now outnumbered men (BIS 2015c: 4; Higher Education Statistics Agency 2015: n.p.). The percentage of non-UK students has doubled over the last 50 years. Whereas in the early 1960s about one-tenth of all full-time higher education students were overseas students, international students account for about one-fifth of today's student population (Committee on Higher Education 1963: §47; UKCISA 2016: n.p.)

3 In 1928, already 15 percent of those aged between 18 and 21 were enrolled in higher education in the US (Perkin 2006: 184). In Britain, the participation rate for full-time

higher education was still 8.5 percent in 1962 with another 5.5 percent in part-time higher education (Committee on Higher Education 1963: Table 5).

4 Whereas Scottish students, for instance, do not pay fees as long as they study at a Scottish university, English students at the same university have to pay fees of up to £9,000. A student from Wales, no matter where he or she studies in the UK, only has to pay fees up to £3,575 with the Welsh government covering the rest (UCAS 2016: n.p.).

5 *The Encyclopedia of Higher Education* lists the following disciplines as undertaking research into higher education: anthropology, comparative education, economics, higher education studies, history, law, linguistics and rhetoric, literature, macrosociology, microsociology, organisation theory, philosophy, policy analysis, political economy, public administration, science studies, social psychology, and women's studies (Clark and Neave 1992: xv). John Brennan and Ulrich Teichler have produced a narrower list of disciplines that comprises education, psychology, sociology, political sciences, economics and business studies, law and history (2008: 261).

6 See, for instance, John Pratt's *The Polytechnic Experiment: 1965–1992* (1997) or William Whyte's *Redbrick: A Social and Architectural History of Britain's Civic Universities* (2015).

7 See, for instance, for book-length studies: Salter and Tapper (1994), Tapper (2007), Palfreyman and Tapper (2014), Shattock (1994, 2012), Lawton (2005), Taylor and Steele (2011), Kogan and Hanney (2000), or Deem, Hillyard, and Reed (2007).

8 Whereas most of these take a biased view and criticise marketisation as a 'distortion' of education (these are discussed in detail in Chapter 17), there is also a theoretically advanced literature on neoliberalism and education that explores the changing 'idea of higher education' in relation to the concept of the student in more detail. See, for instance, Dudley (1999), Bartlett (2003), Simons and Masschelein (2006), Peters (2010, 2011), and Coffield (1999).

Chapter 2

Theorising higher education

To define what a university or a college is and what it is good for is anything but straightforward. Indeed, this question has troubled many writers and caused considerable debate. At least since the nineteenth century, the purpose, structure, nature, and aim of higher education have been contested. But before this debate will be analysed in detail for the period since the 1940s, it is worth asking, from a theoretical perspective, what kind of social phenomenon higher education is.

Higher education as institution

Niklas Luhmann once described the university as an "organised institution" (1992: 90).[1] This formulation can serve as a good starting point to think about higher education as it raises the question of what it means to speak of the university, or higher education in general, as an 'institution'. While the common phrase 'institutions of higher education' or 'higher education institutions' is mostly used in a countable sense and refers to concrete colleges and universities, to describe higher education as an institution is something rather different.

Institutions are relatively enduring patterns that organise social life and regulate human conduct.[2] As Richard Jenkins states, an institution is "a pattern of behaviour in any particular setting that has become established over time as 'the way things are done'" and that "has intersubjective relevance and meaning in the situation concerned: people know about it and recognise it, if only in the normative specification of 'how things are done'" (2008: 157). To speak of higher education as an institution thus implies that irrespective of the specific university or college, there are certain behavioural patterns, meanings, and structures that are similar to all of them. As John W. Meyer et al. point out, "[t]he meaning of categories such as student, professor, university, or graduate, or of topics such as physics or literature, may be locally shaped in minor ways, but at the same time have very substantial historical and global standing" (2007: 187). While concrete universities and colleges may differ considerably, they share meanings, values, norms, and practices that are characteristic of higher education in general and not specific to a particular university or college.

But Luhmann did not only refer to the university as an institution. The university, for him, was a particular kind of institution. It had the features of an 'organisation'. In contrast to an institution, the term 'organisation' describes a more particular type of social structure that has members, explicit objectives, criteria for recruiting members, a division of labour or functional differentiation between members, and recognised patterns of decision making (Jenkins 2008: 167). To speak of universities and colleges as organisations thus highlights that these have particular functions such as producing graduates, that they are characterised by functional differentiations between, for instance, students, academics, and other staff, that they control membership since not everybody can become a student or lecturer, and that they have recognised structures of government, in which each member occupies a specific position.

A defining feature of institutions is their durability and resilience (Scott 2013: 57). Though they also undergo change, institutions are relatively stable and organise social practices over generations. However, this endurance is not simply given but needs to be achieved. As Peter L. Berger and Thomas Luckmann assert, institutions have to be "ongoingly 'brought to life' in actual human conduct" or they will cease to exist (1991: 93). Therefore, they must not be questioned but need to be accepted as legitimate – as being "in accord with the norms, values, beliefs, practices, and procedures accepted by a group" (Zelditch 2001: 33).[3] In an attempt to synthesise various definitions and approaches to the problem of legitimacy, W.R. Scott has distinguished between three forms of legitimacy that correspond to his three-'pillar' model of institutions. According to Scott, the "central building blocks" of institutions comprise regulative elements (explicit rules that regulate behaviour), normative elements (norms and values), and cultural-cognitive elements (shared conceptions of the social world) (2013: 57, 60).[4] Hence, in order to be legitimate, institutions and organisations have to operate within a legally sanctioned regulatory framework, they need a moral basis, and, on the broadest level, they are legitimised by common frames of reference and taken-for-granted understandings (2013: 74). In the case of higher education, universities and colleges, in order to persist, thus have to comply with rules and regulations concerning, for instance, how they spend their funds and treat students. Beyond that, they have to fulfil certain objectives in society and conform to specific values. These could be manifold and include providing training for a job or being the critical conscience of society. On the cultural-cognitive level, universities and colleges are legitimised through the very existence of concepts such as 'higher education' or 'student'.

How central that cultural-cognitive level is for the creation and endurance of institutions has also been emphasised by John Searle. According to Searle, institutions are made up of what he calls 'constitutive rules'. In contrast to rules that regulate existing behaviour, these rules "not only regulate but constitute the very behaviour they regulate" (2005: 9). To take the example of higher education again, before a university or college can have regulations that determine what students have to do in exams or what kind of requirements they have to fulfil in order to get credits, it requires a rule that defines who counts as a student and what a course or an exam actually are. Of course, these rules do not necessarily have to be codified, but there needs to be a collective agreement on what a student, a course, an exam are. Following this fundamental distinction between regulative and constitutive rules, Searle defines institutions as "any system of constitutive rules of the form X counts as Y in C" (2005: 10). In other words, a certain object or person (X) is assigned a collectively recognised status (Y) within a particular context (C). This status carries specific rights and duties, what Searle calls 'deontic powers' (2005: 11). Accordingly, the institution of higher education can be understood as a system of such constitutive rules that define, amongst others, in which context (C) a certain person (X) is considered a student or professor (Y) and the rights and responsibilities this status involves. Though Searle does not use the term, what he actually shows is that at the heart of institutions are processes of 'signification', that is the collective production of meanings.

In order to investigate the role of signification for processes of institutionalisation and institutional change, numerous scholars such as Phillips (2003), Panizza and Miorelli (2013), Phillips, Lawrence, and Hardy (2004), or Schmidt (2008)have turned to the concept of 'discourse'. But though recent years have seen a rising number of publications that claim to study institutions from a discourse analytical perspective, the relation between discourse and institutions is all but straightforward. Not only is the term discourse used in many different ways, but it is also often unclear whether discourse is one type of social practice next to institutions or whether institutions themselves are discursive structures.

Higher education as discourse

The word 'discourse' is commonly used within and without academia, and yet its meaning often stays opaque and is not further reflected. This is quite problematic as the term 'discourse' can refer to quite a number of different things such as conversation and talk, the formal treatment of a subject, an expanded piece of reasoning and argument, or a unit of text (Chafe 2003; Frow 2005: 91; Mills 2004: 2). In the social sciences, the term 'discourse' is often used in a way that broadly follows Michel Foucault's use of the term. This does, however, not mean that there exists a neat definition of 'discourse', as Foucault himself used the term in various and shifting ways. In *The Archaeology of Knowledge* (1969), Foucault suggests that discourses should not be understood

> as groups of signs (signifying elements referring to contents or representations) but as practices that systematically form the objects of which they speak. Of course, discourses are composed of signs; but what they do is more than use these signs to designate things.
>
> (2002: 54)[5]

As Foucault claims here, language and signs in general do not simply denote objects, but they constitute these. Discourse does thus not refer to language or text but rather to areas of knowledge and knowledge production (McHoul and Grace 1993: 31). Following Foucault, Stuart Hall defines discourse as "a group of statements which provides a language for talking about – i.e. a way of representing – a particular kind of knowledge about a topic" (1996: 201), and by providing such a language, discourse does not simply reflect reality but it "structures the way that we perceive reality" (Mills 2003: 55). By organising what can be said, written, or thought about a social object at a certain time, discourse shapes reality and thus exercises power. At the same time, however, discourse is itself the object of power. As Foucault points out, "in every society the production of discourse is at once controlled, selected, organised and redistributed according to a certain number of procedures" (1971: 8). Precisely for this link between knowledge and power, Foucault's notion of discourse has proven so powerful within the social sciences even though it has stayed highly ambiguous and has been used rather differently by various researchers (Mills 2003: 54).

One particularly fruitful strand of research that has been taken up in various disciplines over the last decades is Critical Discourse Analysis, in particular as developed by Norman Fairclough. Building upon Critical Linguistics and works such as Gunther R. Kress and Bob Hodge's *Language as Ideology* (1979) or the collected volume *Language and Control* (Fowler, et al. 1979), Critical Discourse Analysis investigates how texts work with regard to power and ideologies. According to Norman Fairclough and Ruth Wodak, Critical Discourse Analysis

> sees discourse – language in use in speech and writing – as a form of 'social practice'. Describing discourse as social practice implies a dialectical relationship between a particular discursive event and situation(s), institution(s) and social structure(s) which frame it: the discursive event is shaped by them, but it also shapes them. That is, discourse is socially constitutive as well as socially conditioned – it constitutes situations, objects of knowledge, and the social identities of and relationships between people and groups of people.
>
> (1997: 258)

Though Critical Discourse Analysts take up Foucault's concern with power and his claim that discourse is constitutive of reality, their use of the term 'discourse' differs from Foucault in that they primarily focus on the actual use of language (Jørgensen and Phillips 2002: 92). Discourse for them is one 'social practice' that shapes and is shaped by other social structures and institutions. Such a distinction between the discursive and non-discursive has, however, also been evident in Foucault, who differentiates between discursive formations and non-discursive domains such as "institutions, political events, economic practices and processes" (2002: 179–180). While Foucault thus does not postulate that 'everything is discourse', the differentiation between the discursive and the non-discursive has been questioned by writers like Jacques Derrida or Ernesto Laclau and Chantal Mouffe, whose discourse theory will be outlined in more detail below.

In *Hegemony and Socialist Strategy* (1985), Laclau and Mouffe develop a post-structuralist and post-Marxist discourse theory that abandons any distinction between the discursive and the non-discursive. This does not mean that Laclau and Mouffe deny that there is a 'world out there' – a claim that is often brought forward against post-structuralists and social constructionists.[6] As Laclau and Mouffe make clear,

> [t]he fact that every object is constituted as an object of discourse has nothing to do with whether there is a world external to thought, or with the realism/idealism opposition. An earthquake or the falling of a brick is an event that certainly exists, in the sense that it occurs here and now, independently of my will. But whether their specificity as objects is constructed in terms of natural phenomena or expressions of the wrath of God, depends upon the structuring of a discursive field. What is denied is not that such objects exist externally to thought, but the rather different assertion that they could constitute themselves as objects outside of any discursive condition of emergence.
>
> (2001: 108)

Hence, while there is certainly 'a world out there' and objects exist independently of discourse, these do not have any meaning in themselves but are only meaningful within particular discursive frameworks (Howarth and Griggs 2012: 307).[7] Thus, the same object may have rather different meanings depending on the symbolic framework in which it appears. To use an example provided by Laclau and Mouffe themselves, a football exists as a physical object independently of any particular social or cultural system, but this object functions only as a football if it is placed in relation to other objects such as goal post, for example (1987: 82). This set of relations through which the objects are given their meaning is what Laclau and Mouffe refer to as discourse. Seen from that perspective, higher education is likewise a set of relations between signifiers such as 'subject', 'exam', 'lecturer', 'student', or 'essay', and it is only through their relation to each other that they become meaningful.

Laclau and Mouffe's discourse theory is, however, not only valuable because it dissolves the distinction between discourse and other social structures such as institutions but rather for how it conceptualises social change. According to Laclau and Mouffe, meaning is never ultimately stable but always contingent and open for change.[8] To take higher education as an example again, the signifier 'student' has denoted rather different things at different times and in different contexts. While in the past being a student meant to belong to the elect few, this is no longer the case today. Moreover, in the context of 1968, the term 'student' may have been associated with political protests, whereas today students are often compared to consumers. But though meaning is never ultimately fixed, it is not entirely free-floating either. For communication to be possible, meanings need to be fixed to a certain extent. Hence, in order to speak intelligibly about 'students', 'lectures', or 'universities', it is necessary that there is at least partial agreement about what these terms mean. Discourse, in the sense of Laclau and Mouffe, is precisely that partial fixation of meaning within a particular domain – a process that they refer to as "articulation" (2001: 112).[9]

Discourses, according to Laclau and Mouffe, are organised around what they call, in analogy to Jacques Lacan's points de capiton, "nodal points" (2001: 112). A nodal point can be understood as a privileged sign around which other signs are ordered and which limits and fixes the meanings of these signs. As examples of such nodal points, one may think of 'the body' in medical discourse (Jørgensen and Phillips 2002: 26), 'God' in the discourse of Christianity, 'democracy' or 'the people' in political discourse, or 'knowledge' in the discourse of higher education. Nodal points can be imagined as functioning similar to the knots in a net that keep it from disintegrating. But although this is a helpful analogy, it easily disguises that not all nodal points are of similar significance – a point that is not considered in Laclau and Mouffe. Nodal points can be of different power and shift in their relation to each other. As an example, one may think of a political movement for which both 'the nation' and 'God' function as nodal points but where 'the nation' is seen as created by 'God'. Likewise, the nodal points that organise higher education such as 'knowledge', 'truth', or 'prosperity' may not be of equal power as institutions of higher education may be asked to produce knowledge that is of economic use and thus fosters prosperity.

Apart from the construction of nodal points, another central operation for the constitution of discourses is what Laclau and Mouffe call the logics of equivalence and difference (2001: 127–9). The logic of equivalence eliminates differences and creates equivalential identities. Hence, within the discourse of higher education, for example, the signifier 'student' constructs an equivalence between rather different people and fuses their otherwise particular identities. In other words, instead of highlighting that each and every one is different, people that identify as students emphasise what they have in common. Similarly, but with different effects, individuals may identify as 'working class' or as 'women', in which case equivalences are constructed along class or gender lines. Such a relation of equivalence, however, only exists as a negative identity as the logic of equivalence depends on a relation of difference in form of a constitutive outside.[10] In other words, the signifier 'student' can only establish an equivalence between diverse human beings if it is opposed to an outside in the form of the 'non-student', just as the common identity 'women' needs 'men' as its outside. In contrast to the logic of equivalence, the logic of difference breaks up existing chains of equivalence, and instead of emphasising what various people or objects have in common, differences between them come to the fore. In the case of higher education, students may, for instance, not so much identify with their fellow students but with other people of the same class background, locality, gender, or political outlook. In this situation, the equivalence between students as those who are enrolled on a course in higher education is destructed and differences between students are highlighted. Hence, the two logics function in an opposite way, but they are inherently interlinked.

As meaning is never ultimately fixed but stays necessarily contingent, social structures like higher education can never fully stabilise themselves but need to be constantly recreated. The various signs that constitute higher education like 'student' or 'lecture' and the relations between them need to be reaffirmed through articulatory practices. However, as discourses fail to fully constitute themselves and to ultimately halt the flow of meaning, social structures like higher education become the site of conflict as different discourses struggle for hegemony and try to dominate and unify a particular social field through the creation of alternative nodal points and new relations of equivalence.

Power, agency, and the subject

A particularly important contribution of post-structuralist discourse theory has been its conception of power and its reframing of the structure-agency divide. In order to understand how the post-structuralist account of power and agency differs from other more traditional ones, it is worth going back to one of the classic works on power: Steven Lukes's *Power: A Radical View* (1974). In this book, Lukes establishes what has come to be known as the 'three dimensions of power'. The first dimension, he argues, refers to power as it is exercised when one person makes another person do something this person would otherwise not do (Lukes 1995: 11–12). This behaviourist account of power, as it had for instance been proposed by theorists like Robert Dahl, has been criticised by scholars like Peter Bachrach and Morton Baratz, who argue that a second dimension of power consists in the mobilisation of bias and the setting of agendas (Lukes 1995: 21–3). To these two dimensions of power, Lukes adds a third 'radical' dimension because, as he claims, power can also be present in situations in which there seems to be no actual conflict (1995: 24–5). According to Lukes, the differences between these three dimensions can be summarised as follows:

> Extremely crudely, one might say that the liberal takes men as they are and applies want regarding principles to them, relating their interests to what they actually want or prefer, to their policy preference as manifested by their political participation. The reformist, seeing and deploring that not all men's wants are given equal weight by the political system, also relates their interests to what they want or prefer, but allows that this may be revealed in more indirect and sub-political ways – in the form of deflected, submerged or concealed wants and preferences. The radical, however, maintains that

> men's wants may themselves be a product of a system which works against their interests, and in such cases, relates the latter to what they would want and prefer, were they able to make the choice.
>
> (Lukes 1995: 34)

While Lukes thus extends power to the power that a system might exercise and that might not be directly observable, he assumes that this system "works against [people's] interests". It produces a kind of 'false consciousness' (Clegg 2009: 240; Clegg, Courpasson, and Phillips 2006: 210–4). In other words, Lukes relies on an autonomous human being that is eventually able to identify its 'real interests'. Precisely this concept of the autonomous human being has, however, been questioned by thinkers like Louis Althusser or Laclau and Mouffe.

In his classic essay "Ideology and Ideological State Apparatuses" (1971), Althusser abandons the notion of the autonomous individual that can act independently of social structures. Instead, individuals, he claims, are always subjects to ideology. As he argues, ideology constitutes individual persons as subjects as it provides them with social identities:

> ideology 'acts' or 'functions' in such a way that it 'recruits' subjects among the individuals (it recruits them all), or 'transforms' the individuals into subjects (it transforms them all) by that very precise operation which I have called interpellation or hailing, and which can be imagined along the lines of the most commonplace everyday police (or other) hailing: 'Hey, you there!' Assuming that the theoretical scene I have imagined takes place in the street, the hailed individual will turn round. By this mere one-hundred-and-eighty-degree physical conversion, he becomes a subject. Why? Because he has recognized that the hail was 'really' addressed to him, and that 'it was really him who was hailed' (and not someone else).
>
> (1971: 174)

Ideologies thus interpellate concrete individuals, who then recognise themselves and identify with the 'subject positions' that these ideologies provide. Hence, when someone conceives of herself, for example, as 'British', 'women', or 'student', she becomes the subject of specific ideologies. Though Althusser's example of the policeman creates the impression that the individual was actually free to decide whether or not to recognise the hailing and that the individual was autonomous before it recognised itself in ideology, this is exactly what Althusser denies. According to Althusser, "individuals are always-already subjects" (1971: 176). There is no state prior to interpellation. Even before one is born, one is already a subject, for instance of gender ideologies. But this also means that there is no outside to ideology and no possibility for the subject to escape the work of ideology. Ideology functions all too well, and resistance becomes impossible. Indeed, Althusser's only option is to hope for "a scientific (i.e. subject-less) discourse on ideology" (1971: 173).

As radical and fruitful Althusser's theory of ideology has been, it also has a number of shortcomings. What Althusser, for instance, fails to take into account is that the subject is not only the effect of one ideology but is positioned by several ideologies or discourses. The individual subject is an intersection of multiple discursive systems (Eagleton 1994: 217; Haugaard 2006: 57). Hence, someone may identify as 'mother', 'working class', 'student', 'hip hop fan', 'white', and 'Christian' all at the same time. These different subject positions and discourses may not be in harmony. Instead, they can collide. Therefore, social change can occur as competing discourses struggle against each other and new spaces of meaning are opened up.

Moreover, even the positioning of the subject within one ideology or discourse is ultimately bound to fail. As the fixation of meaning is only partial and does never totally succeed, there is always "an ineradicable surplus of meaning or horizon of contingency which contaminates any and all discursive formations" (Ryan 2006: 193). This incompleteness prevents any structural determination of the subject (Torfing 1999: 149, 2009: 119). As Laclau explains:

> The structure will obviously not be able to determine me, not because I have an essence independent from the structure, but because the structure has failed to constitute itself fully and thus to constitute me as a subject as well. [. . .] I am condemned to be free, not because I have no structural identity as the existentialists assert, but because I have a failed structural identity.
>
> (1990: 43–4)

This perspective actually shifts the structure-agency problem:

> In opposition to the postulation of two separate metaphysical entities – agents and structures – we suggest the following: (a) that there are merely relative degrees of institutionalisation of the social, which penetrate and define the subjectivity of the agents themselves; and (b) that the institutions do not constitute closed structural frameworks, but loosely integrated complexes requiring the constant intervention of articulatory practices.
>
> (1990: 223–4)

This post-structuralist view abandons the primacy and pre-existence of either structure or agency and replaces it with "a dynamic account of the relationship between structure and agency" (Howarth 2013: 160). Agency is not possible because there exists an autonomous human being independent of structures, but because the structures always 'fail'. As David Howarth points out, "[i]t is the failure of structures to provide stable points from which to speak or act that opens the space for a more radical form of subjectivity in which social actors are literally compelled to be free, and to identify with new possibilities" (2009: 314).

There is one further aspect in which discourse theory breaks with other accounts of structure, agency, and power. Quite often, power is conceived in rather negative terms as 'power over', that is power as domination and as the enforcement of one's will over others (Göhler 2009: 28) – a notion of power that is also apparent in Lukes's three dimensions of power. Against such a repressive view, discourse theory emphasises the productive nature of power. As discourses "systematically form the objects of which they speak" (Foucault 2002: 54), they not only limit what can be said about an object, but they produce that object and thus enable action. As John Storey argues, "[d]iscourses work in three ways: they enable, they constrain, and they constitute (2015: 133). While they limit the scope of meanings and action, they also create subjects with the power to act. Moreover, as discourses produce subjects they also generate power relations between them. Thus, the discourse of higher education, for example, constructs specific power relations between students, academics, and others, for instance, concerning the question who can decide what is worth studying. But as discourses are never fixed, such power relations are likewise instable – and as this book will show, these power relations between students and others have been a central issue in the debate about higher education.

Analysing higher education and the student

Higher education is a complex and relatively stable discursive structure that regulates behaviour, provides identities, and constitutes relations of power. It is a 'system of differences' that has been institutionalised over time and consists of signifiers such as 'university', 'lecture', 'student, or 'academic'. However, this institutionalisation is never complete but remains partial and thus open for change. As higher education is not an autonomous structure, change is inevitable as different discourses impinge on it, new relations of equivalence and difference are established, and new nodal points gain in power. Thus, the central concepts and ideas that organise higher education and function as nodal points may shift and struggle against each other. Higher education may be asked to produce 'knowledge', transmit 'culture', offer 'moral guidance', boost 'the economy', function as 'critical conscience', train 'democratic citizens', or be a means of 'social change', to name just a few different 'ideas of higher education'. Just as the function and position of higher education has been a site of struggle, the meaning of the term 'student' has likewise been contested, not only in terms of who ought to be allowed to become a student but also with regard to students' position in terms of power.

As this book investigates how the subject position 'student' has been framed within the struggle over higher education, this ultimately raises the question what kind of material such an analysis could be based on. Indeed, as everything is discursive and every social practice can be regarded as an articulation, every practice related to higher education somehow or other contributes to its stabilisation or change. Thus, one could take into account such diverse areas as classroom interaction, architecture, chats, government acts, clothing, campus novels, prospectuses, newspaper reports, exam papers, and so on. There seems to be no limit with regard to what could be analysed. However, these different articulations are by no means of the same kind. Instead, they work on rather different "discourse planes" as they 'speak' from rather different social locations and have different addressees (Jäger and Maier 2009: 46–8). Hence, one can distinguish, for instance, between universities and colleges' self-representation aimed at future students, media reports for the general public, personal observations, literary reflections, or policy documents.

This book focuses on one particular discourse plane, which might be termed 'the debate on the idea of higher education' and which is constituted by texts that explicitly formulate arguments concerning the function, structure, and purpose of higher education. These texts can stem from within academia, students, or politicians, but what unites them is that they put forth a particular 'idea of higher education' and aim for a shift in the discourse.

Notes

1 The actual title of the essay is "Die Universität als Organisierte Institution" (Luhmann 1992: 90–9), which can be translated into 'the university as an organised institution'.

2 Joseph Burke defines an institution as "a set of behaviours patterned according to one or more variously codified and differentially enforced rules whose development can be evolved or constructed or both" (2011: 321). According to W.R. Scott, institutions are "multifaceted, durable social structures, made up of symbolic elements, social activities, and material resources" (2013: 57).

3 One of the most well-known definitions of legitimacy in the context of the study of organisations and institutions has been offered by Mark C. Suchman: "Legitimacy is a generalized perception or assumption that the actions of an entity are desirable, proper, or appropriate within some socially constructed system of norms, values, beliefs, and definitions." (1995: 574) For an overview of various definitions of legitimacy within the context of institutions and organisations, see Deephouse and Suchman (2008: 50–2) and Johnson, Dowd, and Ridgeway (2006: 55–9). Theories of institutional legitimacy often start with Max Weber and his distinction between different forms of legitimate domination. First, Weber claims, domination can be legitimised by the belief in the legality of an order. Second, domination may be legitimised by tradition. Third, domination may be considered legitimate because of the charisma of a ruler or leader (Weber 1978: 216–8). This threefold distinction has become rather popular within the study of institutions even though Weber was not concerned with institutions but with domination. When discussing why social orders are accepted as legitimate, he actually distinguishes between four bases of legitimacy: tradition, affectual faith, value-rationality, and the belief in legality (Weber 1978: 36).

4 Another threefold differentiation has been proposed by Suchman, who distinguishes between pragmatic, moral, and cognitive legitimacy. Pragmatic legitimacy refers to the support of an organisation because it offers something in exchange (exchange legitimacy), is responsive to larger interests (influence legitimacy), and is conceived of as having good intentions (dispositional legitimacy) (Suchman 1995: 578). Moral legitimacy "reflects a positive normative evaluation of the organisation and its activities" (Suchman 1995: 579), while cognitive legitimacy is based on comprehensibility (plausible explanations) and 'taken-for-grantedness' (Suchman 1995: 582).

5 In "Politics and the Study of Discourse", Foucault defines discourse as follows: "discourse is constituted by the difference between what one could say correctly at one period (under the rules of grammar and logic) and what is actually said. The discursive field is, at a specific moment, the law of this difference." (1991: 63)

6 Such a typical criticism is illustrated by Barbara Czarniawska with reference to George Levine, who tells the anecdote of an astrophysicist who asked him at a party whether a deconstructionist would survive the fall from a high tower with the use of deconstruction (2003: 131). For a discussion of this claim towards the 'world out there' see also Gergen (2009: 161–3) and Edwards, Ashmore, and Potter (1995: 26–32).

7 This perspective distinguishes social constructionists like Laclau and Mouffe or Jacques Derrida from the social constructionism of John Searle. While Searle likewise emphasises that social reality is a construct, he claims that this social construct "must bottom out" in something that is not a construction but rather a brute fact (Searle 1995: 191). This position of Searle has raised numerous criticism, for instance by Hund (1998), Page (2004: 268), or Rust (2006: 28–9).

8 In this respect, Laclau and Mouffe follow Jacques Derrida, who argues that meaning is never fixed because language functions as a never-ending chain of signifiers without a centre or transcendental signified (Derrida 1982: 11–25; Laclau and Mouffe 2001: 112).

9 As Laclau and Mouffe explain, "we will call articulation any practice establishing a relation among elements such that their identity is modified as a result of the articulatory practice. The structured totality resulting from the articulatory practice, we will call discourse. The differential positions, insofar as they appear articulated within a discourse, we will call moments. By contrast, we will call element any difference that is not discursively articulated" (2001: 105). A discourse can thus be understood as a reduction of possible meanings by turning the 'elements' of the discursive field into 'moments' through practices of articulation. While the 'field of discursivity' is structured by differential relations but unfixed by a certain discourse, its elements, which are signs with multiple, potential meanings, can become fixed as moments of a discourse if their meaning persists from one articulation to another (Andersen 2003: 50; Torfing 1999: 92).

10 David Howarth refers to the Black Consciousness Movement in South Africa to explain the relations of equivalence and difference. As he argues, in the struggle against apartheid, different sections of the oppressed established an equivalential relation that united different ethnic and social groups by constructing one major relation of difference between the oppressed and the oppressor (2000: 107).

Part I

Higher education for post-war Britain

Chapter 3

Setting the scene

Though this book focuses on the debate on British higher education from the 1940s onwards, many of the issues that have shaped this debate cannot be comprehended without having a rough understanding of the earlier history of British higher education. Therefore, this chapter provides a short overview of the development of British higher education from the foundation of the first universities until the early decades of the twentieth century.

Founded in the twelfth and thirteenth century, the universities of Oxford and Cambridge are not only the oldest universities in Britain, but they are two of the oldest universities in the world and enjoy a worldwide reputation. Apart from their reputation and long tradition, the two universities are also distinct with regard to their structure. Both Oxford and Cambridge consist of more than 30 independent colleges each. These colleges not only offer accommodation to staff and students and facilities such as libraries, dining halls, and common rooms, but they also take care of some of the teaching responsibilities. But though today these features may appear as typical of Oxford and Cambridge, they only developed over time. In the early days, students did for instance not live in the colleges of the university but were accommodated in private lodgings, hostels, or halls. The colleges only began to admit students in the fourteenth century (Anderson 2006: 2). Over time, the colleges' importance increased as they took over most of the teaching functions from the university and controlled admissions. Moreover, they absorbed most of the hostels and halls – not primarily in order to make life easier for the student but rather to impose discipline (Anderson 2006: 6–7). For similar reasons, academic dress in the form of black gowns was introduced in the sixteenth century in order to achieve uniformity and encourage good behaviour (Cobban 1999: 48).

As far as the student body is concerned, students in the Middle Ages differed considerably from students today. Not only were they exclusively male, but they were also much younger. In the late fourteenth century, Cambridge admitted students as young as fourteen (Cobban 1999: 19). With regard to the social origin of the student intake, the universities were not as elitist as one might think. Though there were hardly any poor students, there were also few sons from noble families. Of course, the universities were interested in attracting students of high status, but it was only from the sixteenth and seventeenth centuries onwards that noble sons made up a significant part of the student body (Cobban 1999: 31–4). This change in student intake went hand in hand with a shift in the function of the universities. While in the Middle Ages university education was rather vocational and the universities' primary function was to provide future servants of church and state (Anderson 2006: 4), attitudes towards education changed in the sixteenth century, in particular amongst the English élite, who started to consider education an indispensable attribute of a gentleman (Brockliss 2016: 137). Increasingly, the role of the universities was to offer a moral and cultural education and to provide the aristocracy and gentry with a set of common experiences and values (Anderson 2006: 8).

At the same time, ties between the universities and the state were strengthened. In 1571, the universities had their corporate statues confirmed by Act of Parliament, and from 1604 onwards, they were given two seats each in parliament (Anderson 2006: 9). Moreover, the universities were further bound to the state as they had to conform to the new state religion. At Oxford, all undergraduates over the age of sixteen had to subscribe to the Thirty-nine Articles from 1581 onwards, and while similar subscriptions did not exist at Cambridge, a royal mandate demanded in 1616 that degree recipients at both universities had to subscribe to the Book of Common Prayer and the Thirty-nine Articles (Lawson and Silver 1973: 102). Such restrictions, which limited access to Anglicans, were intact until the second half of the nineteenth century.

While Oxford and Cambridge were still the only universities in England in the early nineteenth century, they were by far not the only universities in the British Isles at that time. In 1592, Trinity College was founded as Ireland's first university, and even before then, a number of universities had been established in Scotland. The University of St Andrews, the University of Glasgow, and King's College at Aberdeen had all been founded in the fifteenth century, followed in the sixteenth century by Tounis College at Edinburgh and Marischal College at Aberdeen. Though at the beginning these universities had problems to establish themselves, as in particular students from the upper strata of Scottish society preferred to study elsewhere (Ridder-Symoens 2003: 439), they eventually thrived, and in the eighteenth century, when student numbers at Oxbridge were falling, the numbers in Scotland rose so that by 1800, Scotland, though only a tenth of the English population, had nearly as many students as England (Anderson 2006: 17).[1] But Scotland did not only have more universities and students, studying in Scotland was also in many ways different from studying at Oxbridge. The Scottish universities offered a four-year general arts course in classics, mathematics, and philosophy, students were accepted at an earlier age, teaching was provided through lectures, there were no religious tests, and the universities were mainly non-residential, which made them much more accessible to less well-off students (Vernon 2004: 34).[2]

After the foundation of the Scottish universities, the university landscape in Britain saw no major changes for a rather long time. Dissenting Academies had been opened in the seventeenth and eighteenth centuries for those who were unable or unwilling to attend Oxbridge. Medical schools and colleges such as the College of Arts and Sciences in Manchester (1783) had been established, and plans had been made for the creation of a university in London (Whyte 2015: 29). But it was not before 1828 that a new university opened. Though Durham University was established soon afterwards (1832), it was the newly founded University of London, which eventually had a major impact on the further development of higher education in Britain. Having no charter, the University of London was established as a joint-stock company and had neither ties with the church nor with the state (Whyte 2015: 41). As the University of London had no religious tests either for students or professors, it provoked strong hostility from the church, which founded the rival King's College, London in 1831 (Anderson 2006: 27). But apart from the fact that King's College had a charter and that staff had to conform to the Church of England, both universities were actually rather similar. They were both open to all students irrespective of religious denomination and in both cases students were living at home or in lodgings (Whyte 2015: 45). As both also had no degree-awarding powers, the state founded a new University of London in 1836 as a solely degree-awarding, non-teaching institution, of which the former University of London, now renamed into University College London (UCL), and King's College became the first affiliated colleges. Hence, the first nonsectarian university with the power to grant degrees was established in England (Halsey and Trow 2009: 82–3). In the following decades, the number of colleges affiliated with the University of London grew, and in 1898 the university was given its federal structure and many of the existing colleges in London became schools of the University of London. However, the University of London was not only decisive for the development of higher education in London. From 1858 onwards, any male student could sit for the degree examinations regardless of location, and thus colleges around the country could offer courses that prepared students for London degrees (Anderson 2006: 68; Whyte 2015: 60).

While a university had thus been established in London, there was still none in Britain's new industrial centres. However, initiatives were taken to more firmly establish higher education in these parts of the country. In 1851, Owens College at Manchester was founded as a non-denominational institution that offered courses in classics, mathematics, natural philosophy, English, chemistry, and history (Whyte 2015: 94). Though not a major success in its first years, the climate changed in the 1860s and 1870s, and Owens College could attract a growing number of students (Whyte 2015: 100) Soon, colleges were established in several other industrial cities such as the College of Physical Science, Newcastle (1871), Yorkshire College of Science, Leeds (1874), Firth College, Sheffield (1879), or Mason Science College, Birmingham (1880). While at first these institutions could not award their own degrees, their dependency on the University of London was gradually loosened once Victoria University was established in 1880 as a federal university with Owens College as its first constituent college, soon followed by University College, Liverpool in 1884 and Yorkshire College, Leeds in 1887 (Anderson 2006: 74). In Wales, colleges were established in Aberystwyth (1872), Bangor (1884), and Cardiff (1883), and in 1893 these became constituent colleges of the new University of Wales. In the following decades, new university colleges were founded at Nottingham (1881), Reading (1892), Exeter (1901), and Southampton (1902), and several of the established colleges were given university charters including Birmingham (1900), Sheffield (1905), Bristol (1909), and, as Victoria University was disbanded in 1903, Manchester, Liverpool, and Leeds. England and Wales thus saw an increase in universities within an extremely short period of time. While in the late 1870s there were only four universities (Oxford, Cambridge, London, Durham), the number had nearly tripled by 1910.

As the number of universities and colleges increased, the role of the state altered, in particular with regard to funding. While Oxford and Cambridge, quite in contrast to the Scottish universities, had been independent from state funding, the new colleges were in need of government funds in order to establish work at university level. Though the state provided funding to these colleges, the grants were often earmarked for vocational courses, technical education, or teacher training (Vernon 2001: 258). Following numerous appeals from the colleges, the Treasury eventually provided a grant of £15,000 a year in 1889 to be distributed to 11 colleges according to the amount of education they provided at university level and depending on how much extra funding they could be expected to generate (Vernon 2001: 259). While these grants directly helped the colleges to become universities, they also made the universities increasingly dependent on the state. After various shuffles between the Treasury and the Board of Education, which supplied grants for technical education and teacher training, and the establishment of several Advisory Committees, the University Grants Committee (UGC) was set up in 1919 to allocate the state grants to the universities and university colleges (Owen 1980: 255–8). Though not on the UGC's grant list at the beginning, even Oxbridge started to rely on state grants and was put on the UGC list in the 1920s (Vernon 2004: 197–8). Over the next decades, the UGC grants rose continuously so that by 1946/47 they accounted for more than half of the universities' income (Halsey and Trow 2009: 97). Though the state thus became the main funder of the universities, the UGC, which was directly responsible to the Treasury, was independent enough to act as a 'buffer' and to secure the relative autonomy of the universities and to protect them from direct government interference (Shattock 1994: 1–3).

The greatest significance of the new universities and university colleges that were founded in the nineteenth century was, however, that they gave recognition to an educational ideal that was different from what Oxbridge stood for. While Oxbridge's educational ideal was the gentleman and teaching focused on a liberal education in classics and philosophy (Halsey and Trow 2009: 84; Tight 2009: 6), the new civic universities developed a greater focus on science and technology, and they often established links with local industry and provided specialist subjects such as chemistry in Manchester, metallurgy in Sheffield, or textiles in Leeds (Anderson 1995: 39). Though not adverse to the arts, the civic universities provided a kind of university education that was more geared to the new urban centres of the country. Moreover, they also offered a rather different student experience. In contrast to Oxbridge with its long history, the new foundations did not have a tradition to look back to. Hence, they invented their own traditions and developed means to create a corporate consciousness. Students started to wear academic gowns to distinguish themselves from the rest of urban society, student societies were founded, common rooms and unions were built, university newspapers were established, and traditions like Rags were created (Whyte 2015: 147, 152–6). But the biggest difference between Oxbridge and the new civic universities including London was that the latter did not offer accommodation and that therefore students lived at home or in lodgings. In order to improve the situation, halls of residence were built – first by private initiative or religious foundations and later by the universities and colleges themselves. In particular for university colleges like Reading, whose local population was too small to supply enough students, halls of residence became vital in order to attract students from further away (UGC 1957: §11). Over the years, these halls of residence came to be seen as an indispensable part of university life – a movement that even spread to Scotland, where a number of halls had opened by 1939 (Anderson 2006: 122).

Last but not least, the new civic universities were so important for the development of higher education because they not only increased the number of university places but also brought higher education closer to the people. Though Oxbridge had embarked on extension courses and other initiatives to provide university education to less well-off students (Whyte 2015: 132), the new civics explicitly tried to cater for a new clientele. As Hastings Rashdall claimed in 1902, the new universities had brought "university education within the reach of localities, of individuals, and of classes which could not otherwise enjoy them" (cited in Whyte 2015: 134). This, however, does not mean that the universities were now open to all and sundry. Though the new universities grew in size and Oxbridge also expanded so that from 1900 to 1938 the number of students at British universities increased from about 20,000 to 50,000 (Committee on Higher Education 1963: Table 3), higher education, and in particular university education, was still the privilege of the few. Even if one adds the 13 000 students in teacher training and the 6,000 students on advanced courses in further education, only 2.7 percent of the age group were enrolled in full-time higher education in Great Britain in 1938 (Committee on Higher Education 1963: Table 4). But not only was access to higher education limited, higher education was also marked by a rather strong class bias. Although the number of students with a working-class or lower-middle-class background had slightly increased after the Education Act of 1902, these students were still underrepresented (Halsey and Trow 2009: 83, Perkin 2009: 64). In order to open higher education to more students from lower socio-economic backgrounds, state scholarships were introduced in the 1920s (Anderson 2006: 118). Though the number of students that entered university on these and other scholarships was considerable in the 1930s (Dyhouse 2002: 14), the class bias nevertheless remained largely unbroken. In 1955, only one-quarter of all university students had a father in manual occupation – a number that was significantly higher in the technical and teacher training colleges where these students accounted for 38 percent and 40 percent, respectively (Anderson 1995: 55). Apart from such differences between the universities and the training colleges, there were also great divisions between the universities themselves as the percentage of working-class students was notably lower at Oxford and Cambridge than at other universities (Anderson 1995: 55).[3]

Moreover, higher education was also marked by a strong gender bias. For centuries, women had been denied access to the universities – a situation that only gradually changed over the course of the nineteenth and twentieth centuries. At Cambridge, for instance, the first women college opened in 1869, though not recognised by the university at that time, and from 1881 onwards, women could take the University of Cambridge exams. However, it was not before 1948 that women were actually awarded full degrees at Cambridge (Leathwood and Read 2009: 48–9). Though Oxbridge had awarded degrees to women from the 1920s onwards, the two ancient university were surely the bastion of men well into the twentieth century. It was again the University of London, which acted as a pioneer when it opened its degrees to women in 1878, but other universities followed swiftly. The Victoria University, when founded in 1880, was open to women as was the University of Wales, founded in 1893. In Scotland, special certificates and diplomas for women had been established in the 1870s, and from 1892 onwards women were fully recognised and had their first degrees awarded in 1896 (Cunningham 1984: 178; Rowold 2010: 20). Over the following decades, female students were increasingly accepted and their number gradually rose so that by 1940 about a quarter of university students were women (Carpentier 2009: 239; Dyhouse 2006: 99).[4]

As far as the position of the students within the universities and colleges in terms of power is concerned, students did not have much of a say in the early twentieth century. As most students were not adults in legal terms, the universities and colleges stood *in loco parentis*, and students were subjected to rules and regulations that not only concerned academic matters but also their social life. This particularly affected students who lived in colleges or halls of residence where visiting times and the like were strictly regulated (Thomas 2002: 293–4). Students also had relatively little power in the government of their universities or colleges. Though Student Representative Councils had been founded in a number of universities and though the charters of most civic universities included student representation on governing bodies to a certain extent, students hardly had any actual power in the governing of their institutions of higher education (Ashby and Anderson: 47–50).

Such was the situation of British higher education in the 1930s and 1940s. While Oxford and Cambridge were in a unique position as far as their national dominance was concerned, numerous universities had opened in the industrial centres of the country, and university colleges existed in places such as Leicester and Exeter, in order to meet local demands for liberal education, professional training, and industry-related courses. Besides the universities and university colleges, there were numerous teacher training and technical colleges, which, though less prestigious, were no less important as they catered for more students from the lower-middle and working classes. In contrast to the universities, for which the UGC not only allocated state funds, but also acted as a buffer towards the state, these colleges were under more direct state control. As far as the student intake was concerned, higher education had considerably expanded in the latter part of the nineteenth and the first decades of the twentieth centuries. But even though access had been opened and the number of students continuously rose, higher education was still a privilege, and in particular the universities were characterised by a strong class and gender bias.

Notes

1 If one takes into account population numbers, the following picture emerges for the period around 1800. Though Scotland had only 1.5 million inhabitants, it had five universities, whereas England and Wales had 9.25 million inhabitants but only two universities (Frijhoff 2003: 78).

2 Though the Scottish universities were also residential in the beginning, students increasingly lived in lodgings or with families from the eighteenth century onwards (Anderson 2006: 18).

3 In 1955, only 9 percent of the students at Cambridge and 13 percent of the students at Oxford had a father in manual occupation, whereas the figure for London was 21 percent, 24 percent for Scotland, 31 percent for the civics, and 40 percent for Wales (Anderson 1995: 55). One of the reasons why Oxbridge remained the privilege of the wealthy was the relatively high cost of an Oxbridge education. Studying at a provincial university amounted to around £130 p.a. (including travel expenses) and at Oxbridge to £160 to £240 for women and £200 to £275 for men. Living at home was thus a major financial relief. According to UGC figures, around half of the students (excluding Oxbridge) lived at home in 1938/39 (Dyhouse 2002: 6).

4 In the 1940s, the percentage of women rose to more than one-third but then returned to the pre-war state of about one-quarter. Since the 1960s, the number of female students has been constantly rising so that by the mid-1990s more than half of the students were women (Carpentier 2009: 239).

Chapter 4

National needs and the provision of manpower

Still in the midst of the war, Britain started to make plans for the post-war period. The Beveridge Report (1942) identified five giant evils – squalor, ignorance, want, idleness, and disease – that needed to be addressed in the future and recommended extensive reforms to the system of social welfare. Even though education did not play a major role in the Beveridge Report, it was indeed the first area that saw major reforms.[1] In 1944, the Butler Education Act raised the school leaving age to 15 and introduced free and universal secondary education (Jones and Lowe 2002: 113–4). Though selection at the age of 11 was strict with students being allocated to different schools depending on their performance in the 11+ examinations, secondary education was nevertheless opened to thousands of women and working-class pupils. The Butler Education Act thus allowed for greater equality of opportunity than had ever been the case before.

In contrast to these massive reforms in the school sector, higher education was barely touched, and no attempts were made "to destroy the universities as 'citadels of privilege'" (Benn and Fieldhouse 1993: 311). Although there was a growing consensus that higher education needed to expand in order to accommodate ex-service men and women as well as the growing number of qualified school leavers (Lowe 1988: 57),[2] the question what kind of higher education system would be best suited for such an expansion was hardly dealt with (Bocock and Taylor 2003: 251). This is all the more striking because the state had by then become the main funder of the universities. While in 1920/21 the parliamentary grant had covered 33.6 percent of university expenditure (excluding new buildings and equipment), this had risen to 52.7 percent by 1946/47 (Halsey and Trow 2009: 97).

One reason for this reluctance to reform the universities might have been the strong link that existed between the universities and the political élites, in particular Oxford and Cambridge (Salter and Tapper 1994: 8). However, this cannot sufficiently explain why the Labour Party, which had such eminent critics of the universities' elitism as R.H. Tawney,[3] did not try to reform higher education after it had come to power in 1945. According to Jean Bocock and Richard Taylor, the lack of interest in higher education actually resulted from Labour's preoccupation with the reorganisation of the school sector

(2003: 250–1). The restructuring of secondary education was considered much more important for the alleviation of social inequalities than a reform of higher education, and many party members believed that a reform of the school sector and financial help to poorer students would resolve problems of inequality in higher education (2003: 250–1).

But even though the government did not put forth any major reforms of higher education, this does not mean that the government did nothing at all. It clearly supported the expansion of higher education and thus raised the number of student grants as well as the UGC grant, which rose from £2.1 million in 1945 to £16.6 million for 1950/51 (Benn and Fieldhouse 1993: 311). Student numbers climbed accordingly from 69,000 students in full-time higher education in 1938/39 to 122,000 in 1954/55, of which 50,000, respectively 82,000 studied at universities (Committee on Higher Education 1963: Table 3). But expansion was not the only concern of the government at that time. Numerous committees were appointed to investigate the provision of higher education in particular subject areas and to make suggestions for future development. Hence, the Goodenough Report advised on medical education (1944), the McNair Report on teacher training (1944), the Teviot Report on dentistry (1946), and the Clapham Report on social and economic research (1946) (Shattock 2012: 12). Of particular interest to the governments of the post-war period was education in science and technology, in which student numbers were relatively low and had even dropped before the war. In the universities, the percentage of students in pure science had fallen from 17.0 percent in 1920/21–1924/25 to 16.3 percent in 1935/36–1938/39 and from 13.5 percent to 9.7 percent for students in technology (Sanderson 1999: 70). As the war had shown how much modern civilisation depended on scientific and technological progress, deficiencies in scientific and technological education became a prime concern in the 1940s (Anderson 2006: 132; Halsey and Trow 2009: 91). Faced with the problems of reconstruction and a relatively weak economy, education in science and technology became of national relevance. Thus, the government commissioned two enquiries: The Percy Report *Higher Technological Education* (1945) and the Barlow Report *Scientific Manpower* (1946).

The Percy Committee had been appointed "to consider the needs of higher technological education in England and Wales and the respective contribution to be made thereto by Universities and Technical Colleges" (Ministry of Education 1945: §1). It recommended amongst others the designation and development of a number of Technical Colleges to offer full-time courses at a standard comparable to university degree courses as well as the creation of a National Council of Technology to coordinate and advise on policy and to secure standards in technical education (Ministry of Education 1945: §29, §35, §53). While the Percy Report focussed on the non-university sector to provide "technical assistants and craftsmen" (Ministry of Education 1945: §4), the Barlow Report, although supporting the call for strong technical colleges, was more concerned with scientists and university expansion. Asked to "consider the policies which should govern the use and development of our scientific manpower and resources during the next 10 years" (*Scientific Manpower* 1946: §1), the Barlow Committee recommended, amongst others, to double the number of science graduates (*Scientific Manpower* 1946: §23). Though the number of students in science and technology actually rose over the next years, the increase was not considered satisfactory. Hence, the White Paper *Technical Education* (1956) suggested further expansion. Similar to the Percy Report, it focused on the non-university sector and argued that "the bulk of full-time or sandwich courses should be carried on in colleges which concentrate on advanced courses of technological level" (Ministry of Education 1956: §65). Following the White Paper, eight (later ten) Colleges of Advanced Technology were designated, which, in contrast to the universities, were under the control of local education authorities (LEAs).

The manpower doctrine

Even though the Percy Report, the Barlow Report, and the White Paper 1956 made different suggestions concerning the type of institution that should carry the bulk of expansion, they all agreed that the number of students in science and technology needed to increase. Indeed, agreement on this point was so strong that the Barlow Report presented it as common sense and stated that "[w]e do not think that it is necessary to preface our report by stating at length the case for developing our scientific resources" (*Scientific Manpower* 1946: §2). Whenever the need for a higher number of scientists, technologists, and technicians was justified, arguments were markedly similar in both reports and the White Paper 1956. The Percy Report, for instance, claimed that

> the *position of Great Britain as a leading industrial nation* is being endangered by a failure to secure the fullest possible application of science to *industry*; and second, that this failure is partly due to deficiencies in *education*.
>
> (Ministry of Education 1945: §2, emphases added)

Likewise, the Barlow Report declared that

> [i]f we are to maintain our *position in the world* and restore and improve our *standard of living*, we have no alternative but to strive for that scientific achievement without which trade will wither, our Colonial Empire will remain undeveloped and our lives and freedom will be at the mercy of a potential aggressor.
>
> The problem of scientific manpower during the next decade falls into two distinct parts. The immediate tasks are to bring back our qualified scientists to civil life from the Forces and from the innumerable civilian occupations in which they have been serving the Forces [. . .]. The longer

> term problem is to provide sufficient qualified scientists to meet *the nation's requirements* during the reconstruction period and thereafter.
> (*Scientific Manpower* 1946: §2–3, emphases added)

The White Paper 1956 quoted the Prime Minister Sir Anthony Eden, who argued:

> The prizes will not go to the *countries* with the largest population. Those with the best systems of education will *win*. [. . .] [I]f we are to make full use of what we are learning, we shall need many more scientists, engineers and technicians. I am determined that this shortage shall be made good.
> (cited in Ministry of Education 1956: §1, emphases added)

And later the reader was informed that

> [t]he management of full employment, with its much greater need for a responsible attitude to work and its challenge to greater output per man as the only way further to *raise living standards*, has brought a sense of our *dependence on education as the key to advance*.
> (Ministry of Education 1956: §159, emphases added)

In all these cases, higher education was framed within a discourse that was structured by the nodal points 'economy', 'living standard', and 'nation'. The dominant argument was that education and training were crucial for economic performance, which in turn was vital to secure a high standard of living and Britain's position in the world – a world that was entirely conceived of in terms of a fierce competition between different nations. Thus, the White Paper 1956, for example, spoke directly of the danger that Britain might be left behind "the U.S.A., Russia and Western Europe" (Ministry of Education 1956: §3).

In order to secure Britain's position in the world and to improve the nation's economic performance, the expansion of higher education, in particular scientific and technological education, was deemed crucial. Hence, the Percy Report again and again referred to the "demand of industry" (Ministry of Education 1945: §41), the "needs of industry" (Ministry of Education 1945: §5), or "the demands of the engineering industry" (Ministry of Education 1945: §7). The Barlow Report spoke of "the nation's requirements" (*Scientific Manpower* 1946: §3) and the "demand for scientists" (*Scientific Manpower* 1946: §5).[4] Likewise, the White Paper was concerned with the "rising demand for scientific manpower" (Ministry of Education 1956: §6). In all these cases, expansion was justified through manpower demands rather than goals such as greater social justice (Benn and Fieldhouse 1993: 301).

This exclusive focus on manpower needs also shaped the concept of the student. The White Paper 1956, for instance, stated that "[i]f talent is not to be wasted, more boys and girls must stay on at school till they are eighteen and aim at studying science or technology at either a university or a technical college providing advanced courses" (Ministry of Education 1956: §16). Students were described here as "talent" that could be "wasted". This formulation is telling as the concern was not that an individual might waste his or her talent, but that the nation could lose potential talent in the form of prospective students. The student was regarded as a resource that actually belonged to the nation.

This conceptualisation of the student as a resource turned up time and again in the White Paper 1956 and it was also dominant in the Percy and Barlow reports. Thus, the Percy Report, for instance, stated:

> While however we recognise that both educational institutions and industry may not have handled their material to the best advantage, we cannot resist the conclusion that the best material is not being offered to either in sufficient quantities.
>
> (Ministry of Education 1945: §41)

Students were described here as "material" that could be "handled" and came around in "quantities". At other points, students were referred to as "resource", "supply", "reserve", or "output"; they were "offered", "provided", or "wasted", and were "available" or in "shortage".[5] All these words stem from the world of industry. The idiom employed was taken directly from the production line. Education was conceptualised within the discourse of industrial production and management. Institutions of education were made equivalent to factories, and students were treated as objects. Within this input-output-model, in which raw material (students) is turned into products (graduates) and production is regulated not through the availability of raw material but through the demand for the final product, students are denied any form of agency. They are neither in a position in which they have an impact on what they become, nor do they have an active role in the learning process or any agency within the higher education system. Instead, they are moulded into whatever the national economy requires.

This form of thinking, in which students only turned up as manpower and resources to the nation's economy, was not yet hegemonic and did not lead to any major reform of higher education. Nevertheless, the idea that higher education was an instrument to achieve economic growth not only stayed influential in the decades to come but gained in prominence from the 1980s onwards – albeit in a modified form. In the 1940s and 1950s, however, the debate on higher education was still dominated by writers from within the universities. These writers by and large showed contempt for a purely economic understanding of higher education and sought to define the idea of the university rather in terms of culture and personal development.

Notes

1 While most welfare policies were implemented after the election victory of Labour in 1945, such as the National Insurance Act (1946), the National Health Service Act (1946), the New Towns Act (1947), or the National Assistance Act (1948), the Butler Education Act was passed in 1944, not only during war times but also under the Conservative-led coalition government. Education was thus of prime importance, and within the following decades it became the second most expensive welfare service (Lowe 1993: 232).

2 Through the Further Education and Training Scheme 44,755 men and women who had served in World War II were given access to universities and university colleges (Vaizey 2012: 34). As the total number of ex-service men and women receiving an award was too high to be accommodated by the universities alone, the grants could be used in technical colleges as well. As a consequence of that arrangement, work of university standard was established in technical colleges (Robinson 1968: 18–9).

3 Already in the years before World War I, R.H. Tawney argued for a much more open and inclusive university system that would allow workers to access higher education throughout their lives (Taylor and Steele 2011: 31–6).

4 In contrast to the Percy Report, the Barlow Report more specifically discussed access to higher education and argued that many more students were capable of entering higher education: "We conclude, therefore, that there is available in our population a large reserve of innate intelligence and that, even allowing for the other factors, there are more potential graduates than we could hope to take into our universities by any degree of expansion practicable within the next ten years. This would still be true if the standard of intelligence at which the individual is regarded as suitable for a university education were materially higher than it is to-day." (*Scientific Manpower* 1946: §28) With this focus on intelligence as the prime access criterion, the Barlow Report subscribed to a meritocratic conception of higher education that ran counter to the prevalent entrance practices of universities. However, the report did not propose a purely meritocratic system. Instead, it pointed out that "[c]haracter, temperament and wider qualities of minds are, of course, as important as intellectual acuity and the test for fitness for the Universities is not intelligence alone" (*Scientific Manpower* 1946: §25).

5 Cf. Ministry of Education (1945: §12, 16, 17), *Scientific Manpower* (1946: §2, 3, 5, 10, 16, 17, 23, 26, 27, 35, 38, 40, 56, 61, 62, 63, 67), and Ministry of Education (1956: §1, 6, 16).

Chapter 5

The idea of the university

In the 1940s and 1950s, the government was by no means the only one who thought that higher education had to change. Academics like Bruce Truscot, a pseudonym for Edgar Allison Peers, or Walter Moberly published books that initiated widespread debates about the function of higher education and its place in modern society. Journals like *Universities Quarterly*, founded in 1946, provided a platform for discussion, and also the UGC increasingly tried to shape the future development of the universities.

What is striking about the debate on higher education in the 1940s and 1950s is how much this debate was confined to the universities. Not only did the most prominent voices come from within the universities, but they were also near exclusively concerned with the universities. This strong focus on the universities actually reflects the strong divide that ran through the higher education landscape in the 1940s and 1950s, with the autonomous universities on the one side and the 'rest' on the other. Indeed, the term 'higher education' only became prominent in the 1960s (Bocock and Taylor 2003: 264). How much this divide between the autonomous universities and the training colleges structured thinking about higher education can also be seen, for instance, in the journal *Universities Quarterly*, which adopted the name *Higher Education Quarterly* only in 1987. But the divide was not only upheld by those writing from within the universities. The Percy Report as well as the White Paper 1956 also made a strict distinction between universities and technical colleges (Ministry of Education 1945: §4, 1956: §28). Even though the universities were themselves structured by hierarchies, the divide towards the non-university sector appeared much more insurmountable.

Out of the numerous publications that contributed to the debate, the following chapter first takes a closer look at five individual voices – Bruce Truscot's *Red Brick University* (1943), Walter Moberly's *The Crisis in the University* (1949), the writings of Michael Oakeshott, F.R. Leavis's *Education and the University* (1943), as well as Eric Ashby's *Technology and the Academics* (1958) – and thereafter explores common themes and topics in the debate on the university with a particular focus on issues such as student power, expansion, and student life.

Bruce Truscot and the 'search for knowledge'

According to Robert Anderson, Bruce Truscot's *Red Brick University* (1943)[1] was the "most influential university treatise of the 1940s" (2006: 124). Written from the distinct perspective of the civic universities, which Truscot termed Redbricks, it was primarily a critique of the unevenness between Oxbridge and the Redbricks.[2] Though Truscot praised a number of features of the Redbricks such as longer terms and often more direct contact between students and academic experts (1951: 36–8), his general tenor was that the Redbricks were in a much worse condition than Oxbridge. This disparity within the English university landscape needed to be overcome so that in the end there were "no longer two large residential universities for those who are either well-to-do or brilliant, and ten smaller universities, mainly non-residential, for those who are neither" (1951: 54). But *Red Brick University* was more than a critique of the unevenness of the English university landscape. Indeed, one of the main problems that Truscot identified was that "the essential and inspiring central idea of the university is apt to be forgotten at Redbrick – or even never heard of" (1951: 75). Hence, Truscot himself took on the task to tell his readers what this idea of the university actually was. A university, he claimed, was "a corporation or society which devotes itself to a search after knowledge for the sake of its intrinsic value" (1951: 65). Although Truscot did not completely reject vocational training, he insisted that this was not the essential task of the university (1951: 68). Truscot thus dismissed the Redbricks' original function, which had been to produce intelligence while, at the same time, being a service to commerce and industry (Armytage 2009: 57–8). But his ideal of a university whose essential task was research was also rather far removed from the Oxbridge tradition and writers like John Henry Newman, who had insisted in *The Idea of a University* (1852) that the main task of the university was "the diffusion and extension of knowledge rather than the advancement" (1996: 3).

As far as the students were concerned, Truscot's ideal of the university assigned them a rather peculiar position. While Newman had objected to a university whose prime task was scientific and philosophical discovery precisely because such a university would not need students (1996: 3), Truscot actually reassured his readers that "[t]here could perfectly well be a university which [. . .] had no undergraduates at all" (1951: 70). However, Truscot nowhere seriously intended to actually ban students from the university. Instead, he emphasised that students needed to subscribe to the idea of the university and identify with it. Although Truscot acknowledged in *First Year at the University* (1946), that for many students the motive for studying was that it would lead "to a good job offering good money" (1964: 133) – a motive that "[o]nly saints and fools disregard" (1964: 133), he also made clear that this motive was in conflict "with the fundamental purposes of university education" (1964: 133). According to Truscot, students had a misguided idea of the university. Not only did they mistake the university for another kind of school, but they also misunderstood the purpose of a university education (1951: 73–6, 188–9). Just as academics ought to search for knowledge for its own sake, the student had the "essential task [. . .] to pursue learning for its intrinsic value" (1951: 73). Students should thus subscribe to the same values as academics and consider themselves as "members of a society with a common aim, toward which seniors as well as juniors are working" (1951: 77). While students and academics were not equal in position, they ought to be united by a common idea and consider themselves part of a community dedicated to learning and the search for knowledge for its own sake.

Walter Moberly and the university as mentor

While Truscot instigated the post-war debate on higher education, Walter H. Moberly's *The Crisis in the University* (1949) was the "first important twentieth-century philosophy of university education" (Silver 2003: 100).[3] Written in the aftermath of World War II and in anticipation of the Cold War, *The Crisis in the University* argued for a university that actively engaged with the major challenges of its time – challenges that for Moberly were less of an economic or technological nature but that arose because "[t]he whole complex of traditional belief, habit, and sentiment, on which convictions are founded, has collapsed" (1949: 16). According to Moberly, this intellectual and moral crisis presented the university with a "stupendous intellectual task" (1949: 293) – a task that the university was, however, unable to tackle as long as it was itself in crisis. Instead of being united by a common idea and purpose, the university was riven by competing ideals, but none of these, neither the Classical-Christian nor the liberal nor the technological-democratic university, was sufficient for the task ahead because, as Moberly argued, "[n]either the technical expert in blinkers nor the 'gentleman amateur,' neither the journeyman nor the dilettante, is equal to the demand of the times" (1949: 170). The solution, however, was not to have future scientists receive some basic knowledge of literature or philosophy. Rather, science and technology needed to be set within a discussion of values and ends. As Moberly told his readers:

> If you want a bomb the chemistry department will teach you how to make it, if you want a cathedral the department of architecture will teach you how to build it, if you want to keep your body in health the physiological and medical departments will teach you how to do so. But if you ask whether and why you should want bombs or cathedrals or healthy bodies the university is content to be dumb and impotent.
>
> (1949: 52)

Hence, the university ought to stop hiding behind a "false neutrality" (1949: 54) and examine the "fundamental questions" about the purpose of life and the world one would like to live in (1949: 107).[4] In contrast to both the manpower doctrine and Truscot, Moberly saw the function of the university neither in producing whatever society or the national economy asked for nor in searching for knowledge for its own sake. Instead, the university should engage with questions of values and ends because, as Moberly claimed, society needed the university "not only as an agent but sometimes as a mentor" (1949: 231). But therefore, the university had to change. Instead of primarily transmitting knowledge, the university ought to make students "exercise their minds on the issues which are really momentous" so that they could "decide responsibly on a life-purpose" and

> disentangle and examine critically the assumptions and emotional attitudes underlying the particular studies they pursue, the profession for which they are preparing, the ethical judgements they are accustomed to make, and the political or religious convictions they hold.
>
> (1949: 70)

Although Moberly himself preferred a university based on a Christian outlook, he refrained from being dogmatic. Whatever beliefs students or academics held, what was most vital was that the university did not stay silent on the important issues of the time but that it helped students develop "their own philosophies of life" (1949: 108). This required not only a change with regard to what was taught but also with regard to the way the university treated the student.

As Moberly claimed, it ought to be a "fundamental educational principle" of the university to regard students not as pupils but as adults (1949: 110). At a time when students were *in statu pupillari* and were not adults in legal terms, this was quite a remarkable proposition. Although Moberly supported the practice to assign students in their first years to 'moral tutors' (1949: 213), he generally rejected the *in loco parentis* system as it prolonged the students' time as mere adolescents and sheltered them from the responsibilities and difficulties of life (1949: 10). Instead, the university ought to recognise the "liberty" and "initiative" of the student (1949: 42). Hence, Moberly appreciated modularisation as practised in the US and the German ideal of *Lernfreiheit* as these would acknowledge the adult status of the students by granting them more liberty through choice but also responsibility (1949: 42).[5]

Moberly's *The Crisis in the University* initiated a widespread debate, and as much as there was agreement, it also raised considerable disagreement.[6] One of the most thorough criticisms was levelled by Michael Oakeshott, Professor of Political Science at the London School of Economics, in his article "The Universities" (1949), which was the starting point for a number of essays on the university including "The Idea of a University" (1950).[7]

Michael Oakeshott and the value of liberal learning

According to Oakeshott, the whole discussion about the university's purpose and function was misguided as it misrecognised what a university actually was. For Oakeshott, a university was "not a machine for achieving a particular purpose or producing a particular result" but "a manner of human activity" (2001: 106). Hence, universities should neither be considered as means to produce manpower nor be called upon to offer moral guidance. Moreover, Oakeshott repudiated the idea that the university needed a common culture or ideal. According to Oakeshott, the "world of learning" needed "no extraneous cement to hold it together" (2001: 109). It was rather like a conversation, and a conversation, he claimed, did "not need a chairman" nor did it have a "predetermined course" (2001: 109).

This ideal of the university as a place where learning was pursued without any particular purpose or function was, however, endangered as it had "got mixed up with notions such as 'higher education,' 'advanced training,' 'refresher courses for adults'" (2001: 116). Quite in contrast to these forms of higher education, a university education, so Oakeshott argued, was not concerned with training for a profession (2001: 113). In contrast to other institutions of higher education that had a clear function in society by training students for a job, the university, as Oakeshott saw it, was a place that was removed from the outside world and led a life of its own.

This was also reflected in the way Oakeshott conceptualised the student. For Oakeshott, the student was "neither a child nor an adult" but someone who stood "in a strange middle moment of life when he knows only enough of himself and of the world which passes before him to wish to know more" (2001: 111). This in-between state – being neither adult nor child – did not by mistake correspond to the student's time at university. As Oakeshott explained,

> [t]he characteristic gift of a university is the gift of an interval. Here is an opportunity to put aside the hot allegiances of youth without the necessity of at once acquiring new loyalties to take their place. Here is a break in the tyrannical course of irreparable events; a period in which to look round upon the world and upon oneself without the sense of an enemy at one's back or the insistent pressure to make up one's mind; a moment in which to taste the mystery without the necessity of at once seeking a solution.
>
> (2001: 113–4)

Being a student thus meant to accept the "gift of an interval" and "the privilege of being a 'student,' the enjoyment of *schole* – leisure" (2001: 114) and to enter a place that was "liberated from the distracting business of satisfying contingent wants" (2001: 115).

F. R. Leavis and the English school

Although F.R. Leavis is probably best known as a literary and cultural critic, he also put forth a particular university ideal that he articulated first in *Education and the University* (1943) and returned to in *Two Cultures? The Significance of C.P. Snow* (1962) and *English Literature in Our Time and the University* (1969).

The idea of the university that Leavis proposed in these texts was based upon a thorough critique of modern, 'technologico-Benthamite' civilisation as he had developed it in *Culture and Environment* (1933) together with Denys Thompson. According to Leavis and Thompson, industrialisation and the change of work and consumption patterns had produced numerous negative effects: Work no longer provided a source of identity; leisure was devoid of meaning and had been reduced to mere distraction; an overemphasis on wealth had replaced the search for well-being; and standardisation had led to a levelling down of quality as well as the suppression of critical voices (1950: 32–37, 57–77). Following this line of criticism, Leavis argued in *Education and the University* (1943) that it was the primary task of a university to counter these developments and to "check and control the blind drive onward of material and mechanical development" (1979a: 16). Thus, the university should be "a spiritual force that can direct and determine" (1979a: 30) and "produce the 'educated man' – the man of humane culture who is equipped to be intelligent and responsible about the problems of contemporary civilization" (1979a: 30).

In many ways, this university ideal resembled Moberly's ideas. Not only did both Leavis and Moberly perceive society as being in crisis, but they also considered the university as a mentor to society and attacked a purely utilitarian understanding of education. In contrast to Moberly, however, Leavis did not postulate a set of common values and even rejected the idea that the university needed a founding philosophy (1979a: 17–18, 20). What he argued for instead was "a humane centre" with which all specialists were "in touch" (1979a: 28). This centre was supposed to be the English School because the study of literature trained "in a way no other discipline can, intelligence and sensibility together" (1979a: 34). Moreover, literary studies, which were based on the study of "a concrete tradition" (1979a: 19), were not, so Leavis claimed, primarily concerned with pure literary judgement but with judgements about life and thus led "constantly outside themselves" (1979a: 35).[8] But besides its intellectual function, the English School also had a structural function. It would order the university around a centre and thus create a hierarchy as the English School would become a university within the university.

Eric Ashby and technological humanism

In contrast to Leavis, Eric Ashby, who was a botanist by training, was one of the most prominent advocates of science and technology. Instead of making the study of literature the centre of the university as Leavis suggested, Ashby's *Technology and the Academics* (1958) argued for a university in which science and technology would play a prominent role. Still, Ashby was no supporter of the manpower doctrine. What he proposed instead was a new humanism for a university in a technological age.

According to Ashby, the universities were still rather ambiguous in their attitude towards technology and had not fully adapted to the scientific revolution

(1958: 66). Although a large number of students actually studied technology, it had "not been assimilated into the ethos of the university" (1958: 66). This did not mean that the universities were not supplying enough technologists or that Ashby thought that their only job was to produce manpower. Indeed, he warned of the danger that the universities might respond "so readily and so efficiently" to the demand for manpower that they would "run the risk of self-disintegration through too facile an adaptation to tomorrow's world" (1958: 88). Hence, Ashby, though he promoted science and technology, by no means subscribed to the manpower doctrine. What he argued for instead was a new idea of the university, in which technology would "become the core of a new twentieth-century humanism" (1958: 85).

In order to establish such a new humanism, the universities, according to Ashby, should abolish the false antithesis between science and humanism and the equally false antithesis between liberal and specialised education (1958: 75–8). While Ashby was in general sympathetic to any attempts which tried to counteract overspecialisation such as broad first year courses or the German *studium generale*, he thought that these models, despite their merits, were still based on the antithesis between liberal and specialised education. What was needed, he claimed, was to "use specialist studies as the vehicle for a liberal education" (1958: 81). Specialist studies should be the core around which relevant liberal studies would be grouped. To illustrate what this might mean in practice, Ashby provided an example for the study of brewing. The study of brewing would not only naturally lead to the study of biology, microbiology, and chemistry, but

> the student could be made interested in the economics of marketing beer, in public houses, in their design, in architecture; or in the history of beer-drinking from the time of the early Egyptian inscriptions, and so in social history; or, in the unhappy moral effects of drinking too much beer, and so in religion and ethics. A student who can weave his technology into the fabric of society can claim to have a liberal education; a student who cannot weave his technology into the fabric of society cannot claim even to be a good technologist.
>
> (1958: 84–5)

This ideal of a technological humanism was rather far removed from writers like Leavis but also from the manpower doctrine.

In contrast to the manpower doctrine, Ashby emphasised that the universities also had a critical function in society. As he claimed, there was "an ambivalence in the position of a university", which had to fulfil and adapt to social needs and yet "must from time to time threaten the stability of society" (1958: 92). Ashby's strongest resistance to the manpower doctrine, however, concerned the way it conceptualised the student:

> It is the unforgivable sin to introduce the concept of man-power into education. For centuries universities have been concerned with individual men, not man-power. [. . .] Universities must be firm even with their friends, in rejecting any implication that they are concerned with man-power. They are not. They are concerned with individual men.
>
> (1958: 92)

As much as Ashby promoted science and technology and hence challenged writers such as Leavis, he sided with them in their rejection of the manpower doctrine, not only because the manpower doctrine had a limited view of the university's function but also because it had an inadequate concept of the student.

The idea of the university and the manpower doctrine

The writers discussed above all put forth rather different ideas of the universities. But as much as the views of Truscot, Moberly, Leavis, Oakeshott, and Ashby differed, there was one common denominator: they all opposed a purely utilitarian understanding of the university as a means of manpower production. All of them formulated ideas of the university structured around nodal points other than 'standard of living' and 'economy'. These included amongst others 'knowledge for its own sake' in the case of Truscot, 'moral values' in the case of Moberly, 'learning for its own sake' in the case of Oakeshott, or 'tradition' and 'culture' in the case of Leavis. And also Ashby, who much more than other writers asserted that the universities needed to adapt to the scientific and technological revolution, argued for a new humanism quite in opposition to the manpower doctrine.[9] While these writers varied in how much they rejected the notion that the university primarily had to train students for a future career, they all agreed that a university education was about more than that.

With this claim, these writers were not alone. Other writers of the time likewise argued that the university should not only produce graduates fit for a job but should provide them with "width of outlook, some tolerance for the divergent interest of their fellow men, and an attitude to life which is permeated by a habit of intellectual honesty" (Mountford 1948: 369), "culture and understanding" (Trevelyan 1948: 480), or "character and personality" (Fulton 1962: 61), and also the UGC stated that while "[n]o university of the future can escape the duty of furnishing the majority of its students with a type of training to some extent specifically related to their future careers", it would "fail of its essential purpose if it did not, by some means or other, contrive to combine its vocational functions with the provision of a broad humanistic culture and a suitably tough intellectual discipline" (1948: 60).

The opposition to the manpower doctrine was not only a question of different values and aims, but it was inextricably linked to issues of power. While the hegemony of the universities was not challenged until the 1960s (Salter and Tapper 2000: 67), the writing was already on the wall with the state providing for more than half of the funding of the universities and calling for a greater focus on manpower production. Accordingly, Moberly warned that the increasing financial dependence on the state would give the government "an irresistible weapon for establishing control of university policy" (1949: 227). In this context, the efforts to define an idea of the university can also be understood as attempts to protect the university's autonomy and its authority. But in order to establish a hegemonic discourse that could counter the manpower doctrine, it was considered vital that all of the university's members subscribed to the same idea of the university. Thus, all the attempts to define an idea of the university were also efforts to create an academic community based on shared values and aims. Precisely for that reason writers like Moberly or Leavis deplored the growing specialisation and fragmentation within the university and argued for common aims, common values, or a common centre such as the English School. Truscot repeatedly emphasised that the university was "a society with a common aim" (1951: 77). And in a way this is also indirectly true for Oakeshott, who, although rejecting the idea of a common purpose and culture, the moment he wrote about the idea of the university and distinguished between education and training, indirectly also emphasised a common idea of the university precisely as that institution that was committed to education and not training.

But what such conscious references to the university as a community actually indicate is that no such community existed at that time. This observation is nothing special to the academic community but a particular twist to any debate about 'community'. As Zygmunt Bauman has pointed out,

> [s]ince 'community' means shared understanding of the 'natural' and 'tacit' kind, it won't survive the moment in which understanding turns self-conscious [. . .]. Community can only be numb – or dead. Once it starts to praise its unique valour, wax lyrical about its pristine beauty and stick on nearby fences wordy manifestos calling its members to appreciate its wonders and telling all the others to admire them or shut up – one can be sure that the community is no more (or not yet, as the case may be).
>
> (2001: 11–2)

Similarly, Gerard Delanty argues that talking about community is both "utopian and nostalgic at the same time" and often part of a "discourse of loss and recovery" (2010: 4). This double perspective is also present in writers like Truscot, Moberly, or Leavis. They not only formulated ideas of the university for the future, but they all shared the assumption that there had been a situation in the past when the role of the university was clearer and society was less in turmoil. Though this is not equally dominant in all of these writers, again and again one can find references to a better past. Truscot, for instance, claimed that "the essential and inspiring central idea of the university is apt to be *forgotten* at Redbrick – or even never heard of" (1951: 75, emphasis added). Leavis recurrently referred to tradition and thought that "society [. . .] *had lost* intelligence, memory and moral purpose" (1979a: 23, emphasis added). Moberly believed that "[t]he whole complex of traditional belief, habit, and sentiment, on which convictions are founded, *has collapsed*" (1949: 16, emphasis added). And Oakeshott stated that "the idea of a university *in recent years* has got mixed up" (2001: 116, emphasis added). Though Moberly, Truscot, and also Leavis aimed at a reform of the university, they all assumed that something had been lost. As much as they tried to formulate ideas for the university of the future, there was always the underlying assumption that there had been better times before society and the university had fallen prey to the rise of modern utilitarian civilisation.

The opposition to the manpower doctrine was by far not the only thing that united writers like Truscot, Moberly, Leavis, and many others. Even though their particular ideas of what a university ought to be like and should achieve differed considerably, there was also a remarkable overlap in the way they conceptualised the student.

The student as agent

In contrast to the manpower doctrine, which saw the aim of higher education in producing graduates that fit in the labour market and conceived of students as a resource, writers like Moberly or Leavis were not only much more concerned with the individual student, but they also emphasised that education was a means to develop agency. Leavis, for instance, argued that university education should produce "'educated man' – the man of humane culture who is equipped to be intelligent and responsible about the problems of contemporary civilization" (1979a: 30). For Moberly, a university education should assist "students to form their own philosophies of life, so that they may not go out into the world maimed and useless" (1949: 108). And Oakeshott claimed that a university education could help students "lead a more significant life" (2001: 115). But though these writers explicitly opposed the manpower doctrine and stressed that a central aim of education was the development of agency, they also mirrored it to a certain extent.

In the writings of Truscot, for instance, one can repeatedly find statements like "we must encourage students to speak" (1951: 78) or "[w]e must try to clarify in the undergraduate's mind the concept of 'general culture' and urge upon him the adoption of a definite policy of self-education" (1951: 79). Similarly, Moberly called upon the university to "stimulate and train" students and to "impress on its students the urgency of deliberation and decision" (1949: 108). In both cases, the focus was not on the student as an agent but on what the university ought to do to the student. Of course, as the audience of Truscot and Moberly was primarily academics and those involved in policy making, it is not surprising that they focused on what needed to be done in order to enable students to become agents. And yet it is striking how little students actually figured as agents in their writings. Even in the case of Moberly, who stressed that students were to be treated as adults, the student was not very present as an agent. The same is true for Ashby and Oakeshott and in a way, also for Leavis. Though Leavis emphasised that students were "educating themselves" and that teachers were only responsible for "instruction and guidance" (1979a: 44), he did not consider to what extent students should have power over their own education and could, for instance, determine for themselves what was worth studying. The critical education that Leavis aimed for always stayed within a paternalistic structure, in which the academic defined "student needs" (1979a: 47). Sometimes he even reduced students to objects, for instance when he wrote about the "the desired student-product" (1979a: 27) – a formulation that actually mirrored the manpower doctrine.

There was thus a considerable overlap between the manpower doctrine and the academic voices as far as the agency of the student is concerned. Though the academic voices did not treat students as a resource and emphasised that education was a means to gain agency, they, similar to the manpower doctrine, did hardly consider students as agents within the university. For them, students were not agents, but only agents-to-become.

Expansion and the 'new student'

The post-war period was a time of continuous expansion with an ever increasing number of students entering higher education. While Truscot, writing in 1943, believed that 16 universities with 3,000 students on average would suffice and hence opposed demands for large-scale expansion as they were, for instance, voiced by the National Union of Students (1951: 273), the general climate was very much in favour of expansion. However, what raised concern was the type of students that expansion was believed to bring into the universities. According to Oakeshott, for instance, expansion posed a threat to the very existence of the university as it opened the universities to students who did not understand what a university was about:

> A university will have ceased to exist [. . .] when those who came to be taught come, not in search of their intellectual fortune but with a vitality so unroused or so exhausted that they wish only to be provided with a serviceable moral and intellectual outfit; when they come with no understanding of the manners of conversation but desire only a qualification for earning a living or a certificate to let them in on the exploitation of the world.
>
> (2001: 117)

For Oakeshott, this utilitarian attitude and the focus on education as a preparation for a job were clearly more prominent in the lower social classes (2001: 152). Likewise Moberly, though much less critical of expansion, also identified a change in the student intake and thought that there was a rising number of students who might be intellectually superior but who did not have "the background of culture which could once be assumed" (1949: 47). This belief that expansion opened the universities to a new type of student was not particular to Moberly or Oakeshott but rather widespread in the 1940s and 1950s. A writer in *University Quarterly*, for instance, assumed that there was a rising number of students "who from lack of ability, intellectual interest or strength of character did no good to the university" ("Notes" 1949: 13). Likewise, the UGC thought that more and more students entered the universities who were "the first of their families to receive a university education" and that these students had "an inadequate framework of general reference into which they can fit their specialised training with a sense of its relevance to the whole" (UGC 1957: §99). In all these cases, the non-traditional or 'new students' as they were later called, that is students from a socio-cultural background without a university tradition, were considered as more utilitarian in their approach to education and as less suited for the university experience than the traditional students.

While this image of the 'new student' was widely shared, reactions varied. Oakeshott, for example, argued that selection ought to be tougher (2001: 151), and J.F. Wolfenden also questioned the appropriateness of entry tests and insisted that selection for university should not be based on academic merit alone (1951: 20–1). However, for many writers the question was not how to restrict access but rather how to integrate the 'new students' into the university community.

Student life and the building of communities

According to Truscot, one of the biggest differences between Redbrick and Oxbridge was the life the student led while at university. In contrast to the Oxbridge student, who entered "a dozen new worlds each more thrilling than the last" (Truscot 1951: 32), the Redbrick student, Truscot claimed,

> goes off five mornings a week to Redbrick University exactly as he went to Back Street Council School and Drabtown Municipal School for Boys [. . .]. Exactly as at those earlier institutions, he climbs the similar flights of dirty, sordid stairs (only there are more of them), sits in a rather larger classroom of the same type and with the same grimy outlook [. . .]. Between four and five o'clock he goes home to the same sort of high tea as he has had all his life and then attempts to settle down to an evening's work, either alone in an unused sitting-room, in his unheated bedroom or, more probably, in the living-room, where Lizzie, at the same table, is wrestling with her algebra, Bertie is continually appealing to him for help with his French, and at all too frequent intervals the wireless is turned on [. . .].
>
> (Truscot 1951: 33)

To improve the situation of the Redbrick student, Truscot promoted the construction of halls of residence. Such halls would not only allow the Redbricks to recruit students from across the nation and offer students more freedom of choice as they were no longer bound to study close to home. But above all, halls would provide a surrounding that would improve the students' academic work, physical well-being, and all-round education, and make it easier for students to enter into the social life of the university (Truscot 1951: 59, 202). Similarly, Moberly claimed that one major drawback of the Redbricks was that most of their students were "not uprooted from their everyday environment" and did not have "the stimulus of a wholly fresh start in new, spacious and exhilarating surroundings" (1949: 207). What the Redbricks lacked, according to Moberly, was an environment that had a positive impact on the student. Though Moberly also recognised a number of problems with the traditional halls of residence as these could, for instance, be too pastoral in approach and were rather expensive (1949: 215–6), he agreed that halls offered more favourable studying conditions than the family home or lodgings and could be "a great humanising force" (1949: 217). Accordingly, Moberly praised the Oxbridge colleges, where "[c]ommon study has been based on common living", where the student "entered into life-membership of a society possessing a remarkable power to enlist his affection and loyalty", and where "its members regarded themselves as sons of an Alma Mater" (1949: 201). Clearly, the ideal was that students, through living together, were socialised into a community with which they eventually identified.

Such a focus on living conditions and social relationships was by no means particular to Truscot or Moberly but extremely widespread at that time. Though it was of no concern for a writer like Leavis, who wrote from a distinct Cambridge perspective, and though Oakeshott argued against halls of residence (2001: 144), the tenor of the time was that common living was an indispensable part of being a university student – despite the fact that only about a quarter of all university full-time students actually lived in halls or colleges (UGC 1957: Fig. 1). The UGC, for instance, stated in 1948 that halls were essential to the university because "the full advantages of a university education are not attainable by a student who does not spend at least part of his university career under conditions of community life" (UGC 1948: 54). The value of halls was also a recurring topic in *Universities Quarterly*. J.W.L. Adams, for instance, highlighted the intellectual and social impact of halls of residence (1948: 243). John Murray claimed that a hall provided "certain moral and social influences" and that living in a community was "an inherent part of education" (1949: 563). Cyril Bibby argued that residence would free students from the confines of their home, foster communal life, and have a positive educational influence (1953: 187–8), and Doris Thoday showed that students living in a hall were more active in university life (1957: 48). Even those who were more critical of the traditional hall, like Ashby, emphasised that it was important that students spent more time at the university and were integrated more fully into university life (1951: 150–3).

Student accommodation became such a central issue that the UGC set up a committee, chaired by W.R. Niblett, to "consider and report on the nature and importance of the role which should be played by halls of residence in the education of university students" (UGC 1957: §1). Published in 1957, the Niblett Report recommended increasing the number of halls "rapidly and considerably" (UGC 1957: §39). As the education of the student would go well beyond the actual classroom, it was considered vital that the student would "mix with his fellows and seniors under conditions which give him great encouragement to appreciate and discuss matters of the spirit and of the intellect at the highest level of which he is capable", and therefore, it was argued, the hall of residence had "a role of great importance to play" in the wider education of the student (UGC 1957: §4). According to the report, a university education could only be successful if the student lived "in civilised conditions outside his lecture hours, is a member of a social group to which he can feel loyalty, and has many personal contacts which will extend his interests" (UGC 1957: §24). Besides offering better study conditions than most students would find at home or in lodgings, halls were thus considered to have a positive educational impact on the student. They were regarded as a means of enculturation – a means to cultivate a certain habitus (Whyte 2016: 159).

This educational and socialising effect of living in a community was considered particularly vital for the 'new students'. Adams, for instance, claimed that "a large number of students inevitably come from a limited social and cultural environment" and that there was thus "a real need to bring them into contact with staff and other students of different interests and experience" (1948: 243). The Committee on the Future of the University College of Hull asserted in 1950 that halls could "compensate for the deficiencies in earlier upbringing and education" (cited in Silver and Silver 1997: 22). In other words, in contrast to the traditional student, the 'new students' needed some additional socialisation. Similarly, the UGC argued that as the number of students grew "the gap between the way of life in the home and the way of life required to foster academic progress was growing wider" (1957: §12). Coming from a background without a university tradition, the 'new students'

> may, despite the enlightened efforts of the schools, be still deeply ignorant of [the university's] real aim and nature. It may seem to them primarily a place where they as individuals will be prepared for posts. They do not see it also as a society where knowledge is advanced and a whole range of intellectual values revealed through a way of life – a society whose standards they must themselves embody if they are properly to have a university education. To accept the idea that university standards should influence their whole personality, their range of interests and their social being, requires a revolution of mind and attitude.
>
> (UGC 1957: §21)

As much as the aim was to provide means that allowed the 'new students' to succeed, this call for "a revolution of mind and attitude" has, as Brian Salter and Ted Tapper have called it, an "unconscious totalitarian flourish" to it (1994: 11).

The underlying attitude is one that Alistair Ross has described as "almost colonialist" as "the universities appeared to see their purpose as being to enculture these individuals and to foster in them the social and cultural attributes of the ruling classes" (2003b: 31–2). The question was not how the university might adapt to the 'new students' but rather how to transform these students and make them fit in. In this respect, the prime purpose of the community was "to socialise students into a moral and cultural order" (Wyatt 1977: 130) and thus to maintain a social and cultural norm through the creation of a rather homogenous student body.

Such an attempt to create a community inevitably entails what Tony Blackshaw calls "the dark side of community" (2010: 151). As much as community is about inclusion, "its companion side is always exclusion and oppression" (2010: 151). This aspect of oppression has also been stressed by Sarah Mann, who argues that the idea of community "suggest[s] a requirement to homogenise one's identity, purpose and value in order to be a member" (2005: 46). The ideal of the university as a community implies that students accept and subscribe to its values and cultures. But this internal homogenisation also depends on the exclusion of all those who do not fit. In other words, the logic of equivalence that constitutes the community requires a constitutive outside in the form of its non-members. The construction of an 'us' is only possible through the construction of a 'them'. This was already emphasised by Moberly, who deplored that Redbrick students were "not uprooted from their everyday environment" (1949: 207). In particular for students who did not come from a cultural background with values similar to those of the university, the integration into the university community was supposed to foster a disidentification with their home culture.

While writers like Truscot or Moberly considered this uprooting from the home culture as a form of liberation as it allowed the student to enter a new world, it is striking how much they ignored the problems that such an uprooting might entail. This is all the more remarkable if one considers that at roughly the same time Philip Larkin's *Jill* (1946), in which scholarship boy John Kemp struggles to find his place in Oxford, vividly portrayed the problems that working-class students encountered in an upper and upper-middle class surrounding. While *Jill* was confined to the Oxbridge experience, Richard Hoggart's widely acclaimed *The Uses of Literacy* (1957) was concerned with the problems that the working-class students encountered more generally. Though he appreciated the gains that higher education offered to these 'scholarship boys', he also pointed out the conflicts and anxieties they experienced. Actually writing about the 1930s, Hoggart argued that these students, while they were "emotionally uprooted from their class" (2009: 263), were at the same time not at home in the middle-class culture they had entered and hence stood "at the friction-point of two cultures" (2009: 264). These problems, that the uprooting from one's home culture might involve and that Hoggart so impressively depicted, were of no major relevance to writers like Truscot, Moberly, or the

UGC. As much as they considered the creation of a social community vital for the education of the student, the entirely positive attitude towards the uprooting of the 'new student' reveals their unrivalled belief in the value and superiority of middle-class culture.

Notes

1 This study uses the 1951 edition entitled *Red Brick University*. This edition consists of the 1943 original plus several chapters from *Redbrick and these Vital Days* (1945). Although the title of the book is *Red Brick University*, the spelling used within the book is Redbrick.

2 Truscot's use of the term Redbrick comprised more than the late nineteenth-century civic universities. Besides Birmingham, Liverpool, Leeds, Sheffield, Bristol, and Manchester, Truscot included Nottingham (1948, University College Nottingham 1881), and Reading (1926, University College Reading 1892). It is never clear though which role the University of London played for Truscot.

3 Though Moberly's book initiated a widespread discussion and was immensely influential and important at his time, it has been hardly ever referred to later, probably because of its outspoken Christian perspective (Halsey 1992: 45).

4 According to Moberly, the university had never been neutral as it had, for instance, reproduced a socially stratified society, nor could it ever be neutral because to refrain from discussing certain topics was always already a judgement (1949: 54–6).

5 While the American degree curriculum was divided into modules, the English universities typically offered highly specialised honours degrees which left much less room for choice, in particular since teaching and exams were separated and the three or four years of study completed with a final examination (Rothblatt 2009: 202–4).

6 *Universities Quarterly* devoted a whole issue to the discussion of Moberly's book. While M.L. Oliphant agreed with Moberly on a number of points, Lionel Elvin criticised Moberly for privileging the Christian outlook and argued that there had always been students who, no matter whether the great issues were discussed in their university courses or not, founded societies to discuss precisely these issues (1949: 31). A.E. Teale approved of many of the problems that Moberly identified but suggested that the problem was "the disproportionate attention given to intellectual growth as compared with moral and aesthetic development, and in the lack of any special provision for a clarification of the values implied in intellectual achievement" (1949: 45). There were also more hostile views. P.M.S. Blackett, for instance, claimed that the universities were in rather good shape and fulfilled their task, which was to primarily produce people fit for their job (1950: 226–36), and Lord Simon blamed Moberly for not addressing the fundamental problem which was to produce more engineers (1949: 76–9).

7 These were later republished together with several other essays as *The Voice of Liberal Learning* (edited by Timothy Fuller) in 1989 and again in 2001. In the following, all references are to the 2001 edition.

8 It is difficult to locate the sciences in Leavis's scheme, and Joe Moran even speaks of the "systematic exclusion of the sciences as representative of the technocratic, utilitarian society he deplored" (2002: 5). However, as Leavis pointed out in a later text, his emphasis on English literature was not supposed to be an affront to the sciences and other specialist studies but rather aimed at the creation of "a strong humane centre" (1979b: 3).

9 What is striking though is that while these writers attacked the utilitarian and instrumental view of education, they did by and large share the manpower doctrine's assumption that the university was of national importance. Although 'nation' was not as strong a nodal point within the ideas from within academia as it was within the manpower

doctrine, its value and organising power was largely unquestioned, and some writers even linked the idea of the university to the nation. When Leavis, for instance, emphasised the value of culture and tradition, he was primarily concerned with the tradition of English literature. Moberly saw the universities as the nation's conscience and claimed that "their basic assumptions" had to be "those of the nation" (1949: 140). These two examples as well as the fact that the other writers did not question that higher education was in a way a service to the nation, suggest that 'nation' was indeed a rather powerful nodal point that defined both the manpower doctrine and the ideas of the university that were trying to counter it.

Chapter 6

The student voice

According to Eric Ashby and Mary Anderson, students were a rather "contented lot" at the beginning of the twentieth century (1970: 51). While they complained about poor facilities and the like, they were by and large unpolitical. But though students at that time were not as politicised as they were in the 1960s, this does not mean that they were totally unconcerned about the society surrounding them. As Georgina Brewis has shown, students had for long volunteered in all kinds of social work. In the late nineteenth century, for instance, students assisted in university settlements, and in the early twentieth century, student rags became a widespread form of fund raising for charity (Brewis 2014: 22, 83).[1] A rather significant moment in the history of student volunteering was the General Strike of 1926, in which thousands of students acted as strike breakers. Though students only accounted for about a fifth of the volunteers, the General Strike had a large impact on the image of the student. As students were highly visible amongst the volunteers, they attracted considerable media attention (Brewis 2014: 74). Thus, even though not all students volunteered as strike breakers and some also sympathised with the workers, students seemed to take sides in what was essentially a class struggle and appeared as being alienated if not hostile to the working-class cause (Saltzman 1994: 117).

In the 1930s and 1940s, students became increasingly politicised. While the National Union of Students (NUS), founded in 1922, still refrained from political activities, numerous political societies, in particular communist and socialist societies, were formed, political student magazines like the left-wing *Student Vanguard*, *This Unrest*, or *Cambridge Left* were founded, and long-established student newspapers increasingly covered political topics (Schüth 2001: 22–3). One of the most publically noticeable actions of student activism at that time came from the Oxford Union, which, in 1933, passed a motion declaring that "this House will in no circumstances fight for its King and Country" (cited in Gevers and Vos 2004: 339–40). Though other unions had discussed comparable motions, the Oxford case caused a moral outrage and made NUS president Denis Follows write to every student union to encourage them to hold similar debates (Brewis 2014: 113). The politicisation of students was further spurred by international events such as Italy's invasion of Abyssinia, Hitler's rise to power, and the Spanish Civil War. In particular the latter had a huge impact as it mobilised a great number of students and established alliances between students of various political backgrounds (Brewis 2014: 123). Students volunteered as fundraisers and became politically active in 'Arms for Spain' campaigns to oppose the British government's policy of non-intervention (Brewis 2014: 125). As a result of these activities, a "corporate student consciousness" emerged, that united students across institutions (Simon 1987: 193). Hence, in 1937, the NUS changed its constitution and allowed the association of training colleges and technical colleges, and by 1945, 66 such colleges had become full members and another seven associated members (Simon 1987: 201).

A particularly significant milestone for the emergence of a common student consciousness was the British Student Congress of 1940. With over 550 student delegates, the congress attracted more participants than any other national student congress in the decades before (Schüth 2001: 105). Though the number of participants at NUS congresses actually grew in the following years, the 1940 congress was of particular relevance not only because it signified a growing corporate consciousness amongst students but also because it marked a shift in the focus of the student movement. While in earlier years, student activism had concentrated on areas outside of higher education, students now increasingly took issue with the nature and purpose of higher education. Hence, the 1940 congress not only passed resolutions that demanded political as well as economic and social equality and condemned imperialism, colonialism, and capitalism (Simon 1987: 199–200), but it also formulated a Charter of Student Rights and Responsibilities.

After emphasising that institutions of higher education should actively contribute to the establishment of a peaceful, democratic, and just society and that university education was no class privilege, the charter set out the following rights and responsibilities:

> THE RIGHT to the free expression of opinion by speech and Press. THE RIGHT to organise meetings, discussion and study on all subjects within the University and College precincts. THE RIGHT to belong to any organisation, whether cultural, political or religions. THE RIGHT to participate to the full in all activities outside the universities, and to collaborate with extra-university organisations. THE RIGHT to a share in the government and administration of the universities. Given these Rights, WE PLEDGE ourselves to fulfil our responsibilities to the community, AND CALL on all students to defend them by their united action, and all sections of the British people, for their support.
>
> (cited in Schlüth 2001: 106–7)

By claiming these rights, the charter challenged the position of the students within the institutions of higher education. Not only did it call for greater freedom for students, but it also demanded the right to partake in the government and administration of the universities.[2] Strikingly, such demands for student power had not yet been central to NUS policy in the 1930s. Indeed, it was often academics like Ramsay Muir, who, when speaking at the NUS conference of 1939, encouraged students to seek greater control of their education (Ashby and Anderson 1970: 75–6).[3] In the 1940s, however, the NUS increasingly took up such demands and began to engage with issues concerning the purpose and structure of higher education. This growing concern with higher education was given its most visible expression with Brian Simon's *A Student's View of the Universities* (1943).

A student's view

Brian Simon, who had been NUS president in 1939/40, began *A Student's View of the Universities* as an official project sponsored by and written on behalf of the NUS (Simon 1987: 202). Due to the outbreak of the war, the project was abandoned, and Simon published the book as a personal statement on the current situation and future development of higher education.[4]

In contrast to writers like Oakeshott, Simon's starting point was not an abstract ideal of the university. Instead, he was concerned with the function of higher education in the reproduction of society. By tracing the history of the universities, selection processes, and employment patterns, Simon demonstrated how strongly the function and organisation of the universities was intertwined with the structure of society and how universities reproduced social inequalities. Hence, he considered a reform of the universities a necessary means for the overall transformation of society and demanded that the universities were "consciously contributing to the rational progress of society" (Simon 1943: 11). Instead of being detached from society, the universities, according Simon, ought to be at the centre of society and lead it towards a better future.

This ultimate aim of social reform was nowhere better expressed than in the concluding passages of *A Student's View of the Universities*. Written in the style of a manifesto, Simon declared that

> the universities, and all that they stand for, can only reach full stature when there is social control over production and distribution, and the progress of society is planned in the interests of the whole people. Under such conditions the universities will draw to themselves the best of the nation's youth, for equality of opportunity will be a reality and no longer a phrase. Apart from training them as efficiently as possible for their jobs, they will equip them with the knowledge and the social and scientific understanding necessary if they are to be acutely aware of the problems facing society, to realize the necessity for action, and to apply their talents in the service of the community.
>
> (1943: 141).

According to Simon, socialism was thus the precondition for the realisation of equality of opportunity and the full flourishing of the universities, which should not only train students for their job but contribute to the improvement of society.

As much as Simon's radical egalitarian and socialist ideal of the universities countered both the 'liberal' idea of education and the manpower doctrine, it actually took up most of the nodal points that organised these ideas. These were, however, reframed within a discourse structured by the two major nodal points: 'the people' and 'equality of opportunity'. Hence, knowledge, technology, and science, he claimed, ought be "used in the interests of the people to raise the standard of living" (1943: 13). Moreover, universities were there for "the development of human personality" and should be "centres of a vital and creative culture [. . .], closely linked with the daily activities and problems, and essentially, therefore, at the disposal of the people" (1943: 141–2). More than with any other writer so far, Simon saw the task of the university in working for the good of the whole people and in bringing about a more socially just society.

In order to achieve these aims, Simon came up with a number of concrete proposals, which supposedly represented the view of the NUS. These contained, amongst others, a reform of university curricula to include more political debates and to emphasise the relation between the studied subject and wider society, a reform of the entrance regulations to universities and colleges, the abolition of fees plus the introduction of maintenance grants for all students, a reform of teaching methods to allow for more discussion and to develop the student's critical faculties, a reform of the examination system, the abolition of the hierarchy and division between universities and technical and training colleges, complete freedom of discussion, and the improvement of student welfare (1943: 128–37).

In retrospect, the most significant proposal was probably to radically open access to higher education. According to Simon, the only criterion upon which access to higher education was granted ought to be "the fitness of the student to benefit from this particular type of education" (1943: 129). This demand was actually shared by the NUS, which had argued since 1938 that "[a]ll people qualified and able to benefit from a course of higher education should be able to do so" (cited in Ashby and Anderson 1970: 102). Students thus called for more equal access well before this became policy in the 1960s. A reform of access criteria was, however, not considered sufficient in order to ensure that all people who were fit enough were actually able to benefit from higher education. It was, so Simon argued, also necessary to institute means that allowed everybody to take equal advantage of higher education irrespective of socio-economic background. Thus, Simon called for the abolition of student fees and the introduction of maintenance grants for all students including part-time students and students in further education in order to enable students from less well-off backgrounds to enter higher education (1943: 129).

As progressive and radical as Simon's proposals were, there was also one striking overlap with writers like Truscot, Moberly, and many others of the time. One of Simon's demand was to drastically reduce costs of residence because "hostels are undoubtedly of value in the social and intellectual life of the university community" (1943: 138). Though not speaking of halls but of hostels, Simon still claimed that universities should be communities and that common living played a vital role in the education of the student. This emphasis on the value of residence and the building of communities is highly relevant as it indicates how dominant the ideal of the university as a social and intellectual community was in the 1940s. The community ideal was not only subscribed to by writers like Truscot or the UGC but also by Simon and the NUS. And yet, though Simon endorsed the ideal of the university as a community, he also departed from it to a certain extent. In contrast to Truscot, Simon saw the university less as a community detached from the outside world. Indeed, he emphatically wrote about moments when the difference between students and non-students had been overcome. Thus, he highlighted how the war effort had "broken down the old traditions of academic isolation" (1943: 121). Though this does not mean that Simon radically wanted to abolish any difference between students and other young people, he clearly welcomed moments when this difference was reduced.[5]

The emphasis on the social life of the student is not the only aspect in which Simon mirrored other writers of the 1940s and 1950s. One of the central issues of the 1940s and 1950s was the expansion of higher education and the supposedly rising number of students from a lower-middle and working-class background. This was also of concern to Simon. Similar to other writers of his time, Simon also thought that students from a lower socio-economic background were rather utilitarian and primarily considered education as a means to enter a particular career. However, while others were focussing on the question how to integrate or exclude these students, Simon was much more concerned with the question from where this different outlook derived. As he compared the social set-up of the student body at Oxbridge and Redbrick, their motivations, and chosen courses of study, he observed that the number of arts students was much higher at Oxbridge than at Redbrick. This unevenness, he argued, was actually the result of the students' unequal economic positions. While many of the Oxbridge students were in such a privileged position that there was "no direct relation between their actual syllabus at the university and their future careers" (1943: 48), quite the opposite was the case for the Redbrick students, who, if they wanted to secure their future, had to choose a subject that was "related to a definite career" and had to direct all their work to this end (1943: 49). Like other writers of his time, Simon thus identified the lower-middle and working-class student as utilitarian, but he emphasised that this utilitarian ethos was the result of specific material conditions.

Last but not least, Simon challenged the position of the student in terms of power. Not only did he demand "complete freedom of discussion, organization, and publicity" (1943: 138), but also that students should be given greater control of their life and be, for instance, represented on all hostel committees (1943: 138). Apart from these rather specific demands, it is striking that, in comparison to the academic voices of the 1940s and 1950s, Simon time and again emphasised that students were active agents in the war effort and that they could also act as agents within the university either

> by expressing a point of view with a united voice, and attempting by negotiations, publicity, and other means to have it accepted by the authorities; [or] by directing day-to-day activity into such progressive channels that they themselves increase the scope and effectiveness of the universities.
>
> (1943: 121)

Quite in contrast to both the manpower doctrine, which denied students any agency, as well as the academic voices, which considered students as agents-to-become, Simon highlighted that students already were agents. But probably the most important aspect with regard to student agency was the publication of Simon's book itself. Although it never reached the publicity of Truscot's *Red Brick University*, it was published by a commercial publisher. What the book thus showed to a wider audience was that students actually had a voice.

Notes

1 University settlements were establishments in poorer urban areas where 'educated men' lived and worked. The most famous university settlement is probably Toynbee Hall, which is located in Whitechapel and opened in 1884. In the following years, the number of such settlements as well as missions greatly increased. By 1911, 45 settlements and missions existed throughout the UK (Brewis 2014: 22–5).

2 Though many charters of universities such as Birmingham, Liverpool, Leeds, or Sheffield already included some form of student participation in university government, this was neither the case in all universities nor did it involve much actual power (Ashby and Anderson 1970: 50).

3 Similarly, Sir Bernard Pares declared at the NUS congress in 1938: "It might be no bad thing for students to approach the University authorities with the motto used by Mansbridge of the W.E.A.: 'This is what we workers want to learn – it's for you to teach how to learn it.'" (cited in Ashby and Anderson 1970: 75)

4 Though Simon predominantly used the term 'universities', he rather followed the understanding of the NUS at that time and included training colleges. Indeed, Simon argued for the abolition of the hierarchy that existed between the universities and the training colleges (1943: 135).

5 The NUS also considered it vital to bridge the gap between the university and the outside world. Thus, they suggested that prospective students do a year of social service before entering university. As this idea was rejected by many students, the NUS rather focused on expanding access for students from a wider range of social backgrounds (Brewis 2014: 153).

Part II

Breaking the ivory tower

Chapter 7

Higher education and the welfare state

While the governments of the 1940s and 1950s had largely refrained from tackling higher education, the situation fundamentally changed in the 1960s. Increasingly, the government attempted to steer the future development of higher education and to exercise greater control. Hence, the UGC, which since its foundation had been directly responsible to the Treasury, was transferred to the newly established Department of Education and Science in 1964 (Scott 2007: 61), and in 1967, the universities had to open their books to the Comptroller and Auditor-General (Salter and Tapper 1994: 42). The universities were thus gradually integrated into the wider educational system and became objects of parliamentary scrutiny. The landmark of this development was the appointment of the Robbins Committee, which conducted the biggest investigation into the state of higher education that Britain had seen so far and which reported in 1963.

But the Robbins Report was by far not the only significant report of the 1960s. Three years prior to the Robbins Report, the Anderson Committee published its recommendations for the reform of student maintenance grants. Though often ignored, the Anderson Report (1960) and the following reform of the grant system mark one of the most important steps in the history of British higher education, in particular for students.

The Anderson report

Set up to "consider the present system of awards from public funds to students attending first degree courses at university and comparable courses at other institutions and to make recommendations" (Ministry of Education 1960: §1), the Anderson Committee recommended replacing the existing and rather uncoordinated grant and scholarship arrangements with a coordinated national system in which the state paid fees for home students and supported them with means-tested maintenance grants (Tapper 2005: 202). The importance of this recommendation and the subsequent Education Act 1962 can hardly be underestimated. Although Malcolm Tight argues that the report "was only recognizing and regularizing long-established trends" as about 83 percent of students already received awards from public funds (2009: 66), the grant system as recommended by the Anderson Report was a major development. Whereas before, students had to apply for grants and could not rely on being awarded one, the new grant system meant that access to higher education made students automatically eligible for funding. Although the grant was means-tested against parental income, higher education was now effectively free for most students (Anderson 2006: 139), and the idea of a ladder to be climbed by individual scholarship students was abandoned. Moreover, the introduction of universal maintenance grants had a major impact on student life. While the number of students studying away from home had already risen in the 1950s (UGC 1957: §13), the introduction of universal grants encouraged this tendency. Increasingly, leaving home and living an independent life became an integral part of being a student (Beloff 1970: 29).

Though the Anderson Committee was primarily appointed in order to solve the problems of the current grant system and to make administrative procedures more efficient,[1] the introduction of universal grants was about more than that. The grants were also supposed to serve a number of educational ideals. First of all, they were a means to foster expansion and equality. Even though the Anderson Report argued against free education without parental contribution as this would "make cheap what should be held valuable" (Ministry of Education 1960: §183) and warned that university education should not be understood as "a kind of national service to which all good students must aspire" (Ministry of Education 1960: §184), it in general approved of the expansion of higher education. Hence, grants were said to be vital in order to "ensure that those qualified to take advantage of these costly facilities are not deterred from doing so" (Ministry of Education 1960: §168). Grants were considered as a means to foster equality by guaranteeing that access to the universities did not depend on the financial background of the prospective student.[2]

The Anderson Committee also took issue with the purpose of university education. Though it recognised that there was a "shortage of particular categories such as mathematicians, engineers, scientists and teachers in these fields", it rejected the idea that the prime function of a university education was to supply the nation with manpower. Instead, it emphasised that "the nation should not depart from the ancient and sound tradition that young men and women go to the university to become all-round citizens and not merely to learn a special skill" (Ministry of Education 1960: §12). This adherence to the values of liberal education was complemented by another well-established university ideal: the university as an academic community. According to the Anderson Report,

> much of the value of higher education lies not only in the instruction the student receives but also in the contacts he makes and the life he leads within the student community outside the lecture room and the laboratory.
> (Ministry of Education 1960: §20)

At this point, the Anderson Report clearly tied in with an ideal well known from Moberly, Truscot, and the halls of residence movement. But in contrast to these writers, the Anderson Report did not argue for a homogeneous student body. Instead, it very much endorsed heterogeneity and claimed that universal grants allowed students from various backgrounds to enter higher education. This heterogeneity of the student body was regarded as being of educational value because "[t]o get the full benefit, it is important that the student body at a university or other institution of higher education should not be drawn from too narrow a field; it will gain richness from a wider one" (Ministry of Education 1960: §20). However, the report's ideal of a heterogeneous community was not without its paradoxes as grants could not only foster heterogeneity but also homogeneity. Maintenance grants not only allowed students from different socio-economic backgrounds to enter higher education and mix, but they also encouraged students to leave their homes and move elsewhere.[3] This principle of delocation, as John Carswell calls it, meant that the student might indeed leave a rather diverse community in order to enter one which was rather homogeneous consisting of people "similar in age, attainments and aspirations" (1988: 26). In this respect, the Anderson Report, while considering it worthwhile to bring students from different social backgrounds together, indirectly supported the ideal of a homogeneous and homogenising community cut off from the wider society.

While the report in many ways emphasised well-established ideals of 'liberal' education with its focus on 'all-round citizens' and 'community' and coupled them with a greater emphasis on 'equality', it also introduced a new concept that had not featured strongly in the debate so far. A central argument in the report was that a universal grant system would allow students to choose their higher education institution more freely as it removed financial constraints (Ministry of Education 1960: §17).[4] While 'freedom of choice' had already been an issue for Truscot, who argued that the building of halls would allow students to study somewhere away from home and hence offer "real freedom of choice" (1951: 59), the student's 'freedom of choice' had not been central in the debate so far. In the Anderson Report, however, it became a major nodal point. Instead of considering students primarily as objects or as agents-to-become, the report thus recognised that students also were agents who made choices, and in order for them to be able to exercise this choice, the state had the responsibility to provide the sufficient financial means. In this respect, the Anderson Report gave the student a much more central position – a direction that the Robbins Report continued.

The Robbins report

In 1963, the so far biggest review of higher education was published under the title *Higher Education: Report of the Committee appointed by the Prime Minister under the Chairmanship of Lord Robbins, 1961–63*, commonly known as the

Robbins Report. The reasons for setting up the Robbins Committee were manifold. Due to the Butler Education Act of 1944, the after-war birth bulge, and the growing trend to stay on at school into sixth form, an increasing number of pupils achieved the minimum entrance qualifications for higher education. But even though the number of qualified school leavers was rising, Britain was still lagging behind other developed countries as far as the provision of higher education was concerned and had no coherent system of higher education (Sanderson 1998: 380–1; Tight 2009: 66). Thus, the Robbins Committee was set up "to review the pattern of full-time higher education in Great Britain and in the light of national needs and resources to advise Her Majesty's Government on what principles its long-term development should be based" (Committee on Higher Education 1963: §1). In its final report, the committee recommended the further expansion of higher education, the creation of a Council for National Academic Awards, the granting of university status to the CATs, the foundation of six entirely new universities, the establishment of several Special Institutions for Scientific and Technological Education and Research out of existing colleges and universities, and the alignment of the teacher training colleges to the universities and hence the UGC – the last three of these recommendations were never realised though.

The most important recommendation of the whole report was that higher education should further expand from 216,000 full-time students in higher education in 1962/63 to 558,000 in 1980/81 (Committee on Higher Education 1963: Table 30). Though student numbers had already been rising for decades, this recommendation made the Robbins Report the landmark of the post-war expansion of higher education. The main significance of the report lay, however, not in its support for further expansion, but in the way this expansion was argued for. Although the report also took manpower demands into account and considered expansion vital for economic growth and for the defence of Britain's position in the world (1963: §32), the proposed increase in places was primarily justified on other grounds. As the report made clear, its guiding principle was that "courses of higher education should be available to all those who are qualified by ability and attainment to pursue them and who wish to do so" (1963: §31). This principle, which is commonly referred to as the Robbins Principle, established a kind of right to higher education as it claimed that everybody who had shown him or herself "qualified by ability and attainment" ought to be granted access to higher education. In order to determine whether someone was indeed qualified, the report proposed that in the future the "assessment of performance" should receive more attention next to "the usual estimate of character and general intelligence" (1963: §229) and that school records as well as aptitude tests should gain a greater relevance for the selection of students (1963: §233).[5]

The Robbins Principle was not only fundamental because it argued for expansion and established higher education as a right for all those qualified, but because it put the student in a central position. If higher education was open "to all those who are qualified [. . .] and who wish to do so" (Committee on Higher Education 1963: §31), it inevitably followed that higher education had to expand if more qualified school leavers wished to enter. Though the report also considered manpower demands and claimed that, if productivity was supposed to rise further, the expansion of higher education was necessary (1963: §192), the main argument was that the state had an obligation to provide for equal opportunities and that expansion should thus follow demand 'from below'. Hence, one of the report's main concerns was to project the number of qualified and willing school leavers (1963: §133–4). Even though the Robbins Report did not really touch upon the power of the universities and colleges to control admission standards (Tapper 2007: 210), the rationale underlying the arguments for expansion was student-centred. Similar to the Anderson Report, which emphasised the students' freedom to choose between different universities, the Robbins Report also granted students a more central role. This rather progressive outlook was, however, complemented by more traditional ideas of the student, which come particularly to the fore when having a look at how the report defined the aims of higher education.

According to the Robbins Report, higher education had four central objectives: the "instruction in skills suitable to play a part in the general division of labour" (Committee on Higher Education 1963: §25),[6] the promotion of "the general powers of the mind" and the production of "not mere specialists but rather cultivated men and women" (1963: §26), "the advancement of learning" and "the search for truth" (1963: §27), and, last but not least, "the transmission of a common culture and common standards of citizenship" (1963: §28). However, these aims were not really reflected in the actual report and remained, as W.R. Niblett described it, "enveloped in an English mist" (1981: 9). There was, for instance, no chapter dealing especially with the research function of higher education, and also the division of labour was not very central. But though these four aims were hardly reflected in the report, they have been prominent in the debate on higher education ever since and were, for example, taken up in the Dearing Report (1997), the second major investigation into higher education in the twentieth century.

With regard to the student, it is actually the fourth objective that is the most interesting. While the report pointed out that "the transmission of a common culture and common standards of citizenship" did "not mean the forcing of all individuality into a common mould" (Committee on Higher Education 1963: §28), this aim clearly situated the report in the English tradition of liberal education with its focus on the education of 'round men' and the transmission of culture. Similar to Truscot, Moberly, and many other writers of the 1940s and 1950s, the Robbins Report emphasised that the transmission of culture was not only a result of what was taught but also a product of "the atmosphere of the institutions in which the students live and work" (1963: §28). As the report later explained, institutions of higher education were "not merely places of instruction" but "communities" (1963: §585). Accordingly, the Robbins Report favourably commented on the collegiate system of Oxford and Cambridge as it united "senior and junior members in a common way of life" (1963: §585). While the report pointed out that it did "not wish to see closed academic communities with staff and students forming a kind of world within the world" (1963: §586), it adhered to the ideal of the academic community based on a common way of life.[7] Thus, it recommended that the proportion of students living in residential accommodation provided by the universities should rise from 32 percent in 1961 to 54 percent in 1980 (1963: §594). Though the Robbins Report recognised that to some students the traditional halls of residence "may seem unduly restrictive" (1963: §591), it emphasised that these halls could offer a "sense of real community" (1963: §591). If students still decided to live in self-contained student flats or were accommodated in study-bedroom blocks, they at least needed, the report argued, "facilities for social life" such as "common rooms, reading rooms, rooms for debate and play-reading, facilities for games, music and acting, and good refectories" (1963: §591). Moreover, the report recommended assigning each new student to a tutor, who would offer "regular personal guidance" (1963: §570), and it suggested that teachers should live close by in order to enable social intercourse between students and teachers that stretched beyond the teaching hours (1963: §586). With such a strong emphasis on the building of communities, social intercourse between teachers and students, and close personal relations, the Robbins Report clearly subscribed to an understanding of higher education and the student that had been typical of writers like Moberly and many others and that had also been endorsed by the UGC.

This belief in the value of traditional university culture also shaped many other aspects of the Robbins Report. While the report was the first major government investigation of higher education and hence "marked a break with the traditional defence of the university sector and its autonomy" (King and Nash 2001: 196–7), the report not only championed the autonomy and status of the universities, but it also refrained from considering whether in an expanded system a different form of higher education might be needed. Although it made a few proposals concerning reformed courses and course structures, no fundamental changes to the nature of higher education were proposed. The idea of the Robbins Report was to provide more higher education, but ultimately it would be "more of the same" (Barnett 1999: 303). In this respect, one can only agree with Michael Rustin, according to whom the Robbins Report's ideal of higher education had the "definitive charter of the bourgeois university" (1986: 39).[8] The report was "a paradoxical mixture of radicalism and traditionalism" as it questioned the exclusiveness of higher education but did not challenge its values (Hampson 1979: 137). In a way, this adherence to traditional values was already present in the report's terms of reference, which exclusively focused on full-time students. Although part-time education had quite a great share in the provision of higher education, it was simply not considered as relevant as full-time education at that time (Carswell 1988). The Robbins Report fully subscribed to this dominant ideal of the full-time student. Nowhere was it suggested that the provision of higher education should move away from the traditional image of the young full-time student.

The report not only adhered to the ideal of the full-time student, it also endorsed a rather traditional and normative image of the student in several other respects. When discussing the fourth aim of higher education – the transmission of a common culture – the Robbins Report explained that

> [t]his function, important at all times, is perhaps especially important in an age that has set for itself the ideal of equality of opportunity. It is not merely by providing places for students from all classes that this ideal will be achieved, but also by providing, in the atmosphere of the institutions in which the students live and work, influences that in some measure compensate for any inequalities of home background.
>
> (Committee on Higher Education 1963: §28)

Hence, the transmission of a common culture was supposed to be particularly important for those students who came from lower classes without a tradition of higher education. Though the transmission of culture was considered a means to achieve equality of opportunity, this was based on a rather normative understanding of culture and the student. As a formulation like "compensate for any inequalities of home background" shows, the cultural background of the 'new student' was not valued in its own right but viewed in negative terms. This normative attitude was even more present when the report discussed the importance of close personal relations between students and academics:

> In the educational revolution that we are living through, there is a special and mounting problem of large numbers of young people coming up to the university without a background of higher education and culture in their homes.
>
> (Committee on Higher Education 1963: §570)

Rather tellingly, the Robbins Report did not describe the 'new student' as a student with a different cultural background, but as a student "*without* a background of [...] culture" (emphasis added). In this respect, the report unmistakeably defended a high cultural position and conceptualised the 'new student' as the traditional student's weaker Other. Behind the aim to transmit a common culture, there was thus a strongly normative image of the student. The 'new student' was supposed to be integrated into the norm. That the norm itself might change was not considered.

Higher education as a welfare service?

Though the Anderson and Robbins reports in many respects only recognised developments that were already under way, they were so central for the debate on higher education because they were the fullest expression of the idea that higher education was not a privilege of the wealthy but rather a right and that the state had the obligation to provide for it. In other words, higher education became part of the British welfare state. However, in contrast to the National Health Service or secondary education, higher education was not a universal right but open only to those qualified, which raises the question to what extent higher education can indeed be said to have become part of the welfare state.

According to Asa Briggs, a welfare state can be defined as a state that uses its power "to modify the play of market forces" by guaranteeing a minimal income, by providing protection in the case of "social contingencies" such as sickness, old age, or unemployment, and by ensuring that all people "without distinction of status or class are offered the best standards available in relation to a certain agreed range of social services" (1961: 228).[9] While it is clear from this definition that social services like unemployment benefit or pensions are part of the welfare state, it is left open whether education is included – whether it is part of the "agreed range of services" – or not. In the British case, education was clearly one of the pillars of the welfare state as it was established following the Beveridge Report (1942). Though the Beveridge Report itself did not make detailed recommendations concerning the education sector, it was actually tackled first with the Butler Education Act (1944). The reforms, however, stopped with secondary education, and higher education seems to have fallen out of the welfare state package at that time.

Although the introduction of means-tested grants following the Anderson Report was not a welfare service in the strict sense as it only applied to students, it was still similar to other welfare measures that tried to compensate for financial inequalities in order to establish positive liberty.[10] The grants that the Anderson Report recommended were supposed to ensure that no potential student was deterred from entering higher education because of financial constraints and that every student could exercise freedom of choice. While the Anderson Report focused on financial support to students, the Robbins Report established higher education as a right for all those qualified by ability and attainment. Although it did not directly speak of higher education as a right, the Robbins Report considered the expansion of higher education in terms of justice. Referring to the birth bulge, it argued, for instance, that "it would be gravely unjust that, simply because so many were born at the same time, a smaller proportion of those qualified should receive higher education than in the age groups coming immediately before or after them" (Committee on Higher Education 1963: §810). Hence, to establish justice and equality, the Robbins Principle suggested access to higher education to be based on meritocratic principles – an ideal which itself was increasingly attacked in the 1960s.

While Michael Young's dystopian satire *The Rise of the Meritocracy 1870–2033* (1958) levelled a far-reaching critique at the very idea of a meritocracy, many on the Left did not attack meritocratic ideas in general but rather the class bias that characterised the education system as established after 1944. From the 1950s onwards, it had become clear that universal access to secondary education with early selection based on merit had not abandoned class bias. Accordingly, future Education Secretary Anthony Crosland argued for a fundamental reform of the education system because

> measured intelligence is not a purely innate characteristic; it is at least partly an acquired one. With this knowledge, the whole discussion of 'equal opportunity' takes on a new aspect. [. . .] For measured intelligence at 11 or 18 is not a fixed quantity, but is partly a function of opportunities in earlier life. The 'strong' definition [of equal opportunity] is therefore that, granted the differences in heredity and infantile experience, every child should have the same opportunity for acquiring measured intelligence, so far as this can be controlled by social action.
>
> (1962: 172–3)

Following this argument, selection at the age of 11 was increasingly abandoned and comprehensive schools were established – a development that was not only driven forward by the central government but also by most LEAs, which already had plans for comprehensives ready even before these were requested by Crosland in 1965 (Tomlinson 2005: 20). It is within this context of the debate on equality and the reform of the school sector that the Robbins Report needs to be located.

The Robbins Report took up this debate when it attacked the idea of a fixed 'pool of ability', that is the idea that the number of people who could benefit from higher education was not only limited but also did not vary much over time. Through massive statistical evidence, the Robbins Report showed that there was a class bias in education that was not the result of varying innate abilities but of an educational system that left behind great "reserves of untapped ability" (Committee on Higher Education 1963: §142). While the report did not deny that human beings varied "considerably in native capacity", it argued that the idea that one could "determine an upper limit to the number of people who could benefit from higher education" was "highly misleading" (1963: §137). As educational performance also depended on nurture and hence the number of people qualified for higher education would rise from generation to generation, the report concluded that

> [i]f there is to be talk of a pool of ability, it must be of a pool which surpasses the widow's cruse in the Old Testament, in that when more is taken for higher education in one generation more will tend to be available in the next.
>
> (Committee on Higher Education 1963: §146)

Hence, the Robbins Report to a certain extent tackled questions of nurture and identified the problems inherent in the existing educational system. However, it did not offer any solutions to the situation other than making access to higher education meritocratic. This, however, fit a particular pattern. As A.H. Halsey has pointed out, "the comprehensive principle tends to become sovereign in any given stage of education only when expansion has taken place in the next" (1973: 206). While in the 1940s the Butler Education Act (1944) established a meritocratic and selective secondary school system on top of a mostly comprehensive primary school system, the whole system moved one step further in the 1960s as the Robbins Report argued for expansion and access to higher education based on merit at a time when secondary education became increasingly comprehensive.

With this partial inclusion of higher education into the welfare state, the position of the student shifted. As higher education was framed in a discourse structured around the nodal point 'equality', the student was to some extent recognised as an agent. Even though the Anderson and Robbins reports in many respects subscribed to a rather traditional image of the student with their focus on full-time education and middle-class culture, they positioned the student no longer just as an object or an agent-to-become but also as an agent within the system of higher education.

Notes

1 There were a number of problems with the old grant system. Thus, students had to wait for the decision on the grant before they could accept the offered place at a university, common standards were lacking, and the grant system actually imposed a second process of selection (Ministry of Education 1960: §16, §36, §45).
2 With respect to the discussions about student loans in the 1980s and later, it is interesting to see that the Anderson Report rejected loans because "[t]he obligation to repay, no matter how easy the terms, must represent an untimely burden at the outset of a career" (Ministry of Education 1960: §24). The same argument was shared by the Robbins Report (Committee on Higher Education 1963: §647).
3 One effect of the growing percentage of students leaving their homes was an accommodation crisis in the 1970s and 1980s with students at times housed, at least temporarily, in gymnasia or libraries (Silver and Silver 1997: 23).
4 The greater freedom of choice for students had a major impact on the universities as the civics, for instance, were no longer bound to their local clientele but could now become national institutions like Oxbridge or London (Anderson 2006: 141). At the same time, the new campus universities of the 1960s were able to establish themselves as national institutions right from the start. At the newly founded University of East Anglia, for example, only 4 per cent of the students came from the region in the early 1970s (Anderson 2006: 138–9).
5 As a further move towards a meritocratic system of higher education, the Robbins Report stressed the role of a central clearing house and recommended the extension of the recently established Universities Central Council on Admissions (UCCA) to cover all universities including Oxbridge (Committee on Higher Education 1963: §227).
6 Although this aim, which linked the Robbins Report to the manpower doctrine and service tradition, was mentioned first, it was not very prominent in the whole report. Though the report favoured a strong sector of technical education, for instance by granting the CATs university status or through the creation of special institutions focussing on science and technology (Committee on Higher Education 1963: recommendations

51, 56), questions of manpower were not central. Indeed, as the report pointed out, this objective was not mentioned first because it was the most important but because it was sometimes "ignored or undervalued" (1963: §25).

7 The Robbins Report also considered the maximum size of institutions of higher education. For universities, a size of 8,000 to 10,000 students was seen as appropriate. A bigger university might run the danger, it was argued, that "both teachers and students feel lost in it" (Committee on Higher Education 1963: §471).

8 The same concern was expressed by Eric Ashby, who argued that the Robbins Report while being concerned with expansion and opening access had "comparatively little to say about whether the system should change and what is to be its function in the society of tomorrow" (1973: 142). Likewise, E.J. Richards criticised that the Robbins Committee had not considered that higher education might "move away one iota from their accepted pattern of three-year courses for 18 year old school-leavers [. . .]. At no point did they suggest that this was only one of the many educational frameworks which might be needed in the future [. . .]." (1975: 5)

9 There has been a debate about whether one should understand welfare services as citizen rights. This understanding of the welfare state was proposed by T.H. Marshall in 1950, who considered the welfare state to be the continuation of the expansion of citizen rights from civic and political rights like the right to vote to social rights in the form of services which are based on citizenship alone (Stephens 2012: 511). Glennerster, however, argues that the welfare state as such cannot be understood as a number of citizen rights in the strict sense since insurance benefits for the unemployed, the sick, and pensioners depended on contributions and not on citizen rights (1999: 15–6).

10 In contrast to negative liberty, which is the absence of interference from others, positive liberty refers to the individual's capacity for self-development. Underlying the idea of the welfare state is the claim that the state ought to provide resources that are considered necessary in order to exercise positive liberty (White 2012: 28).

Chapter 8

Barbarians at the gates

The expansion of higher education was not applauded by everyone. While critical voices could already be found in the 1940s and 1950s, these became much louder in the following years. The most famous attack on expansion was made by Kingsley Amis, who felt the need to speak out against those "who are playing the university numbers racket" (1960: 8). Not having a "little tape-and-loudspeaker arrangement" at hand, he was compelled to use capital letters to tell his readers that expansion was no good because eventually "MORE WILL MEAN WORSE" (1960: 8). As the universities were "already taking almost everyone who can read and write" (1960: 9), he argued, it would simply be impossible to expand without seriously damaging academic standards. Nine years later, Amis diagnosed that by then "more ha[d] meant worse" as the universities had to deal with an "academically-unfit majority, or large minority" (1969: 10). This attack on expansion was waged in *Fight for Education* – the first of the Black Papers, a series of pamphlets, in which writers such as Amis, Bryan Wilson, Robert Conquest, Angus Maude, D.C. Watt, and C.B. Cox took issue with the "disastrous mistakes" that they thought were being made in education (Cox and Dyson 1969: 6).[1] Apart from the comprehensive schools and progressive teaching methods, one of the major issues that raised their contempt, in particular in the first Black Paper, was the expansion of higher education. Wilson, for instance, agreed with Amis that "[m]ore ha[d] meant worse" (1969: 73). Maude warned against the "Trojan horse of egalitarianism" (1969: 8–9). Conquest suggested that one solution to the crisis in the universities was to refuse admission for "students without minimal cultural qualifications" (1969: 20). And Watt thought that the universities had passed over "an opportunity to raise their standards of selection of students in favour of an expansion of numbers" (1969a: 35). Such anti-expansionist attitudes were by no means confined to the Black Papers. F.R. Leavis, for example, insisted in 1969 that

> [n]either democratic zeal nor egalitarian jealousies should be permitted to dismiss or discredit the fact that only a limited proportion of any young adult age group is capable of profiting by, or enjoying, university education. The proper standards can be maintained only if the students the university

> is required to deal with are – for the most part, at any rate – of university quality.
>
> (1979b: 187)

What united all these writers was the assumption that expansion had opened the universities to students who were not of the right quality and that therefore tougher selection was needed.

This anti-expansionist stance was, however, not as backward-looking as it might appear at first sight. As Robert Anderson has pointed out with respect to the Black Papers, "[t]o regard university education as a privilege open only to the clever was a new idea, which would have surprised the nineteenth-century dons who struggled with passmen and 'almost idiots'" (2006: 167). What the Black Papers and other critics of expansion like Leavis were defending was actually a meritocratic education system with strict selection for access into the grammar schools and universities (Lawton 2005: 85). Seen from this perspective, the writers of the Black Papers were certainly not that reactionary as none of them argued that access to the university should depend on social status or be the privilege of those of sufficient financial means. However, if seen in the context of the time, the picture actually changes. At a time when it became increasingly clear that meritocratic education systems reproduced social structures – an insight which led to the establishment of the comprehensive schools and was also underlying the Robbins Report's argument against the pool-of-ability thesis,[2] – the Black Papers defended the meritocratic school system and strict selection. Although they did not propose that access to the universities ought to depend on class background, the ideal of selection that the Black Papers endorsed clearly defended a society that was not only shaped by social inequalities and hierarchies but where education reproduced these inequalities.[3]

Some critics of expansion even went further and not only called for tougher selection based on the student's intellectual abilities but also wanted to take other 'qualities' into account. The idea that a university education required more than intellect was actually nothing new. The Barlow Report, which had favoured expansion, had assured its readers that "[c]haracter, temperament and wider qualities of minds are, of course, as important as intellectual acuity and the test for fitness for the Universities is not intelligence alone" (*Scientific Manpower* 1946: §25). As expansion proceeded, however, several critics bemoaned that apparently intelligence had become the main access criterion for a university education. Oakeshott, for instance, complained in 1949 that entrance tests that focused only on intelligence and knowledge were inappropriate as they did not take into account to what extent the student was suited for a university education (2001: 151). Two years later, J.H. Nicholson suggested that in order to deal with the rising number of possible university candidates, entrance tests should also consider "other desiderata such as sensitiveness, curiosity, adaptability and perseverance, or even a real flair for a subject or a way of life of which they have had little previous experience" (1951: 30), and similarly J.F. Wolfenden argued that selection for university should not be based on intellect alone but also include an assessment of character (1951: 17–20). In similar vein, but much more ferocious in tone, some of the authors of the Black Papers complained that expansion had opened the doors of the universities to students who lacked essential qualities and who better not be there. Amis, for instance, claimed that there was a rising number of students "who do not understand what study is about, and who are painfully bewildered by the whole business and purpose of university life" (1969: 10), and Wilson asserted that expansion had brought students into the universities "who were less adequately socialised" for the university experience (1969: 73). The trouble, according to him, was that "[i]ntellect, untempered by taste, character, disposition or even commitment to academic work" had become the main criterion upon which access to the universities was granted (1969: 76). Such calls for selection based on other qualities than intellect were in fact no defences of a meritocratic system but of one in which access to educational institutions depended, even more than in a purely meritocratic system, on the students' socialisation, disposition, and habitus.

The 'new student' myth

It would be misleading to assume that the Black Papers represented the dominant opinion of the time. There was actually a widespread support for the expansion of higher education. But even though the actual views on expansion may have varied, there was one thing that many supporters and opponents of expansion shared: the belief that expansion would open higher education to thousands of 'new students' who were different to their predecessors and lacked many of their qualities.

As previous chapters have shown, this assumption was, for instance, present in the UGC's report on halls of residence (1957: §21) as well as the Robbins Report, which was concerned about the rising number of students "without a background of [. . .] culture" (Committee on Higher Education 1963: §570). Likewise, Albert Sloman worried about the increasing proportion of students who came "from homes with no tradition of culture or learning" (1964: 11). Lord James, future Vice-Chancellor of the University of York, complained about a growing number of students "without cultural background", who regarded a university education only as a means to obtain a job (cited in Hall 1961: 154). And R.M. Ogilvie claimed that "[i]n the past the majority of people who passed through the universities already came up with a framework of values and standards, often Christian, inherited from their family. The new student is entirely lacking in these" (1962: 95). However, not everyone characterised the 'new students' in such negative terms. Richard Hoggart, who had dealt with the situation of the 'scholarship boy' in his widely acclaimed *The Uses of Literacy* (1957), thought that the working classes possessed a culture that needed to be valued in its own right and which it would be wrong "to turn our noses up at" (cited in Hall 1961: 160), and similarly Michael Young argued that education should "show more respect for the values embodied in working-class life" (cited in Hall 1961: 159).

What, nonetheless, united these writers with those who displayed a more negative attitude towards the 'new students' were two things. First, they all thought that the working-class students possessed cultural values that were different to the traditional student.[4] Second, they all believed that the class intake of higher education was changing. What is striking though is that the class intake did not change that much with expansion. While the number of students from the middle classes rose tremendously, the percentage of working-class students remained rather low (Halsey 1992: 101; Ross 2003a: 61; Sanderson 1998: 381–2). The 'new student' was thus less a reality than a myth (Maton 2005: 694). Indeed, the problematisation of the 'new student' was a symptom for a struggle with a new ethos entering higher education, which, in the end, was not so much caused by a widened class intake but by the changing position of higher education in society. This was also hinted at by Stuart Hall, who claimed that the role of education in society had changed in general as educational qualifications had gained in importance as status symbols and education had become "a prime mechanism in social mobility" (1961: 153).[5] To what extent the 'new student' debate was actually about shifting values comes in particular to the fore when having a look at those instance when the problem was no longer located in the working classes but rather in youth cultures.

Youth culture and the question of student identity

For some writers, expansion was by far not the only threat to university. Another issue that raised major concern was the emergence of distinctive youth cultures. Lord James, for instance, complained not only about the rising number of working-class students but about the influence that youth subcultures had on these students. As their friends were "leaving school at fifteen, earning large wages, buying guitars, taking girl-friends out and living the sort of 'Baby Cham life'", working-class students were said to struggle between youth subcultures and the culture of the university (Lord James in Hall 1961: 155). While Lord James still considered youth cultures a working-class phenomenon, Sloman much more generally criticised that many students were the "products of the current teenage culture, some of whose values are alien to those of an academic community" (1964: 62). For Sloman, youth culture posed a problem quite similar to the 'new student' from a lower social background as both had cultural values that were incompatible with the university.

Youth culture was also an issue for some of the contributors to the Black Papers. 'B', for instance, criticised that the students'

> prime wish seems, sometimes, less to make themselves a part of a better university community than to make the university a better part of the

> youth-culture, to win it for youth-nationalism. Indeed the emergence of a distinctive sectarian culture among students, which sees its interests as aligned rather with other young people rather than those of intellectual culture, is an essential feature of the university's ferment now.
>
> (1969: 61)

As 'B' claimed, one of the problems of the university was that students identified with other young people and did no longer integrate themselves into the university community. This was also considered a major problem by Bryan Wilson. According to him, universities had lost their distinctive culture because students had "been less specifically prepared for an ivory tower experience" and therefore rather identified with youth culture (1969: 73). Students, so he claimed, no longer regarded themselves as part of an élite; they were "no longer a class apart from youth in general" but "completely identified with the younger generation, even if they are a particularly articulate, privileged and readily mobilisable part of it" (1969: 72–3). What writers like 'B' and Wilson thus condemned was that the rise of youth cultures threatened the ideal of the academic community. As 'youth' created an equivalence between students and other young people, the constitutive outside of the academic community broke away as the difference towards the non-academic world was dissolved, and at the same time, 'youth' emphasised differences in values between students and academics along the generational divide.

Precisely in this perception of a threat, there was a striking similarity between the condemnation of youth cultures and the problematisation of the non-traditional student in terms of class. In both cases, these 'new students' were, at least by some critics, seen as 'alien' to the university and as posing a challenge to the ideal of the university as a community of values and thus to the legitimacy of the university's authority.

The 'new student' and the crisis of legitimacy

In contrast to the anti-expansionist criticism of the Black Papers, writers like Moberly, the Robbins Report, or the UGC's report on halls of residence were not concerned with the exclusion of the 'new students' but with the question how these students could be integrated into the university. Hence, their focus was on means to socialise students into a particular culture. While this socialisation of the 'new students' was often regarded as a form of emancipation and as a means to foster equality of opportunity, it can also be seen as an instrument to secure the authority of the university both within society at large and towards its students.

As Pierre Bourdieu and Jean-Claude Passeron have argued, one of the key characteristics of institutionalised educational systems is that they have to reproduce their own conditions of existence (1990: 54). Hence, educational institutions aim to transmit those cultural values that legitimise their existence in the first place. However, as institutions of education are part of the wider society, they are also affected by changes in that society, and tensions may arise between the reproductive tendencies of the educational institutions and more widespread social and cultural shifts that actually question the legitimacy of the educational institution. Precisely that is what the problem of the 'new student' signifies. The supposedly rising number of 'new students' with values 'alien' to the university was considered a problem that endangered the reproduction of the university and that needed to be warded off. No matter whether the 'new students' were to be excluded or integrated, in both cases the aim was to ensure that the students conformed to a cultural norm and that the culture of the university could thus be reproduced. Hence, the problem of the 'new student' points towards the friction between the shifting position of the university in society and the reproductive tendencies of the university. But while writers like Moberly and Sloman, the Robbins Report, and also the UGC still showed a strong belief in the value of the culture that the university stood for, the Black Papers' strong anti-expansionist stance actually reflected the waning authority of that culture.

But as the culture that legitimised the university lost in authority, this also undermined the authority of the academics as representatives of that culture. It was not by chance that the authors of the Black Papers considered the rise of the 'new students' as one of the main reasons for the student protests of the late 1960s. As 'B' claimed, the protests and the rejection of the traditional power structures of the university had arisen because some students were "evidently alienated [. .] from the very idea of the university" (1969: 61). As students no longer subscribed to the culture and values that the university represented, they also no longer 'misrecognised' – in the sense of Bourdieu and Passeron – the power structures of the university.[6]

The debate about the 'new student', whether in terms of class or youth culture, thus points towards an internal as well as external crisis of the university. The 'new student' functioned as a metonymy for various new discursive framings of higher education, and the growing debate about the 'new student' actually signified the diminishing power of the traditional idea of the university as a guardian of knowledge and culture. The problematisation of the 'new students' and the various calls for their exclusion or enculturation were efforts to defend a normative university culture and to reproduce the authority and power of the university and the academic. Hence, what the problem of the 'new student' exposes is how central the concept of the student is to the power structures of higher education and the legitimacy of authority.

Notes

1 The Black Papers also marked the rise of the New Right, which gradually gained in power and finally succeeded with Margaret Thatcher. Although the Black Papers were much more elitist than Thatcherism, their strong anti-progressive stance anticipated much of the cultural-political discourse of Thatcherism (Ball 2006: 30).

2 As Pierre Bourdieu later showed, meritocratic education systems tend to reproduce class inequalities because inherited cultural capital and habitus largely determine success in education. For an overview as well as some criticism levelled at Bourdieu, see Jenkins (2002: 110–20).
3 Strikingly, the Black Papers focused exclusively on the universities as far as higher education was concerned. This not only mirrored the authors' own university background but also the common English ideology of higher education being essentially the universities with some other institutions not worth further ado. Although writers like Moberly, Truscot, and Leavis also focused on the university, the issue is a slightly different one with the Black Papers. After the Robbins Report had popularised the notion of higher education as comprising the universities and other institutions, the exclusive focus on the university within the Black Papers carried a higher significance as it deliberately set the universities apart from other institutions of higher education.
4 The differences in attitude between students of different social background were also an issue in Ferdynand Zweig's survey of Oxford and Manchester students. According to Zweig, the 'new students' who were financed through grants and often had a working or lower-middle class background were "more serious, more anxious and more industrious, more self-conscious and more weary than the student who, kept by his family, took it all for granted and enjoyed himself as much as he could, not worrying too much about exams and his future career" (1963: xv). The changing student intake in terms of class was also a major issue within numerous campus novels of the 1940s to 1970s. Apart from Philip Larkin's *Jill* (1946), which tells the story of 'scholarship boy' John Kemp at Oxford, class was also a central topic in Kingsley Amis's *Lucky Jim* (1954) as well as Malcolm Bradbury's *Eating People Is Wrong* (1959), in which working-class student Louis Bates is depicted as strange and unfitting as his counterpart the African student Eborebelosa as both "came out of as foreign a culture" (Bradbury 1978: 163). As Ian Carter has shown, there are several other novels from Raymond Postgate's *The Ledger is Kept* (1953) to J.I.M. Stewart's *The Man Who Won the Pools* (1961) to Simon Raven's *Places Where They Sing* (1970) that at one point or another touch upon the issue of the 'new student' and class culture (1990: 103–29).
5 Likewise, W.R. Niblett asserted that the values of students in general had shifted. As he stated, students in the early 1960s were "differently orientated from their predecessors" as they were "being civilized in an environment strong in incentives to material success, weaker than used to be the case in incentives to success of other kinds" (1962: 13–4).
6 Misrecognition is used here in the sense of Bourdieu and Passeron, for whom misrecognition is "the process whereby power relations are perceived not for what they objectively are but in a form which renders them legitimate in the eyes of the beholder" (1990: xxii).

Chapter 9

New institutions for new students?

Since World War II, Britain's higher education landscape had not changed much. Although higher education had expanded, the number and type of colleges and universities had by and large remained the same. Apart from the Colleges of Advanced Technology (CATs), which were established in 1956 but were actually based on existing technical colleges, the only new foundation was Keele (founded as University College of North Staffordshire in 1949). In the 1960s, however, things changed tremendously. Seven new universities were founded, 30 polytechnics were created, and, last but not least, the Open University was given its charter in 1969 and soon offered degree courses via distance education.

The campus universities: old wine in new bottles?

When the University of Sussex received its charter in 1961, it was the first of seven entirely new universities and was soon followed by East Anglia (1963), York (1963), Lancaster (1964), Essex (1965), Kent (1965), and Warwick (1965). Like the older Redbricks, these universities had grown from local initiatives (Dormer and Muthesius 2001: 147). But in contrast to the nineteenth-century foundations, which had all started as colleges and were only later granted university status, the new universities of the 1960s were constructed from scratch with university status right from the start. They were thus "born free" (Beloff 1970: 26),[1] and through the introduction of near universal maintenance grants, they could immediately recruit students on a national basis (Fulton 1964: 11).

The seven new universities were not only all founded at roughly the same time, but they also shared numerous other characteristics. They all had a strong focus not only on the pure sciences and the arts but also on the social sciences, which were still not well-established in England at that time (Beloff 1970: 40). Moreover, all seven universities, to a greater or lesser extent, tried to establish what Asa Briggs, at that time Pro Vice-Chancellor of the University of Sussex, called "new maps of learning" (1964: 60). Their aim was not to produce specialists but people able "to compare, to relate and to judge" (1964: 63). As Albert Sloman, Vice-Chancellor of the University of Essex, formulated it, graduates increasingly needed to be experts in a particular field, but instead of becoming mere specialist, they ought to become "experts who see their expertise in perspective" (1964: 10). Hence, all of the seven universities departed from the traditional honours or combined honours degree – whether it was through overlapping major and minor subjects (York, East Anglia, Lancaster, and Warwick), broad-based preliminary courses that shifted specialisation to a later stage (Essex and Kent), or the replacement of departments with schools that put the core subject in a context of other subjects (Sussex) (Corbett 1964: 32; Rich 2001: 50–1).

The most striking commonality between the seven new universities was and still is their architecture and location. More than any other higher education institution, these universities used architecture as an educational device. Architecture was "part and parcel of the institutional and academic concept" (Dormer and Muthesius 2001: 48). While the use of concrete and glass, which also earned them the name Plateglass Universities (Beloff 1970), transmitted a modern ethos in tune with the architectural styles of the post-war period, their location and spatial organisation seemed to be a revival of much more traditional ideals of university education. All seven universities were established not in major urban areas but in the less industrial if not rural spots of England such as Colchester or Norwich (Rich 2001: 49, Birks and Holford 1972: 16), and due to UGC demands, they were built as campus universities located out of town (Cross and Jobling 1969: 173). This remoteness was supposed to help build strong communities and to prevent students from commuting (Sloman 1964: 14), but it also separated the universities from the wider society.[2] As Bernard Crick has argued, the campus universities

> represent an idea of a university as a refuge from the world of productivity, partly monastic in origins and partly arising from Matthew Arnold-like scorn for the common culture and for the new technologies that fed him and his pupils.
>
> (1979: 59)

With their new maps of learning and their plateglass architecture, on the one hand, and their campus structure and detached location, on the other, the new universities were thus both progressive and traditional at the same time. This fusion of the old and the new was nowhere better pronounced than in the case of the University of Essex.

Amongst the seven new universities, Essex occupies a special position. Not only did it arrive at some fame in the student troubles of the 1960s, but it also gained popularity as the most permissive university. Thus, *The Sun* called it "The no-rules university", and the *Daily Mail* spoke of the "Live-as-you-like university" (Beloff 1970: 117). But even before it opened, the university received major publicity through a six-part BBC lecture series, in which Albert

Sloman, Essex's first Vice-Chancellor, set out his vision of the university and spoke in detail about its role and structure.

According to Sloman, the university was a "community concerned with advancing and disseminating knowledge" (1964: 9). This rather traditional ideal of the university structured around the nodal points 'knowledge' and 'learning' was, as Sloman claimed, jeopardised by "rapidly expanding knowledge" and "expanding numbers" (1964: 10). However, as far as the student was concerned, what put pressure on the ideal of the university were not only the increasing number of students but rather the kind of students that entered the university. Like so many others of his time, Sloman was concerned about the rising number of students "drawn from the families of semiskilled and unskilled workers" (1964: 51)[3] and was worried that many students were "products of the current teenage culture" and subscribed to values that were "alien to those of an academic community" (1964: 62). With this problematisation of the 'new student', Sloman sided with the Robbins Report as well as the UGC, and like them, he considered it vital that universities formed communities.

For Sloman, it was an integral part of a university education that the student had the "intellectual and social experience of being a member of an academic community" (1964: 50) – a community that was not only united by shared values but by a common way of life. As a university was not just concerned "with the pursuit of learning but with the fulfilment of lives" (1964: 63), it needed, so Sloman argued, to "provide an experience of living" (1964: 51). Such a focus on the building of communities and the student's social life was not particular to Essex. Speaking about the University of Sussex, John Fulton, for instance, emphasised that the education of the students went beyond formal teaching and that it was essential "to organize the life of the university so as to ensure for its undergraduates the fullest development of their whole personalities" (1964: 20). Likewise, Maurice Hutt claimed that a university was "a place you are 'of' not just 'go to', a community not just a processing plant" (1964: 44). The means that were taken to establish such communities, however, slightly differed between the seven universities, and one of the most radical solutions was tried at Essex.[4]

While the UGC had still favoured the traditional halls of residence in 1957, these were falling in favour in the 1960s, and some universities started to experiment with new forms of residence. Not only were traditional halls of residence rather expensive, but students increasingly preferred other forms of accommodation that allowed them more freedom than the traditional halls offered. Accordingly, Sloman argued that "[p]lans formulated in 1963 for student living must take account too of the greater maturity of young men and women and their legitimate desire for independence" (1964: 12). Thus, Essex did not rely on traditional halls of residence but opted for tower blocks that consisted of student apartments with communal kitchens and living rooms on each floor and that had no resident staff – an option that was also favoured by the NUS at that time (Tapper and Palfreyman 2011: 68). As it was obvious right from the start that accommodation on campus was limited, the question arose how to offer the communal life also to students who could not reside on campus. The solution that Essex opted for was to offer special study rooms for students who lived off-campus. These study rooms were not part of some central learning facilities but integrated into student apartments. The aim was to draw students into smaller communities that might even establish closer ties and feelings of belonging than a hall could offer and which would thus ensure that even non-residential students could "enjoy the communal life of the university" (Sloman 1964: 56). Though the whole experiment did not succeed because often non-residents came in when residents went out and was thus soon abandoned with only six of the planned 29 tower blocks actually built (Birks and Holford 1972: 27), it was a remarkable attempt to bring together traditional ideals and new social and financial realities.

The campus universities that were founded in the early 1960s thus tried to bridge the old and the new. They drew 'new maps of learning' and often gave students more freedom and power in the running of their university than had traditionally been case (Beloff 1970: 69).[5] But at the same time, they represented like no other the idea that the university was a community of its own that was detached from the rest of society. Being a student meant to become a member of a 'total community', which also implied that the ideal student was the young full-time student for whom higher education marked a specific period in life. Hence, even though the new universities modified traditional ideals of the university, they hardly questioned their boundaries. This was eventually left to the government and the establishment of the polytechnics and the Open University.

The polytechnics: the people's universities

While the Labour government readily accepted the Robbins Report's argument for expansion, it rejected many of its other proposals. Neither were teacher training colleges taken out of LEA control and linked to existing universities nor were any new universities founded or existing colleges other than the CATs transferred to university status (Godwin 1998: 171–8). Instead, the government designated 28 (later 30) polytechnics as distinct higher education institutions under LEA control and without degree awarding powers (Palfreyman and Tapper 2009: 43–4).[6] Thus, Labour not only fundamentally restructured secondary education with the formation of the comprehensive schools, but also profoundly changed the system of higher education for the years to come. Indeed, the binary policy, as it came to be called, was not questioned by the following governments and stayed for more than 20 years.[7]

The binary policy was first announced in a speech given by Anthony Crosland, Secretary for Education and Science, at Woolwich Polytechnic in 1965. In this speech, Crosland dismissed the Robbins Report because it allegedly favoured a higher education system based on a "'ladder' principle" as every institution of higher education would eventually seek university status (1974b: 204). Calling upon his listeners to leave behind the "snobbish caste-ridden hierarchical obsession with University status", Crosland suggested that what was needed instead was to strengthen the non-university higher education sector (1974b: 204). Such a strong non-university sector was necessary, he claimed, for four reasons. First, there was "an ever-increasing need and demand for vocational, professional and industrially-based courses" that the universities could not fully satisfy but which needed to be met in order "to progress as a nation in the modern technological world" (1974b: 204).[8] Second, a binary system was said to be less depressing and degrading than a ladder principle (1974b: 204). Third, he claimed that it was "desirable in itself that a substantial part of the higher education system should be under social control, and directly responsive to social needs" (1974b: 204). Fourth, pointing to other countries where a relatively strong non-university sector already existed, he asserted that Britain would actually "not survive in this world" if it downgraded its professional and technical non-university sector (1974b: 204).

While Crosland's first and fourth reasons clearly positioned the polytechnics within the manpower doctrine and thus structured higher education around the nodal points 'economy' and 'nation', the third reason directly tackled questions of power and raised the question of who ought to be in control of higher education. As Lord Annan has argued, the Department of Education and Science (DES) was "appalled by the Robbins report" as its proposals would have meant not only to remove many higher education institutions, including teacher training colleges, from the public to the university sector but also to "encourage every college to abandon the kind of technical education so necessary for the middle grades of industry" and to "drop teaching part-time students" (1982: 5). These worries were not thin air. Once the CATs had been granted university status, they soon started to shed lower level work (Pratt 2001: 21). Seen from the perspective of the DES, the establishment of the binary policy was thus a means to maintain and enlarge control. Hence, the designation of the polytechnics can be regarded as a major step towards greater state intervention in higher education (Tapper and Salter 1992: 15).

Unsurprisingly, the binary policy raised criticism. Thus, D.C. Watt, for instance, accused Crosland of largely ignoring the many activities "pursued at the great majority of British universities" (1969b: 122) – a criticism that Crosland responded to in his Lancaster speech, in which he stated that universities were socially responsive but not under direct social control (1974a: 209). Others like Lionel Robbins condemned the policy as "making the system more hierarchical than ever" (cited in Shattock 2012: 65). Such an interpretation of the binary policy was not only rebutted by the DES in its White Paper *A Plan for Polytechnics and Other Colleges* (DES 1966a: §28) but also by Gerald Fowler, who claimed in retrospect that the aim of the binary policy was

> not to create a depressed, second-class, and under-financed sector of higher education, [. . .] but to give recognition to the possibility that there might

> be more than one valid philosophy of higher education, or such differences of emphasis within a philosophy as to require more than one institutional model.
>
> (1972: 271)

However, the polytechnics were not only supposed to give recognition to a different idea of higher education but also to a different student.

In his Woolwich speech, Crosland claimed that the non-university sector was much more comprehensive than the universities as far as the provision of higher education and student intake were concerned (1974b: 207). This comprehensiveness became an even more important argument in Crosland's Lancaster speech of 1967, in which he spoke of "two categories of students whose importance to the nation can hardly be overestimated" but which were not taken care of by the universities: full-time students below degree level and part-time students at various levels (1974a: 210). By providing courses for these students as well as full-time degree courses, the polytechnics would not only supply the nation with manpower but also provide "opportunities for educational and social mobility" (1974a: 211). The polytechnics were thus supposed to give recognition to a type of student who had so far been largely ignored in the debate in higher education and hence broke with the idea that there was only one proper form of higher education and thus one appropriate student.[9]

But as much as the polytechnic idea appreciated alternative concepts of higher education and the student, it also upheld established values. When Crosland defined the polytechnics as being part of the further education tradition, he approvingly quoted the Association of Teachers in Technical Institutions, which described this tradition as providing education and training for a student whose "primary motivation is the profession he intends to follow" and who "is committed to a profession from the outset" (cited in Crosland 1974b: 205). Thus, he indirectly claimed that the polytechnics were supposed to cater for students who considered education primarily as a means to enter a career. Although Crosland later argued in a slightly different direction in his Lancaster speech, his initial and most important statement on the binary policy constructed an opposition between the utilitarian and instrumental polytechnic student and the academically minded university student. Instead of transgressing traditional ideals, he thus subscribed to the distinction between the liberal universities and the utilitarian rest.

While Crosland, as well as the respective White Paper *A Plan for Polytechnics and Other Colleges* (1966), stayed within established boundaries and subscribed to the division between vocational and academic education, Eric Robinson, one of the advisors to Crosland and a strong supporter of the polytechnic idea, formulated a vision of the polytechnics that went further. The idea of higher education that he put forth in *The New Polytechnics* (1968) challenged the common distinction between academic studies, which were said to focus on the search for truth and the discovery of knowledge, on the one hand and vocational studies, which concentrated on applying knowledge and developing skills, on the other hand. While these two forms of education had traditionally been seen as diametrically opposed, Robinson claimed that only an integrated approach would reflect the demands of modern society:

> It is indefensible that so many students in higher education are prepared for no occupation and that so many are prepared for one and one only. If liberalism in education means the development of the individual to establish and maintain his own values and to be equipped to hold his own against the pressures around him, there has never been a greater need for it than now. But to assume that it is best pursued by ignoring the world as it is and the need to earn a living in this imperfect world is a great mistake. The most illiberal education is the one which makes a student mere fodder for the industrial machine; but the man most vulnerable to the industrial machine is the one who must enter it without knowing or understanding anything about it. To pretend that the real world of 'muck and brass' does not exist is the worst disservice higher education can do a student.
>
> (1968: 116)

What Robinson here proposed was what Patrick Ainley has called a "liberal vocationalism" (1998: 145). This ideal of the polytechnics went far beyond Crosland as it actually challenged established distinctions. The polytechnics as Robinson envisioned them were not offering a second type of higher education next to the universities, but they were bridgeheads to change the whole system. The polytechnics, according to Robinson, were not supposed to "merely fill a niche" that had been neglected by other institutions of higher education, but they had the task to "change the pattern of higher education" (1968: 117). While Crosland as well as the White Paper emphasised the need to provide higher education for a particular type of student, Robinson's aim was to establish "higher education for all" (1968: 12). As he explained in another text, the aim was "to find a new idea of a university and to create new comprehensive universities – much bigger, much less exclusive, much closer to the community as a whole and much less 'academic' than the present universities" (1969: 231). But therefore, higher education had to be fundamentally rethought and needed to abandon some of its traditional ideals. Hence, the elitism of the university as well as its isolation from the whole community needed to be broken down. For Robinson, "[t]he popular university ideal of abstracting the student into an academic community for long continuous periods" was "irreconcilable" with the idea of mass higher education and ongoing education as both meant that higher education needed to have "a large urban and part-time element" (1968: 47). Instead of following the ideal of the "boarding school university", the polytechnic, as Robinson saw it, ought to be the "urban community university" (1968: 48). Indeed, it should become the "people's university" (1968: 49). This did not mean to merely provide higher education for many people. According to

Robinson, the polytechnics ought to fully endorse a new educational philosophy and recognise that "students should come before subjects, before research, before demands of employers and before demands of the state" (1968: 117). As he argued, institutions of higher education needed to "design the courses to suit the student" (1968: 158) and "establish firmly that the college exists for the benefit of students, not *vice versa*" (1968: 159). Moreover, he asserted that institutions of higher education should open their entry requirements (1968: 168–9), offer courses for which there was a need in the community (1968: 170), make courses more flexible (1968: 185), and give students representation on academic boards and on the boards of governors (1968: 178).

What Robinson thus proposed was an idea of higher education that put the student at the centre. Instead of framing higher education in a discourse either structured by the nodal points 'economy', 'wealth', and 'nation' or by nodal points such as 'knowledge for its own sake', 'culture', or 'morals', Robinson put forth a vision of higher education at whose heart were 'the people' and hence 'the student'. These nodal points had already been central to the socialist vision that Brian Simon had expounded in *A Student's View of the Universities* (1943), and they had gained in power in the 1960s, for instance, with the Robbins Report. But while the Robbins Report was first and foremost concerned with opening access and did not consider fundamental changes with regard to the content and form of higher education, Robinson actually went further and argued that the whole higher education sector needed to be restructured.

The Open University

While proposals for a university that used modern technology like radio or television had already been made decades before (MacArthur 1974: 3), the idea really gained ground in the 1960s. In 1962, Michael Young suggested the use of correspondence teaching and teaching via television because, as he argued, "[i]f the student can't come to the lab, then the lab must come to the student" (cited in Stanistreet 2009: 8). At the same time, the Labour Party's Taylor Committee recommended that "as an experiment, the B.B.C. sound radio and television and the ITA [Independent Television Authority] should be required to co-operate in organising a 'University of the Air' for serious planned adult education" (cited in Silver 2003: 200). These proposals also entered Labour's 1966 election manifesto, and after the election victory, the White Paper *A University of the Air* (1966) set out plans to establish a university that would have no entrance requirements and function through distance education. Hence, the Open University, as it was called by then, was finally founded in 1969 and admitted its first students in 1971.

The most important novelty of the Open University was without doubt that it opened higher education at degree level to thousands of students who had formerly been denied access to higher education. Of course, further education for mature students and students without A-level qualifications was not entirely new. The Workers' Educational Association (WEA), numerous LEAs, and also universities had for long offered adult education programmes. But in contrast to these schemes, the Open University was not only supposed to be much bigger in scale, but it was set up as an autonomous university with degree awarding powers – an aspect that had in particular been insisted upon by Minister for the Arts Jennie Lee (Stabler 1987: 230–3).

The University of the Air was supposed to fulfil a number of functions. In his famous 'white heat' speech, Harold Wilson highlighted the impact of scientific and technological developments and argued that without the full embrace of the scientific revolution Britain would become "a stagnant backwater, pitied and condemned by the rest of the world" (1963: 2). Therefore, a number of changes were suggested with regard to the education sector that included the abolition of the 11+ examinations, the expansion of higher education, as well as "plans for a University of the Air" (1963: 4). The University of the Air was thus presented as part of wider educational reforms, all of which were considered means to spur the 'white heat' and ensure Britain's position in the world.[10] This was, however, only one of the numerous tasks that the University of the Air was supposed to accomplish. According to Wilson, the University of the Air would also make "an immeasurable contribution to the cultural life of our country, to the enrichment of our standard of living" (1963: 4). This aim was likewise emphasised in the election manifesto of 1966 (Labour Party 2002: 144) and the following White Paper, which spoke of "the improvement of educational, cultural and professional standards generally, by making available to all who care to look and listen, scholarship of a high order" (DES 1966b: §3). Last but not least, the University of the Air was considered a means to provide greater equality of opportunity. Hence, Wilson argued that the University of the Air was "designed to provide an opportunity for those, who, for one reason or another, have not been able to take advantage of higher education" (1963: 4). The Labour Party Manifesto of 1966 claimed that the University of the Air would "mean genuine equality of opportunity for millions of people for the first time" (Labour Party 2002: 144). And similarly, the following White Paper maintained that through the University of the Air opportunities could be enlarged for those who were "not attracted by traditional institutions or unable for a variety of reasons to take advantage of them" (DES 1966b: §2). The University of the Air was thus given multiple functions and was presented as an intersection of various ideas that had shaped the debate on higher education so far, all with their respective nodal points such as 'economy', 'culture', 'learning', and 'equality'.[11]

As the Open University offered courses at degree level to students without traditional qualification, it departed from the meritocratic principles that had been underlying the Robbins Report. While the Robbins Report had argued that all those qualified by ability and attainment should be allowed to enter higher education, the Open University opened higher education to everyone irrespective of previous qualifications. Now courses in higher education were not only "available to all those who are qualified by ability and attainment to pursue them and who wish to do so" (Committee on Higher Education 1963: §31) but simply to those who wished to do so. As the Labour Party announced in its election manifesto, the aim was to "give everyone the opportunity of study for a full degree" (Labour Party 2002: 144). Although it is debatable to what extent access was really open and how much the social spectrum of the student intake of the first years was actually wider than at more traditional institutions of higher education,[12] the very idea of the Open University discarded the traditional image of the young, full-time, middle-class student with A-levels. Moreover, the Open University opened higher education not only for those who actually enrolled on its courses. While places were limited right from the start and quotas were set for different occupational groups, regions, and courses (Pratt 1970: 375), there was no limitation to the number of people who could make use of the Open University's TV and radio broadcasts. The Open University was thus open "in a goldfish-bowl sense" (Tunstall 1974a: xi).

Besides questions of access, the Open University is so central for the debate on higher education because it challenged one of the most widely cherished ideas of higher education. Using distance learning based on written and audio-taped materials, correspondence, and TV and radio broadcasts, the Open University offered an experience of higher education that radically differed from the traditional universities and colleges. Neither was there much face-to-face interaction between students and teachers or amongst students, nor did the Open University provide an "experience of 'going to university'" (van der Eyken 1974: 30). Though the Open University soon established summer schools and other means to stipulate such an experience and to create communities (Niblett 1974: 98), the social experience of being a student was still fundamentally different from the traditional universities. Unsurprisingly, this aspect raised criticism and contempt. A journalist in the *Times Educational Supplement*, for instance, wrote in 1965 that "a University is not a mode of mass communication, it is a community" (cited in Taylor and Steele 2011: 105).

Moreover, a widespread discussion ensued on the question whether distance education could indeed provide the same as classroom interaction and to what extent it put the learner in a rather passive role and commodified knowledge.[13] Such criticism was discarded by Walter Perry, the Open University's first Vice-Chancellor, who claimed that studying on a part-time basis next to work and often with family responsibilities to attend to would be even tougher than being a full-time student at a traditional university where the student's "life [was] organised for him" (1977: 167). Studying at the Open University required qualities, so he argued, that many young people lacked, which was one of the reasons why the Open University did not accept students below the age of 21 (1977: 57). But as much as Perry emphasised the qualities of the Open University student, he himself considered the Open University a second option only and thought it in many respects inferior to the traditional universities. Hence, he stated that another reason for restricting access to those above the age of 21 was that the Open University, if opened to students below 21, would easily become the "dustbin for all those people who had tried and failed to get into conventional universities" (1977: 58), and that "a young person of 18 would be missing a great deal if he were denied the opportunity of studying in a regular residential university with all that it had to offer in the way of social life and the stimulation of colleagues" (1977: 57). Elsewhere, he declared:

> If I had to choose I would certainly opt for the traditional and normal full-time residential university. But our adult students *cannot* choose. For if he wants a degree he is often offered no choice – it is us or nothing.
>
> (1974: 14, emphasis in original)

Hence, even its first Vice-Chancellor considered the Open University as a poorer option only and subscribed to the traditional ideal of the full-time student, who enjoyed the community life of a residential university. This was by far not the only point at which the idea of the Open University perpetuated traditional ideals.

In contrast to Wilson and other supporters of the University of the Air, Lee and Perry insisted that the Open University needed to be given degree awarding powers in order not to be regarded as "a poor man's University of the Air" (Lee in Taylor and Steele 2011: 105). But the right to award degrees was not only a question of prestige or of being able to offer courses of high standard, it was also justified through the student clientele that the Open University would attract. Although Perry pointed out that some students, in particular "the older ones", might study at the Open University "for reasons of self-fulfilment, or improving their general knowledge and of learning to enjoy life rather more fully", he was convinced that most students would "seek degrees" and "would want primarily to obtain a qualification which would fit them for promotion, for a change of job, for a better job, for more money" (1977: 67). Underlying Perry's argument was thus the well-established differentiation between the traditional university student and the utilitarian 'new student'. But even though the Open University thus partly perpetuated established and normative ideals of the students, it undoubtedly broke new ground by making university education available to a large range of students who had beforehand been denied access.

There was one further aspect with which the Open University explored new terrain and which is particularly noteworthy in retrospect. As the Open University was such a radical and new invention, it was under pressure to display its success. As one of the first publications to do so, Tunstall's (ed.) *The Open University Opens* (1974b) included twelve short chapters of two to three pages in length, in which students reported about their experience of studying at the Open University. It is not so much of concern here that the selection of student voices was done in a rather self-congratulatory fashion. What is actually important is that the student experience was given a central place. Of course, the student experience had been of interest beforehand with publications like

Ferdynand Zweig's *The Student in an Age of Anxiety* (1963) or Peter Marris's *The Experience of Higher Education* (1964). But while these were primarily interested in how students experienced higher education, the *The Open University Opens* made student satisfaction an indicator of quality.

Crushing the hegemony of the university ideal?

In the 1960s, the higher education landscape shifted tremendously. Not only did student numbers further increase, but many new institutions of higher education were created. Seven new universities were built, the polytechnics were established, and the Open University was founded – all of them being manifestations of rather different ideas of higher education. While the campus universities established 'new maps of learning', they were rather traditional as far as the concept of the student was concerned. Students were supposed to become part of a community that was split apart from ordinary society. What Oakeshott had referred to as the gift of the interval in a temporal sense was here given a spatial dimension. But as has been shown, there were also attempts to break away from the traditional ideal of the student and to give students more freedom. These new developments, however, only recognised to what extent the values and wants of those students who entered full-time university education changed. They did not question the hegemony of the ideal of the young, full-time student.

This ideal was tackled by the polytechnics and even more so by the Open University. While the polytechnics emphasised the role of an already existing type of student, the part-time and mature student, the Open University abolished traditional entry requirements and made degree courses available to an entirely new group of people. But as much as the Open University and the polytechnics questioned the traditional ideal of higher education and the student, they only partly challenged the hegemony of the university ideal – indeed, one may even argue that they strengthened it. Though the polytechnics supposedly recognised the relevance of a different type of student, the idea to assign this different student to a particular institution – the polytechnics – meant to leave the universities largely untouched. By institutionalising a different concept of higher education as well as the student, the binary policy indirectly supported the elitism of the universities (Salter and Tapper 2000: 69). While this was actually appealing to many conservatives (Anderson 2006: 156), it was rejected by many on the left, who considered the binary policy an impediment for a thorough reform of the higher education sector as a whole. Hence, John Pratt and Tyrell Burgess claimed that instead of establishing the polytechnics, the government should have supported measures that encouraged vocational work and part-time studies throughout the sector (1974: 184), and similarly, the Communist Party argued that Crosland had not attacked the class bias of the university and had indeed established a worse system while at the same time missing the chance to bring the whole of higher education under public control (Taylor and Steele 2011: 119–20).

The same is in a way true for the Open University. Although it questioned many established beliefs about university education, the notion of the Open University as a second chance university as well as its focus on adult students and students without traditional qualifications indirectly supported the traditional university system. The Open University thus functioned as a kind of "safety valve" as the traditional universities were not required to take in students who did not fulfil traditional entrance requirements and could largely exclude mature students or students who could only study part-time (Trow 1996: 216). These students could be redirected to the Open University instead. While both the polytechnics and the Open University thus challenged the ideal of the young, academically minded, middle-class, full-time student, they also supported it to a certain extent.

Notes

1 In this respect, the University College of North Staffordshire, today Keele University, was an important predecessor because it was founded as a relatively independent institution in 1949 and was thus able to experiment with subject provision and course structures (Shattock 2012: 46; Tight 2009: 59).
2 However, as most universities were still within travelling distance of major urban centres, they faced the problem of the 'weekend exodus' (Birks and Holford 1972: 15). As Beloff remarked, to "visit the universities at weekends [. . .] is to visit a site evacuated as if by the threat of war" (1970: 32).
3 Contrary to Sloman's concerns, the actual student population of the new universities was rather traditional, and at least in the early years, the new universities had a middle-class intake slightly above average (Sanderson 2002: 120).
4 Though the seven new universities were all built as campus universities, their internal structure differed. While three adopted collegiate structures (York, Kent, and Lancaster), the other four universities built different forms of residence that would nonetheless foster the creation of communities (Cross and Jobling 1969: 175).
5 At Essex, for instance, a students' council was installed to direct all student activities and to "represent student opinion directly and informally to the Vice-Chancellor, and formally to the senate" (Sloman 1964: 84). Moreover, students were represented on the university court and on a student affairs committee as part of the senate (Sloman 1964: 84).
6 The binary system was only 'binary' in a very limited sense. The established higher education system consisted of universities, polytechnics, and various colleges. Accordingly, Peter Scott thought it misleading to refer to a binary system as in particular the non-university sector was "a heterogeneous collection of institutions which have little in common with each other except the fact that none is a university in the rather precise constitutional sense" (1984: 156).
7 Although the binary policy rejected many of the recommendations of the Robbins Report, Scott has recently pointed out that there was indeed much common ground. The binary policy agreed with the Robbins Report that expansion was to be aimed for, that there was need for a coordinated system of higher education, and that higher education ought to be financed by the state. These common assumptions may not have

appeared rather noteworthy at the time the binary policy was implemented, but they are if seen from today's perspective as higher education has turned into a market and is primarily funded through student fees (Scott 2014: 162).

8 The White Paper *A Plan for Polytechnics and Other Colleges* (1966) similarly emphasised the "links with industry, business and the professions" (DES 1966a: §4). In practice that meant, for instance, that degrees such as the BA Hons in Criminal Justice Studies and Police Studies as well as Guild craft courses were developed in the 1980s to serve particular employment groups (Pratt 1997: 124).

9 The number of part-time students actually declined in the polytechnics from roughly 74 percent in 1965/66 to about 32 percent in 1991/92 (Pratt 1997: 32), while the number of students on sandwich courses increased from 6 percent to 20 percent over the same period (Pratt 1997: 35). Compared to the universities, the polytechnics provided for a higher proportion of students from a manual background, mature students, students from ethnic minorities, as well as students with non-traditional qualifications (Pratt 1997: 78, 1999: 259).

10 The University of the Air was not only supposed to spur the 'white heat of technology', but it was itself a consequence of the possibilities that the scientific and technological revolution had brought. As the White Paper *A University of the Air* (1966) explained, technological discoveries such as television and radio had made it possible "that the best of our teachers can now be made available to vastly wider audiences" (DES 1966b: §1). This focus on new means of communication was much stronger in Wilson's speech and the White Paper than in the actually established Open University which was more based on reading than TV and radio (Perry 1974: 11; Taylor and Steele 2011: 100).

11 The White Paper *A University of the Air* (1966) provided another argument for the establishment of the Open University. In contrast to the expansion of existing colleges or universities or the building of new ones, the Open University was relatively cheap (DES 1966b: §5). This was also highlighted by Leslie Wagner, who argued that through economies of scale, the lack of student residences, and the possibility to use existing facilities for summer schools, the Open University was much cheaper than other higher education institutions (1974: 21–4). For this reason, correspondence courses were even considered favourably by the Robbins Report, albeit as courses run by the existing universities (Committee on Higher Education 1963: §821).

12 Although the first student intake still consisted of a majority of students with normal entrance qualifications (61.8 percent), the percentage of students with lower qualifications (32.6 percent) was still remarkable and actually rose over the next years to 46.6 percent in 1975 (Perry 1977: 145). As far as class is concerned, only 10 percent of the applicants came from the working classes in 1970, and the number was only slowly rising up to 15 percent over the next five years (Perry 1977: 149–50). This led to the early criticism that the Open University was basically serving the middle classes with the highest intake group being teachers (Pratt 1970: 375). However, at least in its early years the picture is slightly more complex. Social class in higher education is normally measured according to the father's occupation. If this is applied to the Open University, 49 percent of the students in the first years could be said to come from a working-class background (McIntosh 1974: 62). The Open University thus offered possibilities for those who had already moved away from their social origin.

13 See for instance Harris (1976: 48), Wood (1985: 141), or Farnes (1976).

Chapter 10

The 1960s student protests

1968 has become the symbol of worldwide unrest. But while Paris, Prague, West Berlin, or Mexico City immediately come to mind, one would hardly think of cities like London as epicentres of the student protests. Although there were quite a number of demonstrations and sit-ins, most famously at the London School of Economics (LSE), Hornsey, Essex, and Hull, the British protests often appear like "the poorer cousin of the USA or continental Europe's student movements" (Hanna 2008: 1542).[1] However, this widely shared evaluation of the British protests should not disguise the fact that the student movement had a considerable impact on British higher education and society at large, in particular by putting forward and shaping public debates (Hoefferle 2013: 204–5). One of the side effects of the protests was that they fundamentally altered the public image of the students. While higher education and students were still held in high esteem in the 1950s, the student protests of the late 1960s and early 1970s changed this picture tremendously. Thus, the *Sunday Telegraph* now spoke of students as "the waste of public money" and "the insult to the name of education" (cited in Hoefferle 2013: 145).

The student protests of the late 1960s had many causes. The expansion of higher education and the recognition of higher education as a right by the Robbins Report as well as the rise of youth cultures surely contributed to a changing student attitude, in particular towards academic authority (Fraser 1988: 87; Thomas 2002: 291). Moreover, political movements such as the Campaign for Nuclear Disarmament, the Anti-Apartheid Movement, the rise of the New Left, and the Vietnam Solidary Campaign had politicised students (Hoefferle 2013: 45; Nehring 2008: 126).[2] Though these political issues were not directly concerned with higher education, they could lead directly to protests over the nature of higher education. The troubles at the LSE in 1967, for instance, started as protests over apartheid, but soon student rights, freedom of speech, and the disciplinary powers of the school became the main issues (Hoefferle 2013: 76–8).[3]

As far as their demands with regard to higher education were concerned, the protests were anything but uniform. While some protesters, including the NUS for a long time, wanted moderate reforms, others such as the Revolutionary

Socialist Students' Federation (RSSF) called for a revolution of society.[4] Often, rather local issues also played a major role in the protests. Hence, when students at the University of Hull occupied parts of the university in May and June 1968, they formulated demands that addressed, amongst others, residence fees, meal and buttery prices, as well as cooking facilities (Fawthrop 1968: 60). Nevertheless, there were a number of concerns that were shared by protesters across the spectrum. These included the abolition of the *in loco parentis* system, the reform of the examination systems, and greater student participation in the government of the institutions of higher education.[5]

The end of *in loco parentis*

One of the central issues of the protests concerned the disciplinary powers that the institutions of higher education had over their students. As students were not adults in legal terms, universities and colleges were standing *in loco parentis*, which gave them the power to strictly control not only academic matters but also student life. This especially affected students living in halls of residence or colleges and in particular women. Often these students were subject to curfew and other regulations concerning, for instance, visiting times, social gatherings, or entertainment of the opposite sex. Although rules differed between institutions of higher education and though not all of these rules were probably enforced any longer, they were in principle still in effect in the 1960s (Ashby 1970: 13; Thomas 2002: 293–4). Criticism of such restrictions and the tight control of student life was nothing new. Already the Charter of Student Rights and Responsibilities of 1940 had pressed for increased freedoms for students. It was, however, only in the 1960s that students really challenged the *in loco parentis* system and demanded to be treated as adults and hence to be given the same rights as every other citizen.[6]

The case against the *in loco parentis* system was argued on various grounds. One central argument was that treating students like children actually ran counter to the aims of higher education. This argument was by no means new. Walter Moberly had already stated in the 1940s that the *in loco parentis* system needed to be abolished as it prevented students from becoming independent and responsible (1949: 10). On similar lines, student protesters like Linda Tinkham now claimed that the ideal of educating responsible and independent future citizens stood in stark contrast to the way students were actually treated (1969: 86). Apart from this educational argument, the *in loco parentis* system was also seen as a relic of the past that no longer did justice to the position of young people in society. This was backed by the Latey Committee, which reported to the government in 1967 and not only recommended lowering the age of majority from 21 to 18 but explicitly commented on the situation in the universities. While the *in loco parentis* system was "based upon the assumption that those between 18 and 21 need someone to look after them", the Latey Committee was "convinced that they do not" (*Report of the Committee on the*

Age of Majority 1967: §462). Following the publication of the Latey Report, the CVCP also agreed that universities and colleges ought to review their regulations concerning student life (CVCP and NUS 1968: 72), and when the age of majority was finally lowered in 1970, the *in loco parentis* system and the strict regulations of student life lost any legal backing.

The reform of the examination system

An issue that caused considerable discontent amongst many of the student protesters were the existing examination practices. While in some colleges, universities, and polytechnics new progressive forms of assessment such as course work or extended essays were already in use in the 1960s, the typical form was still the written final exam either annually or after three years of study. These traditional forms of assessment came under increasing attack in the late 1960s. Hence, from the eight demands that students at Hull University formulated, the very first one was the "[b]asic reform of the examination system" (Fawthrop 1968: 60).

Criticism of the prevailing examination systems was justified on various grounds. Tom Fawthrop, for instance, argued that the traditional forms of assessment would "not test intellectual ability" and would actually be in conflict "with the liberal aims of education" (1969: 100). Similar to the arguments against the *in loco parentis* system, the examination system was claimed to run counter to the ideals of education that the university supposedly stood for. Again, such criticism was not new. Brian Simon had called for a reformed examination system that tested "adaptability and intelligence rather than [. . .] memory and speed of handwriting" (1943: 134), and also academics like Moberly or Leavis had demanded changes. Moberly had criticised that the student was "like an athlete or racehorse being trained for a series of contests" (1949: 199), and Leavis had accused the examination system of creating a student who studied "single-mindedly and undeviatingly how to come out best in the examination" (1979a: 45). The need for reform was also recognised by the CVCP, which welcomed the fact that many universities and university colleges had introduced alternative assessment methods and suggested that further research and experiment be done in this direction (CVCP and NUS 1968: 70). Though some conservative authors like Kingsley Amis defended the traditional exams, even he conceded that there might be colleges or universities where the traditional examination system was in need of reform (1969: 10).

For some radical protesters, however, a mere reform of the examination system was not enough. What they demanded instead was the complete abolition of any form of examination. According to Alexander Cockburn, examinations, just like the content and organisation of education in general, were part of the "conditioning process" that fitted students into capitalist society (1969: 10). David Adelstein argued that the examination system had the prime function "to atomize and stratify" students and to put a label onto students which allowed employers to judge their value (1969: 74). And likewise Fawthrop claimed that exams were "a mirror image of capitalist society as a whole" (1969: 101). As part of the "conditioning process which induces the acceptance of arbitrary authority", examinations were said to reproduce "the dominant assumption that every society must have its rulers and rules", and therefore the "abolition of exams and of all other forms of grading and stratifying" was a central element in the fight against capitalism (1969: 102). The manifesto of the RSSF was also concerned with exams in its action programme and considered the "[a]bolition of all exams and grading" a necessary step in the fight for the "revolutionary overthrow of capitalism and imperialism and its replacement by workers' power" (1969: 21–2). In order to achieve such a social change, however, another step was considered essential as well: students needed more power in the running of their institution of higher education.

The fight for student power

A central and also the most controversial demand of the student protesters was that students ought to be granted a greater share in the government of the universities and colleges. Though many universities already had some form of student representation on welfare committees and sometimes even on court, council, or senate (Moodie and Eustace 1974: 200–4) and though demands for student participation in university government had already been voiced in the 1940s, they came to the fore in the late 1960s.

When the CVCP met with the NUS in 1968, student power within the universities was one of the central issues. While the CVCP could agree with the NUS that the universities needed to review their regulations concerning student life and that the examination system could do with further reform, it was much more hesitant about granting students power in the government of universities and colleges. Hence, the Joint Statement published by the CVCP and the NUS recommended actual student representation and thus decision making powers as far as student welfare was concerned, but it refrained from doing so when it came to academic matters such as curricula (CVCP and NUS 1968: 68). Though it declared that with regard to academic matters it was "essential that students' views should be properly taken into account", the Joint Statement emphasised that "the ultimate decision must be that of the statutorily responsible body" (CVCP and NUS 1968: 68). In other words, students ought to be consulted but should not be granted representation on the relevant committees and governing bodies. But apart from these actual recommendations, the Joint Statement was actually so important at that time because it recognised the NUS as a partner and thus indirectly acknowledged that students should have some say in the development of higher education.

Only one year after the publication of the Joint Statement, the NUS changed course under its newly elected president Jack Straw and demanded that students were not only granted consultation – that is students having the right to be heard but without effective power in decision making – but were given representation on all governing bodies and thus effective power in decision making (Ashby and Anderson 1970: 119). This new direction was defended by Straw in his Granada Guildhall Lecture of 1969. In this lecture, Straw tried to argue the case for student participation 'from within' as he turned the self-proclaimed ideals of higher education against the authorities themselves. Indeed, as he declared, to deny students participation in government would be nothing but the "failure [of the higher education institutions] to apply their own professed ideals and methodology to themselves" (1970: 7).

According to Straw, the fundamental principle underlying the government of the universities and colleges ought to be that "unless there are some specific reasons to the contrary all members of a given community are entitled in some way to be involved in the government of that community" (1970: 12). With this argument, Straw mobilised one of the strongest ideals in the university debate, that of the 'academic community' – a community based on common values to which both students and academics subscribed. What Straw proclaimed here was that if the university was indeed a community with common aims and values, then it would follow that every member should have a say in its government. In other words, he turned the relation of equivalence between students and academics that the notion of community entailed against the differential power relation between students and academics.

Apart from the reference to the community ideal, Straw claimed that student participation in university government went hand in hand with the aims of higher education. Thus, he argued that if the aim was to produce democratic citizens who were actively involved in the development of society, it was necessary "not only to teach people about the democratic system [. . .] but for them actually to be involved in an experience of democracy" (1970: 22–3). Moreover, as higher education allegedly had a critical function, it was particularly relevant that students could direct criticism at their own institution:

> We are educated to question and criticize within our subjects, yet never are we educated to question either the validity of the subject itself, or the system and structure within which that subject is taught, and which conditions the way in which it is taught. We are taught to be half critical only.
> (1970: 25)

Accordingly, student representation would be a necessary step for universities that took their ideals seriously.

What is striking about these arguments is that Straw tried to justify student participation in university government from within the established discourse of university education by directly referring to some of its central nodal points such as 'community', 'democracy', and 'critical thinking'. However, not all of

Straw's arguments stayed within the established discourse of university education. He also made use of a concept that had so far not turned up in the debate at all: the student as consumer.

In order to counter the common argument that students would lack the experience that qualified them to participate in the government of higher education institutions, Straw claimed that though students might be inexperienced in administration, they had "experience as 'consumers' of education" (1970: 18). By referring to students as 'consumers', Straw introduced a new discourse into the debate. Instead of staying within the educational discourse, he framed higher education within the discourse of shopping and consumption. Straw was not the only one to do so. Colin Crouch, for instance, wrote in a student newspaper in 1966 that students were "consumers of an educational service" and thus had "a right to say whether it is good or not" (cited in Hoefferle 2013: 77). What is interesting here is not whether the consumer analogy was in any way appropriate but that the student protesters made use of the discourse of the market and the consumer analogy well before it became popular in the policy discourse.

The fight for student power: radical positions

While the NUS was primarily interested in a reform of the universities, more radical protesters considered such a reform not as an end in itself but as a means towards the change of society as a whole. For the RSSF, for instance, greater student power was part of a programme that aimed at the "revolutionary overthrow of capitalism" (1969: 21). In contrast to Straw, these radical protest groups did not speak from within the discourse of liberal education but from a socialist standpoint and considered student power as a step towards the final defeat of capitalism. Institutions of higher education were regarded as playing a key role in the reproduction of the social, political, and economic system as they taught highly ideological knowledge and skills, disciplined individuals, and naturalised hierarchies and thus conditioned students for their fixed place in the capitalist system (Adelstein 1969: 76; Anderson 1969: 275; Blackburn 1969; Cockburn 1969: 10; Fawthrop 1969: 101). Accordingly, a change of the higher education system was seen as a necessary requirement in order to change the social system as a whole.

Though most of the radical protesters agreed that a reform of the education system was a crucial step in the demolition of capitalism, there was major disagreement concerning the actual role of the student in this fight against capitalism. While some protesters adhered to traditional socialist ideas and considered the working classes as the revolutionary agent with students primarily assisting in the class struggle, others from the New Left emphasised the particular intellectual contribution that students could make to the revolution. This dispute was not only rather central at the national RSSF conference of 1968, but it was also hotly debated in *New Left Review*.[7] But apart from these disagreements, the consensus was that the student struggle should not be restricted to issues within higher education only and needed to exceed the campus (Adelstein 1969: 80). Instead of being largely cut off from society, students ought to occupy a central role within society.

This concept of the student was quite different to both the manpower doctrine, which saw students as a resource for the national economy, as well as the traditional liberal idea of higher education, which focussed on the university as a community distinct from the rest of society. Even though some writers like Moberly and Leavis had emphasised that students should guide society, they had focused on graduates and considered students as agents-to-become. For radical protesters like David Adelstein, however, students were not merely agents-to-become, but they already were agents. Indeed, students were agents precisely because they were not yet graduates who had already found their position in the system. As Adelstein argued, students could be agents in society because they were "less tied to established institutions" and underwent "a formative period in their lives" (1969: 77). They were supposed to act as a driving force of change because they were in a special situation that allowed them to see society more critically than most others could. In a way, this concept of the student mirrored Michael Oakeshott's idea of the interval but with the decisive difference that this interval was not understood as a retreat from society but as a time of special involvement in society.

This conception of the student as an agent of change also found expression in a rather peculiar analogy: students as class or proletariat. The French sociologist Alain Touraine, for instance, characterised students as a kind of new proletariat and the university as "occupy[ing] the same place as the great capitalist enterprise formerly did" (cited in Jones 1969: 26).[8] Alexander Cockburn saw another similarity between workers and students as both were "often trying to achieve power from below" (1969: 15). Leaving aside the question to what extent students can actually be compared to workers, the crucial issue is what this form of rhetoric was supposed to achieve. Instead of being united in a community with a common culture and common aim, the class analogy depicted higher education as an arena of permanent struggle between different power groups. As Gareth Stedman Jones argued,

> the idea of the university as a community of teachers and taught is now as illusory as the philosophy of the Guild system in the first stages of the industrial revolution. Students and teachers must acknowledge their separate interests and establish new institutions based, not upon the idea of community, but inherent and permanent conflict – just as capital and labour are in structural conflict in the factory.
>
> (1969: 27)

By highlighting that students and academics had disparate interests, the class analogy promoted a new understanding of the student. The traditional ideal of the academic community had set students and academics in a relation of equivalence as both supposedly shared common aims and a common culture. In contrast to that, the class analogy emphasised the unequal positions and interests of students and academics. Hence, it established a relation of difference between students and academics and, based on that difference, created an equivalence amongst students across institution.[9] Instead of identifying primarily with their institution of higher education, students were supposed to consider themselves as one class that was united in solidarity. Thus, the class analogy made the actual social and economic conditions of the student the basis for a common student identity. This was directly addressed by Adelstein, who argued that "[t]he specific demand for student power must rest upon the work conditions of students" (1969: 80). The actual life situation of the student was supposed to provide the common ground to unite students – not only within one institution of higher education but across different institutions.

'Students have no rights'[10]

The demands for greater power caused mixed directions. Though many academics agreed that students had some valuable contributions to make and should be granted representation with regard to issues such as student welfare, the idea that students might also have an actual say with regard to academic matters or be represented on the governing bodies of the universities and colleges was heavily disputed. Some academics like Albert Sloman or Eric Ashby approved of greater student involvement in university and college government – albeit with some areas reserved for academics only (Ashby 1970: 66–70; Sloman 1970: 31, 42–3). Others showed much stronger reservations. While some feared that greater student involvement would protract meetings (Moodie and Eustace 1974: 201), some also regarded the idea that students might have a say in academic matters as an outright attack on the university.

One of the most common arguments against student representation was that students were still learners and thus not qualified to make decisions concerning academic matters. Thus, Kingsley Amis, for whom student participation was "pernicious", claimed that students, as they were still learning, were not in a position to decide on issues such as curricula, methods of assessment, or who should teach them (1969: 9) – an argument that was shared by numerous critics such as C.L. Mowat (1969: 11), Harry Kidd (1969: 141), Imre Lakatos (1969: 28), and Max Beloff (1975: 48). Leaving aside the question to what extent the argument was valid, the important point is that it constructed a relation of difference between the qualified and unqualified, between the academics as those who knew and the students as those who did not yet know.

For quite a number of writers, it was not enough to point out that students were unqualified to participate in government. Hence, they warned of the effects that student participation would have. According to Amis, giving students power with regard to matters such as curricula would lower standards as the demands for participation were an expression of "a simple desire to have less studying to do" (1969: 10). Others went much further and drew horrid images of what might happen if students were actually given greater power. Lakatos, for instance, reminded his readers of "the demands of Nazi students [. . .] to suppress 'Jewish-liberal-Marxist influence'" and of students in the USSR who had campaigned against the teaching of "Einstein's 'bourgeois relativism'" (1969: 27). Such comparisons with Nazi Germany or the USSR were nothing singular but made by a number of writers including Michael Swann (1969: 148), Max Beloff (1975: 49), and William Walsh (1969: 68). In all these cases, the demand for student participation was depicted not only as a threat to the university but to the nation as a whole, and thus the defence of the university against students became a matter of defending the freedom of society.[11] Moreover, the references to Nazi Germany and the USSR constructed a strong relation of difference between students and academics along the lines 'ideology vs truth'. Clearly, students were prone to ideology whereas academics were not, or at least less so. Thus, Beloff, for instance, warned of "manipulated student opinion", which, if students had more power, would pose a "threat to academic freedom" (1975: 48–9). The assumption behind such warnings was that students were blinded by ideologies, quite in contrast to the academics, who were the guardians of truth. Of course, such claims were themselves highly ideological, and they totally ignored the fundamental criticism of the radical protesters that the university itself was an ideological apparatus.

Such depictions of students as a threat to academic freedom did not just draw a line between students and academics but between students and the university. The demand for student power was not presented as a conflict between two groups within the university, but between students and the university. Students were positioned as an outside enemy force that could destroy the university. This attitude was also underlying Lakatos's claim that there were "no arguments for Student Power that would not be arguments for Government Power" (1969: 29). Although he acknowledged that "[s]tudents may be part of the academic community in an important sense in which the Government are not" (1969: 29), he supposed that students were not part of the academic community proper. Similarly, Derek Colville announced in the fourth Black Paper that "[a] university, essentially, is its staff" (1975: 51). These accounts of the university actually abandoned one of the central ideals within the debate about higher education: that institutions of higher education were communities of academics and students. Instead of being part of the academic community, students were positioned outside of it.[12]

The student is like . . .

One of the striking features of the protests and the debate about student power was the use of analogies such as 'class' or 'consumers'. Unsurprisingly, these analogies raised criticism from within academia. In the first Black Paper, for instance, Lakatos argued that students did not see that the actual consumer was the state while they were "the goods to be delivered" (1969: 29). As the state financed education, so Lakatos argued, the consumer argument would actually legitimise increased state power but not student power. Kidd saw a different misconception in the consumer analogy with regard to the actual practices of the student protests. As he claimed, "if consumers are dissatisfied, taking over the shop is not their usual remedy" (1969: 138). What Kidd here pointed to is the power structure that the notion of the consumer actually stands for. Consumers 'consume' a service extended to them. Though they might be asked from time to time whether they liked the service or not, they do not have power over that service but remain in a rather passive, non-powerful position. Thus, the consumer analogy actually appealed to some academics like Eric Ashby and Mary Anderson precisely because it called for consultation and not representation (1970: 138).

The use of analogies was not restricted to students. In order to counter the growing demands for student power, a number of academics also employed analogies in order to define what a university was and what position the student ought to occupy within it. Thus, Kidd not only disregarded the consumer analogy but also offered an alternative: the student as patient. As some protesters had argued that students should be involved in decisions that concerned teaching methods and course content because they were the ones who were most affected, Kidd rebutted this argument by stating that "[a] surgical operation has far more importance for the patient than for the surgeon; but that does not entitle the patient to direct how it shall be performed" (1969: 138). Although Kidd primarily used the analogy of the patient to defend the authority of the academic, whom he compared to a surgeon, he implicitly claimed that students were rather passive beings to whom something was done. Students were not regarded as having a stake in their education but as undergoing a specific treatment – an understanding of education pretty similar to the manpower doctrine, which considered students as objects.

The same analogy was suggested by Ashby and Anderson, albeit in a slightly different way. Though they pointed out that the status of a student was different from the status of the patient in a hospital, they emphasised that there was also much common ground:

> Both the doctor-patient and the teacher-student relationship require at the minimum a voluntary consensus about the purpose of the institution they have voluntarily entered. And this presupposes a clear and limited demarcation of authority; clear, because if doctors and professors do not know more than patients and students, there is no point in having hospitals or universities at all: patients and students might as well stay at home. And a limited authority, because the only expertise of doctor or professor which patient or student is obliged to acknowledge is in the expertise which

> brings the two together. Outside this expertise neither doctor nor professor can claim any authority.
>
> (1970: 143)

While they thus limited the academic's authority to academic matters, Ashby and Anderson insisted that students had to acknowledge the traditional idea of the university and hence the academic's authority.

Another analogy that was used in order to defend the authority of the academic was that of the university as a guild. In contrast to the hospital analogy, which assigned the student a rather passive role, the analogy of the guild gave the student a much more active position. Instead of undergoing surgery, the student was seen as an apprentice who learned a trade. However, the guild analogy was not primarily used to emphasise that students were active, but rather to justify their lack of power. Kidd, for instance, argued that "[t]he scholars are those that have made a substantial part of the ascent; the apprentices are little above ground level. They are not yet of the community of scholars, not qualified to share in its government." (1969: 141) Similarly, Ashby declared that a university was "not a mini-state composed of citizens of equal competence to decide academic policy" but was rather "like a guild of masters and apprentices" (1970: 59). Mowat likewise claimed that universities were similar to

> craftsmen's guilds, in which the masters, journeymen and apprentices were all brethren but not all equal. The apprentice had to serve his terms and learn the mystery before he could work on his own, and only the masters could judge a masterpiece and admit its maker to become one of themselves.
>
> (1969: 13)

The guild analogy was actually not new. Moberly had also described the university as a guild and referred to students as "novices" (1949: 121). But while Moberly had used the guild analogy primarily to argue that the university had values and standards of its own that needed protection against the government and the economy (1949: 120–1), Ashby, Mowat, and Kidd referred to the university as a guild in order to defend internal power structures. While the guild analogy was a variation of the ideal of the academic community as it constructed a strict differentiation between members (academics and students) and non-members (the rest of society), it was specifically used to legitimise differences in power within the community.

There is, however, as with most analogies, an inherent contradiction in the guild analogy. While the analogy was used in order to defend academic authority, it assumed that the sole purpose of higher education was to produce future academics. As Ian Carter has pointed out, a guild only takes in those as novices who will later work within the guild and be its members, often for life (1990:

227). In other words, describing colleges and universities as guilds implies that all students wanted to become future scholars. But despite this contradiction, the guild metaphor was rather popular. One reason for its appeal was probably that it emphasised the long tradition of the university and provided reminiscences of 'Merry Old England'. In this respect, the use of the analogy in the 1960s can also be seen as a critique of a world that was in flux with shifting beliefs and values and a loss of traditional authority. The guild functioned as a metonym for an ordered and stable society that stood in stark contrast to the disintegrating demands of the student protesters – the perceived enemies of traditional values.

A new concept of the student?

With the student protests, the student became visible – not as an individual passing through education but as a collective body with a common consciousness. This emergence of a common student identity was absolutely central to the protests of the late 1960s, and sometimes the creation of a community and the feeling to belong to a common cause might even have been the main motivations for students to join the protests (Crouch 1970: 181; Hoggart 1979: 173; Silver and Silver 1997: 159). The protests were thus both the expression of a growing collective student identity and at the same time a means to foster it. Hence, activists like Gareth Stedman Jones, Anthony Barnett, and Tom Wengraf praised, for instance, the troubles at the LSE because it was here that "for the first time students have shown unprecedented collective solidarity in their role as students" (1967: 4). Of course, it is not the case that nothing like a common student identity had existed before, and authors like Brian Simon, himself NUS president in 1939/40, have highlighted that a common student consciousness actually developed in the 1930s and 1940s (1987: 193). In the protests of the 1960s, however, this common student identity grew, and it took a different shape as it was increasingly founded on an opposition towards the university and college authorities.[13] While the traditional liberal-humanist ideal of the academic community had promoted an equivalence between students and academics based on common values and a shared culture and emphasised the difference towards the non-academic, the student community that emerged in the protests was constituted through the difference between students and academics. Indeed, often the student protests were a direct reaction towards decisions by the authorities that were considered unjust and unjustified (Thomas 2002: 284). The resulting confrontations showed that institutions of higher education were not communities but constituted by differences – differences in power and outlook.

The student protests were thus also the expression of a shifting understanding of higher education. Universities and colleges were now seen in terms of power relations. This focus on power structures was itself a sign of the diminishing authority of the culture that had legitimised the power of the university. Hence, students questioned the position they had been assigned to and demanded more rights and a share in the government of the universities and colleges. By doing so, they rejected the idea of the university as a place of disinterested learning and culture. As Bill Readings has argued, albeit not with a specific focus on Britain,

> what matters about 1968 is that the narrative of *Bildung* – of simple passage from infancy to adulthood, from dependency to emancipation (the Kantian narrative of enlightenment that characterizes the knowledge process itself in modernity) – has been rejected by the students in the name of an uncertainty.
>
> (1996: 147)

Though it would be an overstatement to claim that students totally dismissed the idea of education as leading to emancipation, they clearly rejected "any teleological understanding of being a student under the sign of cultivation" (Masschelein and Simons 2012: 170). They discarded the idea that they were only agents-to-become, that they were agents-in-waiting, agents-in-the-future-but-not-yet. Instead, what the protests highlighted was that students already were agents.

What finally became clear in the late 1960s was thus that it was not self-evident what either higher education or a student were. Not only were the debates about student power questioning the function and structure of higher education, but the enhanced use of analogies in the late 1960s shows that the signifier 'student' had become more and more devoid of any fixed meaning. No matter whether students referred to themselves as class or consumers or whether academics compared students to apprentices or patients, all of these analogies were attempts to define what a student was and to prevent the higher education discourse from disintegrating. What the rising use of analogies, which were all taken from discourses other than higher education, thus indicates is that the discourse of higher education and the concept of the student had become rather unstable – an instability that provided fertile ground for the reconceptualisation of the student as a customer within the growing discourse of marketisation from the 1980s onwards.

Notes

1 Similar judgements can be found in contemporary evaluations like Beloff (1970: 61) and Crouch (1970: 97), but also in more recent ones like Tight (2009: 71), Kundnani (2009: 207), Jones (2010: 8), and DeGroot (2013: 355–6).

2 The New Left was not necessarily at the centre of the protests and in many respect the student protests and the New Left stayed rather distinct (Davis 2008: 53). However, several of the radical and leading figures of the protests such as David Adelstein, Robin Blackburn, or Tom Fawthrop showed strong alliances with the New Left and also published articles in *New Left Review*.

3 The protests actually started over the appointment of a successor to Sydney Caine as Director of the LSE. After Walter Adams had been nominated, demonstrations started because of Adams' alleged links to the racist regime in Rhodesia, where he was director of the University College. The troubles, however, really started after the LSE authorities took disciplinary action and suspended David Adelstein, president of the Students' Union, and Marshall Bloom, president of the Graduate Students' Association. Detailed but rather subjective accounts of the events at the LSE are provided in Crouch (1970) and Brewster and Cockburn (1967), who actually took part in the protests, and Kidd (1969), who had been the Secretary of the LSE at that time.
4 As the NUS for long confined itself to matters such as hall management, catering committees, and student grants and was politically rather uncommitted (Ashby and Anderson 1970: 62, 94, 103), politically more radical students, for whom the NUS was "the student's muffler" (Widgery 1969: 129), founded the Radical Student Alliance (RSA) in 1966 followed by the Revolutionary Socialist Students' Federation (RSSF) in 1968. Although it is difficult to judge whether these organisations were ever the 'leaders' of the student movement, they managed to politicise the NUS, which in 1969 changed its Clause Three so that from now on it could take a stance on any political matter relating to students (Hoefferle 2013: 108).
5 Another issue that sparked protests was the government's announcement in 1966 to increase fees for overseas students. This decision was criticised not only by students but also by Vice-Chancellors and staff, who considered the rise in fees as an act of discrimination against students who often had limited access to higher education in their home countries (Hoefferle 2013: 70–1, Jones 1969: 45).
6 Demands to abolish the *in loco parentis* system can for instance be found in Jones, Barnett, and Wengraf (1967: 6), Fawthrop (1968: 60), Adelstein (1969: 79), and Jones (1969: 46).
7 See in particular Shaw (1967), Brewster (1967), Adelstein (1967), but also Fernbach (1969), Cockburn (1969), and Triesman (1969). For the RSSF conference, see University of Sussex Socialist Cub (2008) as well as Walsh (2008). For a further discussion of the relation between Old and New Left and the debate on the role of the student within the revolutionary struggle, see Hoefferle (2013: 99).
8 The class analogy as used by Touraine was also criticised by some protesters themselves. According to Jones, it misconceived the location of power for much of it would actually be located outside the higher education institutions (1969: 27–8).
9 Harold Silver as an academic teacher saw this problem already in the mid-1960s. Hence, he suggested salaries for students, which would turn them into employees of the universities. For as long as students received grants and were thus 'paid' from outside the university, they would always stay outsiders to the university (1965: 411).
10 The declaration that "[s]tudents have no rights" was allegedly made by Sydney Caine, Director of the LSE, to students who protested against the appointment of Walter Adams as his successor (cited in Brewster and Cockburn 1967: 16). Eric Ashby, however, argues that these words were never spoken like that and are a myth (1970: 50).
11 Of course, students marching under the banners of Mao or students who tried to prevent speakers of different outlook from giving talks lend themselves to such a comparison. At Sussex, for instance, an official of the US Embassy was covered in red paint, and at Essex, Conservative MPs were molested and a scientist from the government's research centre for biological warfare was hindered from speaking. Similar scenes occurred at Manchester but also in Oxford and Cambridge (Crouch 1970: 100–2).
12 Another widely used strategy was to divide the protesters into two distinct groups: those who wanted to improve the university and those who allegedly wanted to destroy it. This division can be found in numerous texts of the time such as Lakatos (1969: 29), Ashby and Anderson (1970: 123–8), Gross (1969: 63), or Sloman (1970: 30). There were, of course, differences between student protesters. However, the crude distinction

between two types of protesters was primarily a rhetorical strategy to dismantle the claim for student representation as it allowed to ignore large parts of the protest.

13 That there was indeed such a shift in identity could even be recognised in Oxford. While at the beginning of the 1960s students had still worn gown at tutorials and during dinner to denote their membership to a college community, they had ceased to do so by the end of the 1960s, and instead had started to identify with students elsewhere and no longer as 'elitist' members of an ancient institution (Hoefferle 2013: 175). This change in attitude was also reflected in some campus novels. While in Kingsley Amis's *Lucky Jim* (1954) one can still read of a "late group of students most of them wearing the yellow and green College scarf" (1976: 13), the students in Malcolm Bradbury's *The History Man* (1975) no longer wear clothes that identify them as members of a particular university but rather dress like young people in general. This is particularly evident when the conservative student George Carmody is marked as different from the other students precisely because he wears "a university blazer, with a badge, and a university tie" (Bradbury 2012: 141).

Part III

Marketisation and the student as customer

Chapter 11

Thatcherism and New Public Management

Due to a relatively slow economic growth in the decades after World War II and the economic crisis of the 1970s, confidence in the welfare state faded away and liberal economic values gained in power. Following the election victory of the Conservatives in 1979, the new political outlook could soon be felt in higher education as public funding for higher education was cut so severely that some higher education institutions came close to bankruptcy.[1] While the first years of the Thatcher government were primarily marked by the cuts, the government started to radically restructure higher education from the second half of the 1980s onwards. The UGC was replaced by funding councils; the binary system was abolished and the polytechnics were given the chance to become universities; and last but not least, top-up loans were introduced to gradually replace parts of the maintenance grants for students.

Higher education and manpower needs

While the UGC in its 1984 strategy paper still pondered the aims of higher education as defined in the Robbins Report and claimed "that there are common values which education seeks to transmit and which help to give society its cohesion and stability" (1984: §10), government bodies like the DES already spoke a different language at that time. The Green Paper *The Development of Higher Education into the 1990s* (1985), for instance, declared that it was

> vital for our higher education to contribute more effectively to the improvement of the performance of the economy. [. . .] [U]nless the country's economic performance improves, we shall be even less able than now to afford many of the things that we value most – including education for pleasure and general culture and the financing of scholarship and research as an end in itself.
>
> (DES 1985: §1.2)

Though the Green Paper stated that it did not want to devalue the humanities and the cultural benefits of education, it made clear that the economic case was absolutely central. Consequently, institutions of higher education were asked to focus on the "the production of qualified manpower" (DES 1985: §2.1) – in particular "innovators and entrepreneurs who will create new jobs and those who achieve vocational qualifications, for which there is a market need" (DES 1985: §2.2). This economic view of education was further strengthened in the White Paper *Higher Education: Meeting the Challenge* (1987), which straightforwardly argued that higher education had "a crucial role in helping the nation meet the economic and social challenges of the final decade of this century and beyond" (DES 1987: iv). Thus, higher education was supposed to "serve the economy more effectively, pursue basic scientific research and scholarship in the arts and humanities, have closer links with industry and commerce, and promote enterprise" (DES 1987: iv). Though the White Paper stated that answering the needs of the economy was "not the sole purpose of higher education", it made it absolutely clear that this was the goal that needed to be "vigorously pursued" (DES 1987: §1.5). Higher education was thus near entirely framed around the nodal point 'economy' and was primarily considered as a means of manpower production.

While such an economic view had already been subscribed to by earlier governments and had, for instance, been dominant in the Barlow and Percy reports of the 1940s, the Thatcher government departed from earlier variants of the manpower doctrine in two decisive ways. First, the manpower doctrine as advanced under the Thatcher government was not confined to specific subjects or institutions, as had been the case in the 1940s or with the polytechnics. Instead, the whole of higher education was now subsumed under the economic imperative (Wolf 1998: 221). The biggest difference between earlier manpower models and the manpower conception of Thatcherism, however, was their concept of the student. While the manpower doctrine of earlier decades had regarded students as a resource and required higher education to turn out particular graduates, the economic view of higher education as it arose since the 1980s went further and demanded a change in attitude of both students and higher education institutions. Institutions of higher education were now supposed to counter "'anti-business' snobbery" and to foster the "entrepreneurial spirit" (DES 1985: §1.6), while closer links with business were considered essential "to foster the positive attitudes to enterprise which are crucial for both institutions and their students" (DES 1987: §1.5).[2] At the core of the new manpower doctrine was thus the idea not just to produce enough graduates to meet the demands from the economy and industry but to create particular students with a certain outlook. Just as the Robbins Report and earlier advocates of liberal education had sought to transform students in the name of culture, they were now to be transformed in the name of the economy.

Expansion and the reformulation of the Robbins Principle

After the Robbins Report had argued for an increase in student numbers, the following expansion even surpassed its projections. Instead of the suggested

344,000 places for full-time students in 1970/71, more than 430,000 full-time students were enrolled in higher education by that time, and another 140,000 students were studying part-time (Halsey 1992: 101). The situation, however, changed in the late 1970s when the number of school leavers declined. As the demographic changes were running counter to the growing demand for qualified manpower, a more rational planning of student numbers set in and access to higher education was rethought (Kogan and Hanney 2000: 72).[3]

The Robbins Report had argued that access to higher education should depend on "ability and attainment" (Committee on Higher Education 1963: §31). This principle was now questioned. The UGC and the National Advisory Board for Local Authority Higher Education (NAB), for instance, argued that "A-levels are not always good predictors of achievement in higher education" (UGC 1984: §8). Consequently, they redefined the Robbins Principle as: "Courses of higher education should be available for all those who are able to benefit from them and who wish to do so" (UGC 1984: §8) – a formulation to which the Green Paper 1985 immediately added that "the benefit has to be sufficient to justify the cost" (DES 1985: §3.2). But the UGC and NAB not only reformulated the Robbins Principle, they also shifted the focus with regard to the social groups that were supposed to be given equal access to higher education. The Robbins Report, though it recognised the low number of women in higher education (Committee on Higher Education 1963: §124), had primarily been concerned with equality in terms of class. In contrast to that, the UGC and NAB argued that it was important to provide places for students "not only from different social classes, but also from different ethnic groups" and to ensure that "opportunities for women [were] as good as opportunities for men" (UGC 1984: §11). While the Robbins Report had mainly been concerned with class bias, the UGC and NAB now also tackled the concept of the students in terms of ethnicity and gender.

The White Paper 1987 went even further than the UGC and NAB and not only reaffirmed the reformulated Robbins Principle but also asked all institutions of higher education, including the universities, to recognise non-traditional qualifications gained through access courses or vocational qualifications as alternatives to the traditional A-levels (DES 1987: §2.9).[4] This strong commitment to widening access was not legitimised through nodal points such as 'equality' as had been the case in the Robbins Report. Instead, it was justified only through the economic relevance of higher education. While the UGC strategy paper of 1984 still considered widening access a question of equality and social justice, the White Paper 1987 argued for expansion predominantly in terms of manpower. Further expansion was said to be necessary in order to "take greater account of the country's needs for highly qualified manpower" (DES 1987: iv). Expansion and widening access were not means to foster equality but to boost the economy. While the Robbins Report had considered expansion as an answer to a rising demand from below, the Thatcher government focused on output and the demand for the graduates. Questions of equality, social change, or social justice hardly entered the picture, and the student was primarily regarded as a resource to the nation.

In order to satisfy the manpower demands, institutions of higher education were not only supposed to take in students without traditional qualifications, but they were also asked to increase their provision of continuing education for adults. Though the Robbins Report had already stated that in the future it would be increasingly important to provide courses for adults "to bring them up to date in their subjects" (Committee on Higher Education 1963: §513), continuing education only became a major topic in the 1970s and 1980s. In its discussion document *Higher Education into the 1990s*, the DES suggested that in order to counter the demographic trends the higher education system "might reach out to embrace different types of students and to meet fresh needs such as that of recurrent or continuing education" (DES 1978: §7). This focus on continuing education was also taken up by the UGC, which emphasised that education in later life was necessary as the changing world of work required to update one's "skills and attitudes" (1984: §4) and because education made a "contribution to personal development and social progress" (1984: §5). In contrast to the UGC, the White Paper 1987 argued that

> [m]any individuals want or need education in middle life, sometimes because they had no earlier opportunity and sometimes to make good deficiencies in their previous education. Overlapping with them are the many who need updating, retraining or new skills – for example in business management – in order to remain competent members of Britain's increasingly technological workforce.
>
> (DES 1987: §2.26)

While the DES did not deny that continuing education could contribute to personal development, it considered the increasing provision of education for adults a necessary measure to keep Britain's manpower competitive.

Within the strong economic rationale that underlay Thatcherite policies, higher education was thus increasingly opened to non-traditional students both in terms of age and qualifications. But the concept of the student not only widened, the position of the 'new students' that would enter higher education also shifted in terms of power. In contrast to the Robbins Report, Truscot, Moberly, or Sloman, who had all been concerned with transforming the 'new students' in order to integrate them into academic culture, the White Paper 1987 argued that "institutions of higher education will have to adapt their teaching methods and the design of their courses to accommodate new types of student" (DES 1987: §2.15). This marks a decisive shift in power. Instead of transforming the 'new students', the government called for higher education to adapt to the 'new students'. This loss of authority of the institutions of higher education was part of a fundamental reconfiguration of the relation between the state and higher education.

Performativity and New Public Management

In the 1980s, the economic view of education did not only become increasingly hegemonic, but it also changed significantly as new nodal points such as 'quality' and 'market' gained in power. This new market discourse formed the bedrock for the restructuring of higher education. Following the principles of New Public Management, which meant that private-sector management technics were increasingly applied to the public services in order to achieve cost effectiveness and value for money (Ferlie, Musselin, and Andresani 2008: 335; Salter and Tapper 2000: 70), higher education governance and funding were radically transformed.

The beginning of this new era was marked by the Jarratt Report (1985), which evaluated university management on business lines and treated universities as "first and foremost corporate enterprises" (CVCP 1985: §3.41). Hence, the universities' prime task was said to be to generate "value for money" (CVCP 1985: §2.4). By applying management strategies to universities, the report endorsed strategic and long-term planning and called for clearly defined "[o]bjectives and aims" (CVCP 1985: §3.30), the use of "performance indicators" (CVCP 1985: §3.30), stronger "measures of output" (CVCP 1985: §3.33), and "monitoring procedures" (CVCP 1985: §3.37). Traditional administrative and governmental structures were to be replaced by a top-down approach with professional management as means of government instead of academic consensus (Anderson 2006: 170; Deem, Hillyard, and Reed 2007: 61). For the Jarratt Report, the university was no longer a place of culture and learning, but a business that had to perform. Strikingly, the report was not published by the government but by the CVCP. Quite in contrast to the UGC, which was still reluctant in the mid-1980s to commit itself to the new economic ideology, the CVCP actually took the lead in the restructuring of higher education under market principles (Salter and Tapper 2000: 71). But soon, the language of output measures and performance indicators that the Jarratt Report introduced found strong resonance in the emerging debate on 'quality', and in the following White Papers one could increasingly read of "performance indicators" (DES 1987: §iv), "quantifiable outcomes", and "calculations of value" (DES 1991: §80). Higher education was now legitimised not through reference to 'knowledge' or 'culture' but by what Jean-François Lyotard has called 'performativity'.

In his seminal study *The Postmodern Condition: A Report on Knowledge* (1979, English 1984), Lyotard has argued that the status of knowledge had changed in Western societies as technical developments like computerisation had led to a quantification and commodification of knowledge and information had increasingly turned into the basis for power. Thus, higher education was no longer legitimised by any grand narrative or notions like 'culture' or 'knowledge for its own sake' but only through "the logic of maximum performance" (1984: xxiv). Hence, "[t]he desired goal becomes the optimal contribution of higher education to the best performativity of the social system" (1984: 48) – a goal that is to be achieved through the constant monitoring and regulation of higher education's performance and efficient functioning. As Stephen Ball has pointed out, performativity is "a technology, a culture and a mode of regulation that employs judgements, comparisons and displays as means of incentive, control, attrition and change based on rewards and sanctions (both material and symbolic)" (2003: 216). Such technologies and control mechanism were increasingly instituted in the 1980s, for instance in the form of performance-based research funding through the Research Assessment Exercise (RAE) or quality audit.[5]

As part of this rising dominance of 'performativity' and New Public Management, the higher education system was fundamentally restructured. In 1988, the polytechnics were taken out of the control of the LEAs and placed under the newly established Polytechnics and Colleges Funding Council (PCFC). At the same time, the UGC, which had so far acted as a buffer between the government and the universities, was replaced by the Universities Funding Council (UFC). According to the DES, the creation of the UFC was supposed to "clarify responsibilities, improve financial accountability and increase effectiveness" with the government "provid[ing] planning guidelines for the university system" (1987: §v). This was a total change in the understanding of the university. Even though the UGC had increasingly steered university development in the 1970s and 1980s, it had not been a planning body, quite in contrast to the new funding councils, which much more actively tried to shape the future development of higher education (Palfreyman and Tapper 2014: 5–14; Tapper 2007: 29–31). The university that had once been self-governing was now explicitly governed by the state (Shattock 2006: 134, 2008: 181–2). This trend towards greater government control continued after the polytechnics had been granted university status in 1992 and the now unified system had been placed under the newly created Higher Education Funding Councils (HEFCs) for England, Wales, and Scotland. Within the first two months of their existence, the HEFCs were given a whole series of guidelines asking them to develop new funding methods, to specify what was expected of higher education institutions, to increase accountability, and to more strongly relate funding to performance assessment (Alexander 2000: 423). But while the HEFCs were thus becoming a means to further increase government control, the DES actually justified the abolishment of the binary divide as a means to foster "greater competition for funds and students" and hence to achieve "cost effective expansion" (1991: §17). The abolishment of the binary divide followed a typical market ideology, in which competition was considered as leading to lower prices.

As this short historical sketch of the restructuring of the governance and funding structures of higher education shows, the New Public Management of the Thatcher and Major governments did not mean that state control was minimised. Instead, it was extended in order to create a market from above. As the introduction of management-like governance structures, performance measurement, and monitoring undermined traditional power structures, power shifted towards the government and the funding agencies.

New Public Management and the student

As New Public Management principles gained in dominance in the 1980s, the student initially played only a marginal role. In the Jarratt Report, for instance, students were only indirectly referred to with phrases like "measures of output" (CVCP 1985: §3.33) or "performance indicators" (CVCP 1985: §3.30). Similarly, the White Paper 1991 was concerned with "quantifiable outcomes" in the form of "[p]erformance indicators and calculations of value added" (DES 1991: §80). Students were not present as agents but only as objects that could be measured and quantified in order to determine the institution's performance.

However, there were also occasions when students turned up in a rather different role. They were not only objects through which the performance of the institutions of higher education could be measured but also one of the beneficiaries of the government's planned reforms. Thus, the White Paper 1991 claimed that

> [t]he new framework proposed in this White Paper will enable institutions to make yet more effective responses to the increasing demand for higher education. This will bring benefits for the individuals who study as well as for the economy and society as a whole.
>
> (DES 1991: §3)

Moreover, the White Paper argued that the government wanted to "ensure that this education is increasingly relevant to students' various needs. This will benefit both the individuals who participate and the economy and society as a whole." (DES 1991: §106) The government thus depicted its reforms as being in the interest not only of the economy, but also of the students.

Last but not least, students also appeared as agents within the emerging higher education market. While the government still believed that "student demand should not be the sole determinant of the shape of expansion", it suggested that students ought to be "a major influence" (DES 1991: §20). However, the focus was less on what students actually wanted but rather on students as a financial resource over which institutions of higher education had to compete. Thus, the White Paper 1991 argued that "the real key to achieving cost effective expansion lies in greater competition for funds and students" (DES 1991: §17) and that the binary divide needed to be abolished so that "all institutions will compete for funds and students on an equal basis" (DES 1991: §24). Of course, there had always been a certain competition for good students as well as for students as a financial resource. But now this became a much stronger steering element in the system – not least because tuition fees rose and funding increasingly depended on student numbers.[6] As Kenneth Baker, then Secretary of State, explained, this shift in funding was supposed to give "a new and proper emphasis to market forces" as a greater share of the universities and colleges' funding would "depend on the attractiveness of what they have to offer and their ability to market it" (cited in Pritchard 1994: 256) – an objective that was further promoted through the introduction of the bidding system and fees-only students.[7]

Within the rise of New Public Management, the student was thus placed in multiple positions. Students were considered as measurable objects through which to assess the performance of the institutions of higher education; they were depicted as the beneficiaries of the market reforms; and they were regarded as a resource over which to compete and hence as agents which could shape the provision of higher education.

From grants to loans

For the students, one of the most fundamental reforms of the Thatcher era was the substitution of parts of the maintenance grants, as introduced after the Anderson Report (1960), with loans. Already in 1964 the Treasury had discussed plans for loan schemes, and in 1969 Shirley Williams, Minister of State for Education and Science, had suggested to reduce or even remove maintenance grants and to establish a loans system instead (Hillman 2013: 255, Shattock 2012: 144). While the debate was thus not new, it was the Conservatives under Thatcher who finally took action. As soon as the Conservatives came to power, they abolished subsidies for overseas students and froze the maintenance grant for home students (Brown and Carasso 2013: 8; Watson and Bowden 1999: 243).[8] Following the White Paper *Top-Up Loans for Students* (1988), the maintenance grant for home students was in parts replaced by a loan, which in the long run was supposed to cover about 50 percent of maintenance costs (DES 1988: §1.3). This was a fundamental shift in student funding that abandoned established policies. With the introduction of top-up loans, students were asked to contribute to the costs of higher education for the first time since the 1960s. The introduction of top-up loans thus broke with the principle that the state should be the main funder of higher education.

According to the White Paper 1988, arguments in favour of loans were numerous. Besides the point that a loan system would supposedly "increase the resources available to students" and reduce parental contributions as well as public expenditure (DES 1988: §1.1), the central argument was that grants ought to be partly substituted with loans in order "to share the cost of student maintenance more equitably between students themselves, their parents and the taxpayer" (DES 1988: §1.1). Loans were thus presented as an instrument to achieve fairness. The rhetorical strategy that was employed in this argument is decisive. Instead of referring to society or the community, the word 'taxpayer' was used which reduced society to an accumulation of individuals primarily characterised through their act of paying taxes. This economic and individualistic view of society persisted throughout all further elaborations of the loans argument. Thus, the White Paper maintained that "economic analysis suggests that, in financial terms alone, higher education would be worthwhile to the student even if no maintenance grant were available" (DES 1988: §2.25) and that the financial benefits for the individual graduate were effectively higher than those for society (DES 1988: §2.26). Underlying the loans argument was thus an economic view of higher education that no longer focused on the benefit of higher education for the nation but primarily highlighted the individual economic benefit that higher education offered to the graduate. The economic view of higher education that had still characterised the Green Paper 1985 and the White Paper 1987 was now given a decisive twist as the focus shifted from the nation to the individual – a shift in focus which determined policy for the decades to come.

As far as the concept of the student is concerned, the introduction of loans was, however, not only important because it shifted the focus onto the individual economic benefit of higher education. Loans were also perceived as an instrument to actively change how students understood themselves and the purpose of higher education. According to the White Paper 1988, loans could "increase economic awareness among students" (DES 1988: §1.1). In other words, loans were hoped to transform the student's idea of higher education towards a more economic and utilitarian perspective. With the introduction of loans, the government thus took active measures to shape the student's understanding of education – a development that continued under New Labour and which also motivated the Higher Education Charter of 1993.

The Charter for Higher Education

The reform of public services under New Public Management principles reached a new level when John Major launched the Citizen's Charter programme in 1991. In the following years, dozens of charters were published that covered all kinds of public services and that redefined the relation between citizens and public service providers and specified the standards that citizens could expect. Accordingly, the Department for Education also published a charter for higher education under the title *Higher Quality and Choice*.

As the charter informed its readers, its declared aim was to "ensure high standards of service in higher education" (DfE 1993: 1). Therefore, it described in detail what kind of higher education services could be expected by employers and students, who were now referred to as "the customers of higher education" (DfE 1993: 1). Though the charter emphasised that students also had responsibilities such as attending courses and handing in work in time (DfE 1993: 13), the focus was primarily on the rights of the students. Thus, students were said to be entitled to, for instance, getting information about course content, assessment, and quality, fair treatment with regard to applications, or careers guidance (DfE 1993: 4–11).

Apart from laying down these concrete rights and responsibilities, the charter was significant because it redefined the relation between academics and students as a contractual relationship between customers and service providers. This reconfiguration shifted responsibilities. With regard to teaching, students were, for instance, told:

> You should know in advance how your course will be taught and assessed. You should receive a high standard of teaching and research supervision. This includes effective management of your learning by teaching and other staff.
>
> (DfE 1993: 12)

Not only were students said to be entitled to a high quality of teaching, but it was suggested that their learning could be managed and that it was supposedly managed by teachers and other staff and not the student. As the charter implied, the student as a customer was not an agent of his own learning.

With this reconfiguration of students as customers who were entitled to high quality services and this shift of responsibilities towards the institution of higher education, the Charter for Higher Education marked a further step in the marketisation of higher education and actually foreshadowed what became the central tenet of New Labour's higher education policy.

Notes

1 As the UGC decided not to cut evenly across institutions and subjects, some institutions like Salford, which suffered grant reductions of 44 percent, Keele (35 percent), or Bradford (33 percent) were hit much harder than others like Loughborough (7 percent), Bath (7 percent), and York (2 percent), (average of 17 percent) (Stewart 1989: 226).

2 One such measure to promote entrepreneurial thinking was the Enterprise in Higher Education initiative that was set up by the government in 1987 (Pring 1993: 61).

3 In 1978, the DES offered three different projections of student numbers which ranged from a participation rate of 15 percent to 21 percent, with a mid-way projection at 18 percent for 1992 (DES 1978: Chart 1). As part of these calculations, the DES suggested a shift in entrance patterns as well as continuing education (DES 1978: §7). These projections were taken up by the UGC, which proposed a modest expansion from 560,000 places in higher education (full-time and sandwich) in 1983/84 to 600,000 in 1989/90 (UGC 1984: §1.3-1.12).

4 Access courses had existed since the 1970s, but they were now officially recognised and valued as one of the three routes into higher education. But although there were about 400 access courses in 50 LEAs by 1989, access to the universities stayed rather restricted (Thompson 2012: 55). As selection and admission were left in the hands of the individual higher education institution, the number of mature students and students without traditional qualifications stayed relatively low (Parry 2005: 176).

5 While there had been calls for more selective funding since the 1960s (Kogan and Hanney 2000: 93), the introduction of the RAE by the UGC in 1986 made competition for funding an integral part of the university system (Tapper 2007: 188). Although definitions and assessment procedures of the RAE were altered over the years, it continued even when the UGC was no longer there. Indeed, the importance of the RAE even

rose. While in the first RAE 14 percent of the state funding for research were allocated according to RAE results, this later increased to 30 percent in 1989 and 100 percent in 1992 (Willmott 2003: 133). For an overview of the development of quality control from the Academic Audit Unit, set up by the CVCP in the belief that self-regulation was infinitely preferable to external evaluation, to the Higher Education Quality Council to the Quality Assurance Agency see Tapper (2007: 167–84), Salter and Tapper (2000), Naidoo (2000: 29–32), and Bradney (2001).

5 Before the White Paper 1991 was published, tuition fees had rapidly increased from £607 per student in 1989/90 to £1675 in 1990/91 with a further increase in 1991/92 leading to about 50 percent of teaching costs being covered by fees in contrast to only 15 percent in 1989 (DES 1991: Annex I: 3). Though these fees were still paid by the state, the funding of universities increasingly depended on student numbers.

7 Through the increase of student fees and the possibility to take in fees-only students beyond the number agreed with the funding councils, expansion was achieved at lower costs and students were increasingly seen as an income (Bathmaker 2003: 177). Under the bidding system, higher education institutions had to compete for funding by offering bids below the core unit cost. While the bidding system had great impact with the polytechnics and colleges, the universities refused to bid in order to keep unit costs high (Kogan and Hanney 2000: 92; Shattock 2008: 193). The bidding and fees-only systems were soon brought to a halt because expansion turned out to be much faster than projected and thus too expensive (Cutler and Waine 1997: 78; Williams 2004: 247–8). Nevertheless, the idea that students were 'customers' and had to be competed for in a market was established.

8 The announcement to increase student fees for overseas students caused considerable protest and criticism. While some feared that it would reduce the universities' income, others were worried about the effect that these fees could have on educational opportunities for foreign students in particular those coming from the Commonwealth (Brown and Carasso 2013: 74; Shattock 2012: 160). In retrospect the increase of fees for international students can be regarded as a kind of trial run for the implementation of students fees for home students in the 1990s and the gradual marketisation of higher education.

Chapter 12

Towards the learning society

After a phase of massive expansion in the late 1980s and 1990s during which funding per student had fallen so drastically that Vice-Chancellors were threatening to introduce top-up fees (Lunt 2008: 742), a National Committee of Inquiry into Higher Education (NCIHE) under the chairmanship of Sir Ronald Dearing was appointed in 1996 to find solutions to the funding problem and to formulate strategies for the future development of higher education (Shattock 1999: 9–10; Sutherland 2008: 49). Even though the committee had been set up under the Conservative government, it did not publish its report *Higher Education in the Learning Society* (Dearing Report) until New Labour had come to power – a decision that was made in order to keep higher education and student fees out of the election campaigns (Ryan 2005: 91).

The Dearing Committee conducted the largest review of higher education since the Robbins Report of 1963. But in contrast to the Robbins Committee, which had spoken from within academia and whose members came mostly from the higher education sector, the Dearing Committee also included members drawn from industry and banking – a fact that already shows that the situation of higher education and its position within society had changed (Barnett 1999: 293–4).

The actual recommendations of the Dearing Report included, amongst others, the further expansion of higher education and a stronger commitment to widening participation, greater investment in the provision of Communications and Information Technology, the foundation of an Institute for Learning and Teaching to accredit training programmes for higher education teachers, the continuation of the RAE albeit with a number of reforms, and above all the proposal to have students contribute to the costs of higher education (NCIHE 1997: Annex A). Apart from these recommendations, some of which are discussed in more detail below, the Dearing Report formulated a grand vision: Britain ought to become a learning society.

The aims of higher education and the learning society

According to the Dearing Report, higher education had four main purposes:

- to inspire and enable individuals to develop their capabilities to the highest potential levels throughout life, so that they grow intellectually, are well-equipped for work, can contribute effectively to society and achieve personal fulfilment;
- to increase knowledge and understanding for their own sake and to foster their application to the benefit of the economy and society;
- to serve the needs of an adaptable, sustainable, knowledge-based economy at local, regional and national levels;
- to play a major role in shaping a democratic, civilised, inclusive society.

(NCIHE 1997: §5.11)

In many ways, these four objectives were an updated version of the objectives that the Robbins Report had identified. But though there were obvious similarities, there was also considerable divergence, in particular with regard to the fourth aim of higher education.

In contrast to the Robbins Report, for which the "transmission of a common culture and common standards of citizenship" was one objective of higher education (Committee on Higher Education 1963: §28), the Dearing Report abandoned such a normative view and recognised that the UK had become a society of many diverse cultures – a society in which there was actual "debate about the basis for any system of values" (NCIHE 1997: §5.38). Nevertheless, the Dearing Report identified a number of common values underlying higher education, such as "a commitment to the pursuit of truth", "freedom of thought and expression", or "a willingness to listen to alternative views and judge them on their merits" (NCIHE 1997: §5.39). Furthermore, higher education was supposed to, together with others, "act as the conscience of the nation" (NCIHE 1997: §5.40). While the Dearing Report thus abandoned the normative perspective of the Robbins Report, it still emphasised that there was a set of values that was common to higher education and worth promoting.

Apart from the similarities and differences with the Robbins Report, the most remarkable aspect of the four aims of higher education that the Dearing Report defined was definitely that they did not follow the understanding of higher education that had characterised the policies of the Thatcher and Major governments. Instead of framing higher education predominantly in a discourse organised around the nodal point 'economy', the Dearing Report claimed that higher education was also about self-fulfilment, the search for knowledge for its own sake, as well as the shaping of "a democratic, civilised, inclusive society" (NCIHE 1997: §5.11). But while the objectives of higher education that the Dearing Report defined considerably departed from the view of higher education that had been promoted by the government in the 1980s and 1990s, the picture actually changes if one has a look at the broader vision that the Dearing Report formulated: the creation of a learning society.

'Lifelong learning' and 'the learning society' became popular concepts with the UNESCO in the 1960s and 1970s (Tight 1998a: 474). As the UNESCO's Faure Report *Learning to Be: The World of Education Today and Tomorrow* (1972) claimed, the traditional understanding of learning as being confined to an early stage in life needed to be abandoned because

> only an over-all, lifelong education can produce the kind of complete man the need for whom is increasing with the continually more stringent constraints tearing the individual asunder. We should no longer assiduously acquire knowledge once and for all, but learn how to build up a continually evolving body of knowledge all through life – 'learn to be'.
>
> (Faure et al. 1972: vi)

For the Faure Report, lifelong education was thus both the answer to a changing lifeworld and the realisation of liberal, democratic, and emancipatory ideals of education. In order to make such an education reality, it was necessary, so it was argued, to fundamentally restructure the institutions of education, including higher education (Faure et al. 1972: 161). Such a total restructuring of the education system, however, never occurred, at least not in Britain. Even though there was an established system of adult and part-time higher education through the Workers' Educational Association (WEA), the Open University, the polytechnics, but also the University of London or Birkbeck College (Kogan 2000: 346), these forms of education always stayed inferior to initial full-time higher education. As Mary Henkel points out, "the concepts of the learning society, the knowledge society and lifelong learning were relatively slow to emerge as significant influences in UK national goals for higher education" (2001: 277). Although the higher education sector was asked in the 1980s to increase its commitment to 'continuing education' as it was then called, the concept of lifelong learning only gained in popularity in the 1990s, in particular when 1996 was designated as the European Year of Lifelong Learning (Duke 1999: 21). But it was not before Dearing and the 1997 election campaign that 'lifelong learning' and 'the learning society' became prominent ideas in the debate on education (Bartlett 2003: 191).

In contrast to the liberal and democratic ideals of the Faure Report, which had emphasised "the fundamental solidarity of governments and of peoples", the "belief in democracy", and "the complete fulfilment of man, in all the richness of his personality" (Faure et al. 1972: v–vi), the Dearing Committee envisioned a rather different learning society. As it explained in the very first paragraph of its report:

> The purpose of education is life-enhancing: it contributes to the whole quality of life. This recognition of the purpose of higher education in the development of our people, our society, and our economy is central to our vision. In the next century, the economically successful nations will be those which become learning societies: where all are committed, through effective education and training, to lifelong learning.
>
> (NCIHE 1997: §1.1)

Again, as in the four objectives that the Dearing Report defined, education was said to have multiple functions as it contributed to the quality of life, the development of the people, society, and the economy. But strikingly, the term 'learning society' was only mentioned in the third sentence where it was exclusively linked to the two nodal points 'economy' and 'nation'. This predominance of the economic conception of the learning society became even more explicit soon afterwards, when the Dearing Report argued that the creation of a learning society was vital not only because it enhanced "the quality of life" but in particular "to sustain a competitive economy" (NCIHE 1997: §1.10). While earlier projects of adult and continuing education had considered education as "a key agency for emancipating, informing and empowering the disadvantaged" (Watson and Taylor 1998: 145), the Dearing Report's vision of the learning society, though it also recognised these various functions of education, was primarily an economic one, in which the people appeared as the nation's "only stable source of competitive advantage (other than natural resources)" (NCIHE 1997: §1.11). It was the manpower doctrine expanded to every citizen at every stage in life.

Expansion and widening participation

The concept of the learning society as a society in which education continued throughout life fundamentally reconfigured the concept of the student. While the Open University and initiatives like the WEA had already offered forms of lifelong education, these had always been an additional option and thus indirectly reaffirmed the traditional ideal of the student as a young person, for whom higher education was a particular period in life. In the learning society, however, higher education would not be confined to a particular stage in life but rather a continuous process. The vision of the learning society thus ultimately broke with the traditional "'frontend' model" with childhood and youth as the time of education and adult life as a time of work (Tight 1998b: 261).

But the Dearing Report's vision of a learning society not only widened the concept of the student in a temporal sense. It also called for expansion and widened participation for social groups that had so far been under-represented in higher education. As far as expansion is concerned, the report devoted a whole chapter to analyse the future demand for higher education. The main argument for expansion was based on manpower demands. Though the Dearing Report also took into account demand from school leavers, the central justification of further expansion was that "higher level skills [were] crucial to future economic competitiveness" (NCIHE 1997: §6.8).[1] Quite in contrast to the Robbins Report, expansion was not considered in terms of equality and fairness but primarily as a precondition for economic growth. However, notions of equality and justice came into play in the arguments for widening participation. Thus, the report argued that higher education ought to "promote greater equality of social and economic opportunity" (NCIHE 1997: §5.41) and that "it should be an objective of policy to see that those groups who are currently under-represented in higher education come to be properly represented: as participation increases so it must widen" (NCIHE 1997: §7.21).

Compared to the Robbins Report, there were two fundamental differences with regard to widening participation policies. While the Robbins Report had primarily focused on class, the Dearing Report had a much wider perspective and also took age, gender, ethnicity, locality, and disabilities into account (NCIHE 1997: §7.4–7.19). Moreover, whereas the Robbins Report concentrated on expansion and believed that widened participation would follow from opening access to all those qualified, the Dearing Report emphasised that measures needed to be taken to actively draw students into higher education. Such measures had been established in the years before as HEFCE had started to fund selected widening participation initiatives (Lewis 2002: 208). The Dearing Report reaffirmed these policies and argued that higher education needed "to take active steps to encourage access by under-represented groups" (NCIHE 1997: §5.41).[2] In this respect, both reports differed considerably. While the Robbins Report answered to a rising student demand, the Dearing Report wanted to actively create such student demand. The student was not the agent of expansion but rather its object.

Putting the student at the centre

The vision of the learning society not only tackled the concept of the student with regard to who participated in higher education, but it also repositioned the student in terms of power and agency. Already the Faure Report of 1972 had emphasised that in the learning society the student would occupy a new role because

> the act of teaching gives way to the act of learning. While not ceasing to be taught, the individual becomes less of an object and more of a subject. He does not receive education as if it were a gift or a social service handed out to him by his guardians, the powers-that-be. He assimilates it by conquering knowledge and himself, which makes him [the] supreme master and

> not the recipient of acquired knowledge. [. . .] Education [. . .] is no longer focused *on* the learner, nor anyone, nor anything else. It must necessarily proceed *from* the learner.
>
> (Faure et al. 1972: 161, emphases in original)

For the Faure Report, it was thus the learner who was at the centre of education, which not only meant to focus on the learner but that, as an independent and self-directed individual, the learner ought to steer the learning process.

The Dearing Report also claimed that its vision of the learning society would put "students at the centre" (NCIHE 1997: §8.4). But what this actually meant differed significantly from the ideas of the Faure Report. In the Dearing Report, putting the student at the centre was not so much about making the student an agent in his or her learning as about making teachers and institutions of higher education adapt to changing student demands. Hence, the report claimed that in the future teachers would "have to respond to a changing – and more discerning and demanding – student population" (NCIHE 1997: §8.1) and that "institutions [ought] to be more responsive to student requirements" (NCIHE 1997: §120). Moreover, the Dearing Report suggested that "informed student demand" should increasingly "shape the balance of subjects" (NCIHE 1997: §6.50) and that "student choice should be the main shaper of the system" (NCIHE 1997: §5.52). These are just a few out of numerous examples. The underlying logic was always that higher education had to adapt to the needs of the student and that students' choices should increasingly determine the provision of higher education.

But what the Dearing Report presented as putting the student at the centre actually meant to place the economy at the centre. According to the report, the learning society was not a society in which people wanted to learn throughout their lives but "a society in which people in all walks of life recognise[d] *the need* to continue in education and training throughout their *working lives*" (NCIHE 1997: §1.10, emphases added). For the Dearing Report, it was the changing world of work which in the future would "require people to re-equip themselves, as new knowledge and new skills are needed for economies to compete, survive and prosper" (NCIHE 1997: §1.12). While the report argued that in the future higher education had to increasingly respond to student needs, the assumption was that these needs arose primarily out of economic interests. The same rationale lay beneath the suggestion that "student choice should be the main shaper of the system" (NCIHE 1997: §5.52). As the Dearing Report argued:

> The future demand for those with higher education qualifications will be shaped by the changing structure of the national economy and the labour market, which in turn will be responding to changes in the world economy and the associated competitive challenges. *These forces will find their response in the choices made by individuals* about participation in higher education and

> in employer demand for lifelong learning opportunities on behalf of their employees.
>
> (NCIHE 1997: §6.4, emphasis added)

The assumption was that students would base their choices primarily on economic considerations. However, in order for student choice to respond properly to the economic forces, it needed to be ensured that students made the right "informed choices" (NCIHE 1997: §5.69).

While better information for school leavers had already been an issue in the Robbins Report, the difference between the two reports lay in the information that they believed prospective students required. When the Robbins Report claimed that school leavers needed better information, this information was primarily supposed to be "about the courses available in higher education" (Committee on Higher Education 1963: §225). According to the Dearing Report, students needed not only information about course options, but in particular information detailing the likely costs of higher education as well as future employment prospects (NCIHE 1997: §6.50, §22.18). Again, the assumption in the Dearing Report was that students primarily made, or ought to make, choices based on economic considerations, and as it was these choices which were supposed to shape the system of higher education, what appeared as the centrality of the student was actually the supremacy of the economy. Though the Dearing Report also emphasised that students entered higher education for other reasons than economic ones, the predominant assumption was that economic advantages were, or ought to be, the students' prime motivation. This assumption also underlay the most central argument of the Dearing Report: that in the future students should contribute to the costs of higher education.

Tuition fees and the student as investor

One of the most important recommendations of the Dearing Report was to make students contribute to tuition costs. While the Robbins Report had discussed student fees but finally rejected them (Committee on Higher Education 1963: §647), they had later become a topic again and were in particular supported by the CVCP in order to even out cuts in government funding (Shattock 2012: 198). Even though the proposals of the Dearing Committee were not realised in the end and New Labour opted for a rather different fee system, the Dearing Report marked a turning point as from that time onwards the idea that students ought to pay part of their tuition gained more widespread political acceptance (Wagner 1998: 76).[3]

The report devoted several chapters to the funding of higher education in general and one chapter in particular to discuss the question who should pay for higher education. In this chapter, the report made the case for student fees through a detailed discussion of the various benefits of higher education. Though the Dearing Report did not disregard the numerous economic as well as non-economic benefits of higher education for society at large and therefore concluded that the state should stay the prime funder of higher education (NCIHE 1997: §18.18–23), its central argument was that the individual student benefitted the most from higher education and should thus provide some of its funding. Given the "overwhelming evidence" that graduates were "the main beneficiaries from higher education in the form of improved employment prospects and pay", the report concluded that "graduates in employment should make a greater contribution to the costs of higher education in the future" (NCIHE 1997: §18.24). Student fees were thus presented as a matter of fairness: those who benefitted should pay.

Though this argument – that everybody who benefitted from higher education should share the burden of financing it – was emphasised the most, it was by no means the only reason why fees were recommended. Indeed, the report made several suggestions concerning the various other functions that fees would serve. Thus, it was suggested that when students paid fees, institutions of higher education would be more responsive to student demand since part of their funding depended on attracting students (NCIHE 1997: §22.15). However, as student choice would have the same impact on provision if fees were paid by the state, this was more of a rhetorical move than a proper argument.

But the introduction of fees was not only supposed to have an impact on the institutions of higher education. Fees were also believed to have a transformative effect on the students. Paying fees was believed to make students "more demanding of institutions" (NCIHE 1997: §20.68). Similar to the White Paper *Top-Up Loans for Students* (1988), which had claimed that the substitution of grants with loans would change the students' self-understanding, the Dearing Report proposed that fees would have an influence on how students understood higher education and how they perceived of themselves:

> As a result [of contributing to tuition costs], we expect students of all ages will be increasingly discriminating investors in higher education, looking for quality, convenience, and relevance to their needs at a cost they consider affordable and justified by the probable return on their investment of time and money.
>
> (NCIHE 1997: §1.21)[4]

Though not central to the report's main argument for fees, this was the most radical idea behind the report's proposal to introduce fees – the effect they were intended to have on the student. Tuition fees were supposed to establish a logic that equated students with 'investors' and universities and colleges with 'service providers' and thereby change students in their self-understanding and make them see themselves as human capital – a line of thought that was not only continued but further advanced under New Labour.

Notes

1 Note that the Dearing Report did not speak of a need for higher 'education' but for higher-level skills. Education was here substituted with skills.

2 The report recommended, for instance, special funds for projects that addressed "low expectations and achievement" and tried "to promote progression to higher education" (NCIHE 1997: §7.27).
3 The Dearing Report actually argued for a graduate contribution based on an income contingent contribution scheme with a flat rate fee, i.e. not varied by subject, covering 25 percent of average tuition costs (NCIHE 1997: §112). The Dearing Committee thus rejected variable fees and fees paid up front as they were later introduced under New Labour. For a more detailed discussion of the fees regulations see Barr and Crawford (1998: 72) and Shattock (2008: 198).
4 Moreover, the Dearing Report suggested that in the future a higher part of tuition funding should be transferred to the student, for instance, in the form of vouchers as this "would encourage the student to see him/herself as an investor in receipt of a service, and to seek, as an investor, value for money and a good return from the investment" (NCIHE 1997: §22.19).

Chapter 13

Higher education and the Third Way

After 18 years in the opposition, Labour returned to government with a landslide victory in the 1997 general election. Under the leadership of Tony Blair, Labour had embarked on a new course and departed from its traditional socialist policies. New Labour, as it was then called, followed what has become known as the Third Way – a position which supposedly stood in the middle between liberal economic policies (first way) and left-wing socialist policies (second way). As Tony Blair claimed, "New Labour is neither old left nor new right [. . .]. Instead we offer a new way ahead that leads from the centre but is profoundly radical in the change it promises" (cited in Arestis and Sawyer 2005: 177). New Labour thus abandoned its Clause IV and subscribed to capitalism and free market enterprise.[1] Social problems were supposed to be resolved not through the strong state but by "governing by and through the market" (Peters 2010: 18). Hence, New Labour continued Thatcherite policies with their focus on economic efficiency and competitiveness, albeit with a stronger emphasis on social justice and policies which attempted to resolve the most destructive social effects of marketisation (Bevir 2005: 86; Naidoo 2000: 25–6).

The purpose of higher education

According to New Labour's White Paper *The Future of Higher Education* (2003), higher education was

> a great asset, both for individuals and the nation. The skills, creativity, and research developed through higher education are a major factor in our success in creating jobs and in our prosperity. Universities and colleges play a vital role in expanding opportunity and promoting social justice.
>
> (DfES 2003: 4)

This single paragraph perfectly encapsulates New Labour's understanding of the aims and purposes of higher education. Higher education was considered to be of value both to the individual and the nation, and it had the double function of creating prosperity and bringing about a more socially just society.

That education was vital in order to achieve greater prosperity was emphasised time and again by New Labour. In the foreword to the Green Paper *The Learning Age* (1998), David Blunkett, Secretary of State for Education and Employment, emphasised that learning was "the key to prosperity" (DfEE 1998: 7), and in a speech given at the University of Greenwich, the site of Crosland's famous Woolwich speech, he stressed that higher education had an important role "in securing economic competitiveness" (2000: §11). Likewise, Tessa Blackstone, Minister for Education, argued that higher education was crucial because it produced "innovation and ideas, skills and knowledge", which were "the tools for success and prosperity" (2001: 176). New Labour thus framed higher education within the same economic discourse that had been at the heart of the education policies of the Thatcher and Major governments. But while New Labour's emphasis on education as a means to achieve prosperity mirrored Thatcherite thinking, it also diverted from it in a number of points. New Labour, much more than Thatcherism, stressed the individual economic benefit of higher education. The White Paper 2003, for instance, highlighted that higher education was "a great asset, both for *individuals* and the nation" (DfES 2003: 4, emphasis added), and quite similarly, the Green Paper 1998 stated that education was key to prosperity "both for *individuals* and the nation" (DfEE 1998: 7, emphasis added). New Labour thus continued a development that had started a few years earlier and further shifted the nodal points of the manpower doctrine. 'Economy' and 'prosperity' were no longer set just in relation to 'nation' but were increasingly defined through 'the individual'.

According to the White Paper 2003, higher education was not only there to create prosperity, but it was also a means to expand opportunity and promote "social justice" (DfES 2003: 4). With this emphasis on the social function of higher education, New Labour more clearly departed from Thatcherism and subscribed to traditional leftist ideals. What is striking though is how this function of higher education was actually interpreted. Hence, the White Paper 2003, once it had stated higher education's "vital role in expanding opportunity and promoting social justice", continued by claiming that higher education had many benefits for the individual as graduates got "better jobs and earn[ed] more than those without higher education" (DfES 2003: 4). This line of argument was taken up later again, when the White Paper stated that higher education was "at the heart of building a more socially just society" because education was "the best and most reliable route out of poverty and disadvantage" (DfES 2003: 68). The same rationale was present in Blunkett's Greenwich speech, in which he argued that in a knowledge-economy, higher education became "a potentially powerful instrument of social justice, since it serves not only as a driver of wealth creation, but as a critical determinant of life chances" (2000: §66). In all these cases, social justice was primarily understood in economic terms and the 'social' was equated with the 'economic'. But this was only one of the decisive reconfigurations of the notion of 'social equality'. Instead of aiming for 'equality', New Labour wanted to 'expand opportunities'. This discursive change shifted the responsibility for success or failure increasingly onto the individual and away from the social system. As Sara Hale has pointed out, "[w]here there is the rhetoric of equal opportunity, individuals can have their lack of progress and feeling of personal failure compounded by the implication that it is 'their fault', when the reality is much more complex" (2006: 94). Accordingly, New Labour's Green Paper *The Learning Age* (1998) declared that while citizens can expect rights from the state, they were also responsible "for their own future" (DfEE 1998: 8) and that it was time to revitalise "a culture of self-improvement" (DfEE 1998: 14). New Labour's understanding of society was no longer that of a community, but rather that of "a collective form of self-help" (Davies 2005: 9). Instead of speaking of social structures such as class, New Labour put the emphasis on the individual (Taylor 2005: 112). In this respect, New Labour showed a strong liberalist bend and clearly departed from traditional left-wing understandings of social equality.

Expansion and widening participation

One of New Labour's most ambitious aims with regard to higher education was to raise the participation rate of those aged between 18 and 30 to 50 percent.[2] Such a further expansion of higher education was justified by the White Paper 2003 on two grounds: the economic case and the individual case. According to the White Paper, the economic case for expansion was "extremely strong" (DfES 2003: 57) as there was a growing demand for "a more highly-skilled workforce" and hence the need to expand (DfES 2003: 58). The economic rationale also informed the individual case for expansion. Hence, the White Paper argued that "[f]or the individual, the economic benefits of higher education are well-documented – quite apart from the opportunity for personal and intellectual fulfilment" (DfES 2003: 59).[3] Though the White Paper did not deny that some people might gain "personal and intellectual fulfilment" from higher education, these benefits were devalued as they were not measurable – in other words, they did not fall under the performativity regime.

Strikingly, there was no social case for expansion offered in the White Paper. Indeed, society and the social were only mentioned twice in the arguments for expansion. First, society was referred to under the economic case for expansion and the reader was informed that "[s]ociety [was] changing" as the "economy [was] becoming ever more knowledge-based" (DfES 2003: 58). Here, society was equated with the economy, or at least this aspect was the only aspect of interest. The second time society was referred to in any way, the White Paper argued that "[h]igher education also brings social benefits – there is strong evidence that suggests that graduates are likely to be more engaged citizens" (DfES 2003: 59). However, as Darryll Bravenboer has pointed out, these benefits were subsumed under the individual case for expansion (2009: 108). Benefits to society as a whole were largely excluded, and society was primarily understood as an agglomeration of individuals.

The expansion that New Labour aimed for was not to be achieved simply by further opening access and having student demand drive expansion. Accordingly, New Labour emphasised the need to actually create such a demand in the first place. This had already been an issue in the Dearing Report, but it became a much more central policy under New Labour. As the White Paper 2003 declared, in order for education to be "a force for opportunity and social justice" it was not enough to prevent "active discrimination" (DfES 2003: 67). What was necessary was "to make sure that potential is recognised and fostered wherever it is found" (DfES 2003: 67).[4] Thus, more people, it was argued, needed to "be encouraged" to enter higher education (DfES 2003: 69), for instance through programmes like AimHigher (DfES 2003: 67). Instead of reacting to student demand as the Robbins Report had done, New Labour pursued policies that HEFCE had adopted in the 1990s and tried to actively create demand for higher education. But as much as this focus on demand creation differed from earlier policies that had concentrated on opening access, there was a striking overlap concerning the image of the student who was believed to enter higher education as a result of further expansion.

Already the Thatcher government had argued that institutions of higher education needed "to adapt their teaching methods and the design of their courses to accommodate new types of students" (DES 1987: §2.15). This policy was also endorsed by the Dearing Report, and likewise New Labour emphasised that "institutions and ways of doing things [would] need to change in response to the needs of learners" (DfEE 1998: 18) and that higher education ought to be "better tailored to individual need" (Blunkett 2000: §56). One proposal was therefore to offer a new type of course in the form of a two year Foundation Degree. These degree courses were supposed to "offer rigorous specialist subject knowledge underpinned by a broad base of academic learning" (Blunkett 2000: §34). They were said to be "employer-focused" qualifications (DfES 2003: 42) and "work-focused degrees [. . .] that offer specific, job-related skills" (DfES 2003: 60). The Foundation Degrees were thus primarily proposed to meet demands from employers (Doyle 2003: 283–4). But as the Foundation Degrees were planned to carry "the bulk of the expansion" (DfES 2003: 7), New Labour's argument for Foundation Degrees actually assumed that the 'new students', whom expansion and widening participation would bring into higher education, were utilitarian in ethos and focused primarily on work and vocational qualifications. This has also been pointed out by Irene Brew-Riverson, according to whom the idea underlying the Foundation Degrees was "that certain courses with lower status are more suited to particular groups of people" (2012: 80). Likewise, Carole Leathwood and Paul O'Connell have argued that New Labour endorsed a discourse in which the working classes were represented "as naturally practical, good with their hands and ideally suited to 2-year foundation degrees" leaving the traditional 3-year degrees for the middle classes (2003: 613). Precisely in this respect, New Labour actually subscribed to one of the most dominant motifs within the struggle over higher education: that students from lower classes were primarily interested in higher education as a means to get a job.

Teaching, learning, and skills

New Labour was not only concerned with expanding and widening participation but also with teaching and learning. The White Paper 2003 devoted a whole chapter to these issues and made several proposals how to improve teaching and learning in higher education. More striking than the actual measures that were suggested, however, was how learning and what it amounted to were conceptualised. When the White Paper asked universities to review how they recorded student achievement and "to develop more sophisticated ways of *measuring 'value added'*" (DfES 2003: 48, emphasis added), learning was regarded as a measurable process and, continuing the line established with the Jarratt Report, students were considered as objects within a performativity regime. In addition to that focus on performativity, the White Paper was also explicit about what students ought to learn. A central task for higher education was thus the "development of skills for the workplace" (DfES 2003: 41). Graduates were supposed to have acquired "the right skills to equip them for a lifetime in a fast changing work environment" (DfES 2003: 44), and "good-quality courses" were defined as courses in which students developed "the higher-level skills" that they needed "during their working life" (DfES 2003: 47). As these few examples illustrate, for New Labour higher education was primarily about providing students with the skills that prepared them for the workplace.

This strong focus on skills marked a shift in thinking about higher education – a shift that can best be seen if having a look at both the Robbins and Dearing reports. While the Robbins Report had considered the "instruction in skills" as one aim of higher education (Committee on Higher Education 1963: §25), the term 'skills' had otherwise not been that prominent in the whole report. In contrast to that, the term turned up much more frequently in the Dearing Report. According to Ronald Barnett, this change in language indicated that higher education had shifted from being understood

> as a process that has its location in a given culture that lends itself to 'instruction or guidance' to a culture in which teaching acts will now be made explicit, formal and routine, so that they are susceptible of 'training' and 'skills'.
>
> (1999: 299)

However, the Dearing Report most of the time positioned 'skills' next to 'education' or 'knowledge' in phrases like "skills, knowledge and understanding" (NCIHE 1997: §5.18) or "[t]he education and skills of our people" (NCIHE 1997: §5.28). New Labour's White Paper 2003 hardly did so any longer and spoke near exclusively of skills. Higher education was explicitly regarded as skills development and as a means to fit students into the world of work and to provide them with the means to increase their human capital.

Apart from the strong emphasis on skills, New Labour also promoted a rather particular interpretation of the learning-teaching nexus and hence the relation between students and teachers. Tellingly, the chapter on teaching and learning in the White Paper 2003 was entitled "Teaching and learning – delivering excellence" (DfES 2003: 46). Leaving aside the question of what 'excellence' meant in this context, the crucial point is that both teaching and learning were considered as something that could be 'delivered'. Teaching and learning were seen as a service that was offered by "higher education providers" (DfES 2003: 49). This conception of the learning process not only put universities and students in the position of consumers and service providers, but it also meant, as learning was 'delivered', that the student was not an agent in the learning process and that responsibility for the student's learning success lay with the institution alone.

Fees, choice, and power

The most controversial education policy of New Labour was the introduction of student fees in 1998. Against the Dearing Report's recommendation to set up a system of income contingent graduate contributions that would cover about 25 percent of average tuition costs (NCIHE 1997: recommendation 79), New Labour decided for income tested up-front fees – that is fees paid at the beginning of each year of study – of £1,000 (Barr 2005: 254; Sutherland 2008: 49–50). Though these fees were actually introduced throughout the UK, the recently established Scottish Parliament soon departed and abolished fees for Scottish students studying in Scotland in 2000 (Bruce 2016: 61). But also in the rest of the UK, the fee system as established in 1998 did not survive for long. Following the White Paper *The Future of Higher Education*, the Higher Education Act 2004 allowed universities to charge variable fees of up to £3,000 per year.[5] These fees were not paid up front but were covered by a loan, which students only had to repay once they earned more than £15,000 per year. At the same time, contributions towards tuition fees for the poorest students were increased to £1,200, the means-tested grant was raised to £1,500, and higher education institutions that wanted to charge the maximum fees of £3,000 were obliged to provide minimum bursaries of £300 (Greenbank 2006: 159). The new fee system was introduced in England and Northern Ireland for the academic year 2006/07 and one year later in Wales with the exception that Welsh domiciled students who studied in Wales were eligible for a fees grant and thus did not have to pay higher fees (Brown and Carasso 2013: 96).

The basic argument for the new fee system followed the Dearing Report. Hence, the White Paper 2003 claimed that graduates gained substantial financial benefits and had wider career opportunities than non-graduates and that it was thus only fair if students made a higher contribution to the funding of higher education (DfES 2003: 83). As these benefits for the individual differed between universities and courses, the White Paper concluded that the contributions that graduates made should also vary (DfES 2003: 20). Moreover, the new fees were presented as offering greater freedom to both universities and colleges, which could now raise their own funding (DfES 2003: 77), as well as to students, who, because fees would not be paid up-front, would no longer have to rely on their parents (DfES 2003: 18).[6]

Apart from these references to fairness and freedom, the most important idea behind the new fees system was that it allegedly enhanced the role of student choice as a driving force within the system of higher education. While the Dearing Report had already considered student choice an important element in the shaping of the higher education system (NCIHE 1997: §6.45, 5.52), this idea became absolutely central to New Labour's higher education policy. As the White Paper 2003 argued, the new fees made "student choice a much more powerful force" (DfES 2003: 84) that would "increasingly work to drive up quality" (DfES 2003: 46). The underlying rationale was that as an increasing part of the universities' funding depended on fees and as students would choose high quality courses, universities and colleges would have to raise the quality of what they offered or otherwise they would suffer financial losses. Hence, students would become major agents within the system through the choices they made.

As student choice was supposed to become a much more powerful instrument in the system of higher education, students needed, so it was argued, sufficient information that allowed them to exercise choice and "become intelligent customers" (DfES 2003: 47). According to the White Paper 2003, such information ought to include course data as well as, for instance, whether the university was a centre of excellence, the quality of its facilities, entry requirements, and employment records (DfES 2003: 47). But students did not only need information to make their choices. The White Paper 2003 also had a clear idea of what kind of choices students should make and assumed, for instance, that "students choose the good-quality courses that will bring them respected and valuable qualifications and give them the higher-level skills that they will need during their working life" (DfES 2003: 47). In other words, students were expected to focus primarily on skills and qualifications that were needed in the labour market and thus to choose their courses according to what the economy valued. Following the logic that student choice ought to shape the system of higher education, this would mean that universities and colleges, as they were required to react to student choice, would increasingly offer courses for which the economy called. Hence, while students were positioned as agents within the system of higher education through the choices they made, they were supposed to act as agents on behalf of the economy.

The idea of higher education that New Labour promoted not only emphasised the role of student choice but also that students were entitled to a certain quality of provision. Blunkett, for instance, claimed that students needed to "be confident of the quality of higher education they *can expect* to receive" (2000: 28, emphasis added). The White Paper 2003 stated that students were "*entitled* to high quality teaching" (DfES 2003: 46) and that they had "*the right* to good teaching" (DfES 2003: 49, emphases added). Moreover, the reforms that the White Paper 2003 proposed were supposed to "give students a greater voice" by improving means of redress for student complaints (DfES 2003: 49). All these references to student empowerment were not just by-products of the suggested reforms. While the Dearing Report had justified fees primarily through the private economic benefit and the concept of equity, New Labour framed the introduction of variable fees in a discourse that represented the reforms as an empowerment of the student.

But students were also empowered in another sense. For the information that was considered necessary to allow prospective students to act as customers was not to be provided only by the universities, external examiners, or bodies like HEFCE but also by students themselves. Thus, the White Paper 2003 suggested that a nationwide survey of student views – what came to be known as the National Student Survey (NSS) – ought to be conducted annually and provide prospective students with information (DfES 2003: 46). Hence, students were not only empowered through their choices but also because their evaluations of the institutions of higher education were supposed to influence demand and therefore provider behaviour. This, however, also meant that students indirectly supported the new fee system by providing the information that was considered necessary for its functioning. Students were empowered, but they also became allies in the new market system of higher education.

Notes

1 While Clause IV of the Labour Party Manifesto had aimed at "common ownership of the means of production, distribution and exchange", the revised version of 1995 no longer spoke of common ownership but of "a dynamic economy, serving the public interest, in which the enterprise of the market and the rigour of competition are joined with the forces of partnership and co-operation" (cited in Pearce and Stewart 2002: 569). For a more detailed discussion of the revised Clause IV, which can be seen as the birth of New Labour, see Bochel et al. (2005: 281–3).

2 When New Labour came into office the age participation rate in Great Britain for those under 21 stood at 33 percent. In 1999/2000 this had slightly fallen, while the age participation rate for those 17 to 30 was measured at about 39 percent (National Audit Office 2008: 11–2).

3 The White Paper 2003 not only emphasised the individual economic benefit of higher education, but it was anxious to persuade its readers that the benefit was still there. Hence, it repudiated Kingsley Amis's phrase that 'more will mean worse' albeit in a manner that clearly displayed its strong economic rationale. While Amis had been concerned about the standards of higher education, the White Paper 2003 interpreted this entirely in economic terms and informed its readers that expansion had not led to a decline of the average salary premium (DfES 2003: 12).

4 Though Kenneth Baker's White Paper 1987 had emphasised the need to open higher education to non-traditional students, and special funds for widening participation had

been set up, New Labour was much more taking the initiative (Tapper 2007: 215). The funding councils were thus supposed to reward the "successful outreach to the disadvantaged or under-represented" (DfEE 1998: 61), and higher education institution were asked by HEFCE to develop "an integrated approach to widening participation" which focused on the "student life-cycle" and thus included not only admission but also continuing support (HEFCE 2001: 15). Following the White Paper 2003, institutions of higher education were further required to enter Access Agreements with HEFCE (DfES 2003: 8), and the Office for Fair Access (OFFA) was created to control institutional measures for widening participation (Davis 2012: 25).

5 With the White Paper 2003 and the introduction of top-up fees in 2006, Labour actually acted against their election manifesto. Accordingly, the funding reforms were highly contested and passed Parliament only on its second reading with a majority of five votes and 71 Labour MPs voting against it (Miller 2010: 86–7).

6 Strikingly, such references to the freedom of the individual were also fundamental to the Anderson Report (1960) but with totally opposite results. While the Anderson Report argued for the introduction of universal maintenance grants in order to allow students more freedom, the White Paper 2003 used the same concept of freedom to argue for a new fee system.

Chapter 14

The triumph of the market

When the financial crisis hit Britain and deficits rose in 2009, the funding of higher education came under scrutiny again. Thus, Labour launched a review to reconsider higher education funding, which was eventually published when the new coalition government of Conservatives and Liberal Democrats was already in power. The Browne Review (2010) and in particular its recommendation to remove the fees cap caused massive student protests in November and December 2010. But despite the mass protests, the House of Commons largely accepted the review's proposals.[1] Consequently, teaching grants were reduced by 80 percent, and the fee cap was raised to £6,000 and £9,000 for higher education institutions that would install specific widening participation measures (Callender 2012: 84).[2] These new funding arrangements, however, only applied to England but not to Scotland, Wales, and Northern Ireland where the state continued to fund parts of tuition.[3]

As radical as the measures of the coalition government were, in particular the reduction of the teaching grant and the rise of fees, they were actually continuing developments initiated under Thatcher and New Labour. Since the introduction of loans to top up maintenance grants in 1989, students had continuously been asked to increasingly contribute to the cost of higher education. The funding reforms following the Browne Review reinforced these policies by further substituting public funding with student fees. Hence, Andrew Vincent calls the Browne Review "a symptom or pathology of an ideological hegemony" that had established itself over the last thirty years (2011: 336). However, the coalition government did not just maintain the neoliberal take on higher education as it had been advanced under New Labour, but it actually went much further in its embrace of the market.

The slashing of teaching grants – save a few subjects such as medicine, the laboratory sciences, engineering and some other "strategic and vulnerable" subjects (BIS 2011: 15) – and their replacement with student fees meant that, as far as teaching was concerned, higher education was essentially privatised (Shattock 2013: 29). This was a decisive break with the welfare state and the post-war consensus that the state had an obligation to fund higher education. Even the Dearing Report, which had established the principle that students should pay for their tuition, had unmistakably stated that "the state must remain a major source of funding for higher education" (NCIHE 1997: §18.21). This principle no longer applied to the Browne Review and the White Paper 2011. Apart from grants for a few selected subjects and for poor students, the provision of higher education was no longer a responsibility of the state (Williams 2011: 1).

This radical restructuring of higher education funding had two aims. First, the scrapping of the teaching grant was supposed to make it easier for private higher education providers to enter the market. As David Willetts, Minister of State for Universities and Science, explained to Universities UK in February 2011, the teaching grant gave "publicly-funded HEIs a significant advantage" over private providers and was "one of the main barriers to alternative providers" – a barrier that the funding reforms would remove (2011: n.p.). Second, the greater dependence on student fees was claimed to put 'students at the heart of the system' and to enhance the power of student choice.

The benefit of higher education and the power of student choice

Following the policy established by New Labour, the Browne Review as well as the following White Paper *Higher Education: Students at the Heart of the System* (2011) primarily emphasised the private economic benefit of higher education. Though the Browne Review claimed that higher education was central for the "nation's strength in the global knowledge based economy" (Independent Review 2010: 2) and later also added that higher education "helps to create the knowledge, skills and values that underpin a civilised society" (2010: 14), it made it absolutely clear that the public benefit of higher education was "less than the private benefit" (2010: 21). This focus on the private benefit of higher education was the basis for the recommended funding reforms. Following the logic of the Dearing Report that those who benefitted should pay, the Browne Review as well as the White Paper 2011 justified the rise in student fees as a matter of fairness as those who benefitted most from higher education would contribute most to its costs (Independent Review 2010: 21; BIS 2011: 4). Besides this logic of fairness and the strong focus on the private benefits of higher education, the Browne Review and the White Paper 2011 also reinforced New Labour's logic that variable fees enhanced the power of the student.

According to the Browne Review, the funding reforms "put students at the heart of the system" as their choices would more than ever before "shape the landscape of higher education" (Independent Review 2010: 4).[4] After discarding "central planning" as a means to drive up quality (2010: 8), the Browne Review argued that only a complete market, in which the funding of teaching depended entirely on fees, could ensure that quality improved. According to the review, "[i]ncreasing competition for students will mean that institutions will have stronger incentives to focus on improving teaching quality. If they are not able to attract enough students, their funding will decrease." (2010: 48)

This belief in the power of the market was actually more important to the rise of student fees than the argument concerning fairness. This could, for instance, be seen in the Browne Review's dismissal of a graduate tax as a possible means to fund higher education. A graduate tax was rejected, amongst other reasons, because it would not place the emphasis on student choice and would not make higher education institutions dependent on the student's willingness to pay (2010: 10). The main aim of the funding reforms was neither to improve the financial situation of the institutions of higher education or the state nor to establish a fairer funding system, but to change the position of the student within the system of higher education. The crux was not that students could choose or that their choices were meaningful to them but that higher education institutions had to react to student demand:

> The changes we are making to higher education funding will in turn drive a more responsive system. To be successful, institutions will have to appeal to prospective students and be respected by employers. Putting financial power into the hands of learners makes student choice meaningful.
>
> (BIS 2011: 5)

Supposedly, student choice was meaningful only if institutions of higher education had to respond to it.

Similar to New Labour's White Paper 2003, which had argued for variable fees and also wanted to strengthen the role of student choice in the shaping of the system of higher education, the Browne Review and the White Paper 2011 did not simply promote enhanced student choice but 'informed choice'. But while they continued the argumentation of the White Paper 2003, the provision of information to guide student choice became even more important. Already New Labour's *Higher Ambitions* (2009) had emphasised that in order to have student choice shape the provision of higher education, the choices that students made needed to be "well-informed by objective information about what different courses involve, and their implications for future career prospects" (BIS 2009: 70). Following this line of argument, the White Paper 2011 proposed the introduction of the Key Information Set (KIS). Hence, all universities were asked to provide information such as "student satisfaction", "[p]roportion of time spent in different learning and teaching activities", "[d]ifferent assessment methods used", "[p]rofessional bodies that recognise the course", as well as information on costs and employment including the kind of employment taken up by graduates and their salary, and information on the student union (BIS 2011: 28–9). Similar to the White Paper 2003, the idea was that student choice needed to be carefully guided and that students should primarily understand higher education as an investment and a means to improve their employment prospects. Indeed, when it came to the purpose of higher education, employment was the only information with which students ought to be provided. That the underlying rationale was actually that students ought to base their choices primarily on employment prospects was clearly pointed out in the Browne Review, which argued that "improved employability" was "a key selling point of a course" and that courses that delivered "improved employability [would] prosper" while others would "disappear" (Independent Review 2010: 31). Students were supposed to consider higher education as an investment to improve their 'employability'. But this focus on employability also meant that it was not students who were 'at the heart', as the title of the White Paper 2011 proclaimed it, but rather employers and the labour market. As the Browne Review argued, if students were provided "with clearer information about employment outcomes", this would actually "close the gap between the skills taught by the higher education system and what employers need" (Independent Review 2010: 28). Clearly, students were supposed to choose, but in such a way as to fulfil the needs of the employers.

The student experience

While the Browne Review and the White Paper 2011 intensified the policy that had been established under New Labour and framed higher education within a discourse structured by the nodal points 'choice', 'competition', 'quality', and 'private economic benefit', they also put great emphasis on another concept that had not been central before: 'the student experience'.

Though it was by no means new to speak of 'the experience of higher education',[5] 'the student experience' only came into use as a set phrase from the 1990s onwards with publications such as Susanne Haselgrove's collected volume *The Student Experience* (1994). The phrase also appeared a few times in the Dearing Report, which argued, for instance, that "[i]n the future, the contribution that all staff make to the quality of the student experience will need to be recognised and rewarded" (NCIHE 1997: §14.59). But it was only in the 2000s and 2010s that 'the student experience' became a major catchphrase in the policy discourse. Thus, New Labour's *Higher Ambitions* contained a whole chapter entitled "The student experience of higher education" (BIS 2009: 70), and with the Browne Review and the White Paper 2011, which used the phrase five times in its executive summary alone (BIS 2011: 3–9), 'the student experience' turned into a central nodal point within the policy discourse. Apparently, it was only when the student became a customer that 'the student experience' started to be of major interest.

What is striking though is that while 'the student experience' was often referred to in policy papers, it was hardly ever defined what 'the student experience' actually comprised. In *Higher Ambition*, the chapter on 'the student experience' contained arguments for quality control (BIS 2009: 79), it suggested that "[a]ll universities should publish a standard set of information setting out what students can expect in terms of the nature and quality of their programme" (BIS 2009: 74), and it argued that "students' own assessments of the service they receive at university" ought to be central to the "judgement of the success of our higher education system" (BIS 2009: 70). The Browne Review, though not defining what 'the student experience' was, maintained that, in order to attract students and charge high fees, universities needed to provide a "high quality student experience" (Independent Review 2010: 10). Likewise, the White Paper 2011 repeatedly emphasised that 'the student experience' needed to improve, but it also more clearly stated that this included "teaching, assessment, feedback and preparation for the world of work" (BIS 2011: 4). Moreover, KIS was said to illustrate the quality of 'the student experience', which thus comprised, amongst others, student satisfaction with course quality, teaching, feedback, assessment methods, library and IT provision, as well as accommodation costs, fees, and employment prospects (BIS 2011: 28–9). But while it often remained fuzzy what 'the student experience' actually was, its real significance lay in the way it was framed in the policy discourse.

As Duna Sabri has argued, 'the student experience' as used in the policy discourse homogenised the experience of different students and thereby ignored to what extent the students' experiences of higher education were constrained "by class, ethnicity, gender, race, religion, sexual orientation, or responsibility for dependents", how much their experiences depended on particular personal relationships with academics and with each other, and that their experiences necessarily differed as they took place in rather different institutions (2011: 664).

Moreover, it was assumed that 'the student experience' could actually be measured and hence be objectified and that an important indicator of the quality of higher education services was how students evaluated them. There was, however, a logical problem underlying this assumption. This became most apparent when the Browne Review argued that while students' expectations had increased due to the rise in fees, it was "by no means clear that the quality of the student experience has improved" because results in the NSS did "not indicate significant change" (Independent Review 2010: 23). What was mixed here was the quality of provision and how this quality was 'experienced'. As the expectations of students had supposedly increased, it could well be that improved quality was not recognised or even disregarded – in particular as the NSS has always been based on a different student cohort.

Last but not least, the notion of 'the student experience' as employed in the policy discourse actually positioned students outside of their own experience. Thus, when the White Paper 2011 claimed that "institutions must deliver a better student experience" (BIS 2011: 4) and that all universities needed to "offer a good student experience" (BIS 2011: 5), it suggested that 'the student experience' was a service that was delivered by universities. 'The student experience' did not refer to the actual experience of the student but rather to the services provided by the university. In this respect, the market discourse fundamentally reframed what 'experience' referred to. Peter Marris's *The Experience of Higher Education* of 1964 was, for instance, concerned with students' attitudes, their social life, and social groupings. Similarly, Haselgrove's *The Student Experience* of

1994, though also investigating the services that universities offered, was interested in how students actually 'experienced' higher education. In the market discourse, however, 'experience' became a service and part of a market transaction. Though one might not go as far as Thomas Docherty, who claims that 'the student experience' was there "in order to ensure that [. . .] students do not have any experience" (2011: 50), the market discourse framed 'the student experience' in such a way that 'experience' became a service that students received and was nothing they actually created themselves.

The teaching excellence framework

While the Browne Review and the White Paper 2011 proposed the complete transformation of higher education into a market, the story does not end here. In 2015, the Conservative government published the Green Paper *Fulfilling our Potential: Teaching Excellence, Social Mobility and Student Choice*, and after a period of consultation, the reforms that the Green Paper proposed were translated into the White Paper *Success as a Knowledge Economy: Teaching Excellence, Social Mobility and Student Choice* (2016). In many respects, the two papers continued established policies. Hence, there was the need to "provide greater focus on graduate employability, widen participation in higher education, and open up the sector to new high-quality entrants" (BIS 2015a: 7), competition between universities was said to raise quality as students acted as informed customers (BIS 2016: 11), and measures were proposed to make it easier for new providers to enter the market (BIS 2016: 18). Moreover, plans were made for the creation of a new Office for Students to "put the interests of the student at the heart of our regulatory landscape" (BIS 2016: 15). As before, higher education was framed in a market discourse that was structured around nodal points such as 'employability', 'competition', and 'choice'.

But the government did not only continue established policies of marketisation, it also made a new departure when it announced its plans to set up a Teaching Excellence Framework (TEF) in order to raise teaching standards. According to Jo Johnson, Minister of State for Universities and Science, teaching had so far "been regarded as a poor cousin to academic research" (BIS 2015a: 8). The TEF, so it was argued, would correct this ill by assessing teaching quality, the quality of the learning environment, as well as student outcomes and learning gains (BIS 2015a: 32). Its results would not only provide further information to guide student choice, but they would also be translated into different maximum fees that institutions could charge (BIS 2016: 13, 19). The TEF thus marked a policy shift from quality assurance to a more competitive model in which teaching quality would correlate to funding.

Though the Green Paper claimed that its reforms would "reshape the higher education landscape to have students at its heart" (BIS 2015a: 7), it was actually not the students who were the most central when it came to the TEF. According to the Green Paper, the TEF would supposedly serve three interest groups as it would "deliver better value for money for students, employers and taxpayers" (BIS 2015a: 7). What is striking though is that these three groups were not of equal importance in the Green Paper. Not only was the term 'employer' used more than 40 times in the paper, but again and again it was emphasised that there was strong demand for graduates from employers. Hence, it was stated, for instance, that "[e]mployers want highly skilled graduates who are ready to enter the workforce" (BIS 2015a: 10), that the TEF would "provide better signalling for employers as to which providers they can trust to produce highly skilled graduates" (BIS 2015a: 13), and that it would "help employers to identify and recruit graduates with the skills they require by providing better and clearer information about courses and degree outcomes" (BIS 2015a: 18). In these cases, students were primarily positioned as resources of which employers could make use. Students were not customers but manpower. How much that thinking in terms of manpower actually lay behind the proposal to introduce the TEF became nowhere more apparent than in a rather telling metaphor. According to the Green Paper, the TEF was set up not only to ensure better quality for students and taxpayers but also because "employers need[ed] access to *a pipeline* of graduates" (BIS 2015a: 18, emphasis added). What thus lurked behind the TEF was the rationale of the manpower doctrine.

The TEF has been interpreted by some critics such as Roger Brown as "the latest stage in this process [of marketisation]" (2015: n.p.). However, it can also be read in a rather different way as actually signalling the partial failure of marketisation. The guiding rationale of marketisation that underlay the policies of New Labour and the following governments was that student choice coupled with financial power would force institutions of higher education to offer better quality. This idea had been central to the White Paper 2003, which argued that student choice would "increasingly work to drive up quality" (DfES 2003: 46), and also the White Paper 2011, which asserted that higher fees would "in turn drive a more responsive system" (BIS 2011: 5). If this policy had worked out and transformed higher education into a market where competition led to improved quality, it would not have been necessary to consider the introduction of the TEF. In this respect, the claim that the TEF would, "for the first time, link the funding of teaching in higher education to quality and not simply quantity" actually acknowledged that the market, in which students acted as customers, had not properly functioned (BIS 2016: 6). In other words, as the TEF would provide "additional incentives to drive up teaching quality" (BIS 2015a: 12), it was conceded that the market that was entirely governed by student choice had not delivered what it had promised.

Notes

1 Although the funding reforms passed parliament, the Liberals did not support it throughout. In the House of Commons vote on 9 December 2010, 27 Liberal Democrats voted for the proposals while 21 voted against and eight abstained (Johnston 2013: 201).

2 At the same time, the repayment threshold for tuition fee loans was raised from £15,000 to £21,000, tuition fee loans were extended to part-time students, and maintenance grants for students from low-income families were increased albeit with the upper threshold lowered from £50,000 to £42,000 (Callender 2012: 84).
3 While the Scottish government allowed Scottish institutions of higher education to raise their fees for students from the rest of the UK, Scottish students were still entitled to free tuition when studying in Scotland (Bruce 2016: 62). Northern Ireland did not raise the fees cap for home students but did so for students from the rest of the UK, and the Welsh Assembly decided that Welsh institutions of higher education could charge fees up to £9,000 but at that same time extended the fees grant that ensured that Welsh domiciled students only paid £3,465 (Brown and Carasso 2013: 96).
4 Likewise, the White Paper 2011 declared that the reforms "put students in the driving seat" (BIS 2011: 2) and "put more power into the hands of students" (BIS 2011: 14).
5 See, for instance, Peter Marris's *The Experience of Higher Education* (1964), which investigated student attitudes and student life.

Chapter 15

Neoliberal governmentality and the student

With the crisis of the Keynesian welfare state in the late 1970s and 1980s, neoliberalism was on the rise, and higher education was gradually transformed into a market, in which universities and colleges were supposed to compete for funding and student choice ought to determine the shape of the system. As David Blunkett stated in his Greenwich speech, "[t]he 'do nothing' university will not survive – and it will not be the job of government to bail it out" (2000: §87). Institutions of higher education were now expected to behave like businesses and to become, in the words of Burton R. Clark, 'entrepreneurial'.[1] This call for entrepreneurialism was embedded in a turn to performativity. Through performance indicators, RAE and REF, quality assurance, TEF, and the NSS, higher education was rendered 'legible' – a precondition for higher education to become governable (Walters 2012: 62) – and performativity became the prime legitimation for higher education. Higher education was no longer legitimised by a discourse structured around nodal points such as 'truth' or 'culture'. Instead, it was framed in a discourse that emphasised 'quality', 'added value', 'choice', 'competition', and the 'student experience'.

As part of this development, students were increasingly positioned as customers whose choices were expected to shape the provision of higher education. Institutions of higher education were no longer regarded as authorities but as service providers that had to answer to student demands. However, in a complete market situation, it would not only be the institutions of higher education that would lose in authority and power. If the provision of teaching only answered to student demand and was financed exclusively by student fees, government and its funding bodies would actually have no control over higher education either. Thus, a chasm emerged between the government's aim to use higher education to provide manpower and a system that was supposedly governed by students and their wants. Hence, measures needed to be taken to ensure that students actually made the 'right' choices and considered higher education as an investment. In other words, particular students needed to be produced through a specific 'governmentality'.

Neoliberal governmentality

Governmentality is a concept that Michel Foucault developed in a number of lectures in the late 1970s and which can best be defined as 'the art of government' (Lemke 2001: 191). Government in this context does not refer solely to political structures such as state departments or what is often referred to as governance. Rather, it should be understood in a very broad sense as "the conduct of conducts" that covers "not only the legitimately constituted forms of political or economic subjection but also modes of action, more or less considered and calculated, that were destined to act upon the possibilities of action of other people" (Foucault 2003: 138).[2] Government thus comprises all forms of power that aim at the regulation of conduct, in particular the regulation of one's own behaviour (Hindess 1996: 105). Such an attempt to regulate behaviour is precisely what distinguishes neoliberalism from, for instance, classical liberalism and what is at stake in the marketisation of higher education.

While in classical liberalism the state was regarded as the supervisor of the market and was supposed to intervene as least as possible, under neoliberalism the market becomes the organising principle of the state (Lemke 2001: 200). As has been shown above, this belief has shaped higher education policies since Thatcher. But neoliberalism does not only differ from classical liberalism in the roles it assigns to the market and the state. In contrast to classical liberalism, the assumption underlying neoliberalism is no longer that the market is an order of interaction that arises naturally. Instead, the market must be artificially constructed. Neoliberalism in this sense is not an economic theory trying to describe the world but rather a political and ideological project. According to Simon Clarke, "[t]he point for neoliberalism is not to make a model that is more adequate to the real world, but to make the real world more adequate to its model" (2005: 58). Therefore, it becomes vital to produce particular subjects and subjectivities. While classical liberalism was based on the assumption that individuals were autonomous human beings, in neoliberalism "the state seeks to create an individual that is an enterprising and competitive entrepreneur" (Olssen and Peters 2005: 315).[3] The neoliberal project, which started under Thatcher and was driven forward by all following governments, needs to be understood precisely as such an attempt to construct self-interested and competitive individuals who understand themselves as customers and as investors in their own human capital.

Of course, students may always have considered education as an investment of time, effort, and also of money – at least as long as the state did not provide for tuition and maintenance. That students may act like customers and consider the university as providing a service is also not new. In 1829, students at University College London demanded that one of their professors ought to be sacked because he was not offering value for money (Whyte 2015: 64). What was new about the development that started in the 1980s and 1990s was that the government actually tried to influence how students understood themselves and higher education.

As the preceding chapters have shown, the government not only emphasised that individuals were self-responsible for their future and should thus invest in it, but it actually set up means to shape the students' self-understanding and turn them into entrepreneurial subjects. The White Paper 1987 demanded "to foster the positive attitudes to enterprise which are crucial for [. . .] students" (DES 1987: §1.2). The introduction of student loans was supposed "to increase economic awareness among students, and their self-reliance" (DES 1988: §1.1). The Dearing Report favoured the introduction of fees as these would encourage students to see themselves as "discriminating investors" (NCIHE 1997: §1.21). The White Paper 2003 argued that students needed to be provided with information in order to "become intelligent customers" (DfES 2003: 47), and the White Paper 2011 promoted the introduction of a Key Information Set to guide student choice. As these examples show, the assumption was not that the market would simply answer to student demand, but means were established to make students consider themselves as investors in their human capital in order to make them function properly in the market. Students, so it was thought, needed to be 'taught' how to understand higher education – as an investment in their own human capital. Otherwise the whole project of marketisation would be at risk because students may make choices "for reasons that have nothing to do with quality or value for money" (Thompson and Bekhradnia 2010: 18). The choosing subject of neoliberalism is not the naturally given *homo economicus* but the successfully interpellated subject who 'recognises' him or herself as an investor and entrepreneur. Precisely for that reason, New Labour's *Higher Ambitions* proudly proclaimed that "[t]he introduction of variable fees for students has rightly sharpened attitudes to the value for money higher education represents as a personal investment" (BIS 2009: 70). Fees seemed to function the way they were supposed to as they turned students into investors.

But students were not only supposed to consider education as an investment to increase their human capital. They were also obliged to make that investment. This was particularly well pronounced in the context of lifelong learning. For the Dearing Report, for instance, the vision was "a society in which people in all walks of life recognise *the need* to continue in education and training" (NCIHE 1997: §1.10, emphasis added). As the report argued, there was "*the need* for individuals *to be committed* to lifelong learning" and hence "[e]ducation and training *must be embraced* by people at all levels of achievement" (NCIHE 1997: §5.12, emphases added). Quite in contrast to the ideal of the learning society that had been proposed in the 1970s as well as the tradition of adult education, the learning society of the Dearing Report was not just opening opportunities. Instead, lifelong learning was an obligation for the individual. In similar fashion, the Green Paper 1998 stated that "[t]o realise our ambition, we *must* all develop and sustain a regard for learning at whatever age" (DfEE 1998: 7, emphasis added), and the White Paper 2003 claimed that "[t]oday's generation of students will *need* to return to learning" (DfES 2003: 15, emphasis added). Learning was thus considered a lifelong requirement.[4] As Janice Dudley aptly put it, "learning has become a 'life sentence'" (1999: 90). This compulsory learning throughout life in combination with the creation of free, self-responsible, and entrepreneurial learners was and still is central to neoliberal governmentality and marked the transformation of Foucault's disciplinary societies into what Gilles Deleuze has called 'the societies of control', in which one no longer moved from one space to another and always started again, but in which one was "never finished with anything" (1992: 5).[5]

Marketisation and student empowerment

One of the central nodal points of the discourse of marketisation has been 'choice'. The Dearing Report, for instance, claimed that "student choice should be the main shaper of the system" (NCIHE 1997: §5.52), and since New Labour the logic that student choice should determine what is provided in higher education has become established as the core logic of the policy discourse. But choice was not only at the centre of marketisation, it was also exclusively defined in terms of the market. Instead of seeing choice as a liberal value that encompasses self-direction and the exercise of freedom, choice was completely equated with market exchange (Clarke, Newman, and Westmarland 2008: 249). This limitation of meaning can best be seen if the notion of choice as used in the discourse of marketisation is compared to earlier uses of the concept of choice as they appeared within the debate on higher education. Walter Moberly, for instance, was a great supporter of the German idea of *Lernfreiheit* – the freedom of learning – and modularisation as practised in the US because this would promote self-directed learning and taught the student to act responsibly (1949: 42). Such an educative function of choice was nowhere present in the market model. Indeed, choices that students might make during their time in higher education were not of importance at all. Choice was only of value at one point: when students decided to which college or university to apply. But even then, choice was not important because it was of educational value but because it could steer the market system.

Choice was also a central nodal point in the Anderson Report (1960), and like the market model of higher education, the Anderson Report focused on choice at the access point, that is the choice which college or university to attend. The Anderson Report argued in favour of grants in order to enable students to make choices between different universities without being confined by financial constraints. The market model as established under New Labour and the coalition government worked with a totally different understanding of choice. While the Anderson Report was concerned with enabling people to make choices, the market model not only assumed that people could indeed exercise choice but it focused on using choice as a means to regulate the provision of higher education. As student choice was coupled with funding, it was argued, universities and colleges would be required to offer good quality. Hence, the White Paper 2011 claimed that "[p]utting financial power into the hands of learners makes student choice meaningful" (BIS 2011: 5). But of course, students had also made choices regarding courses and institutions in the past, and surely these choices had been quite meaningful to them even without paying fees. What has been at stake in the discourse of marketisation was, however, not whether these choices were meaningful to the student, but that they were of greater consequence within the system of higher education. At the centre was not the student, as was the case in the Anderson Report, but rather the market. And yet choice was presented as if it was primarily in the interest of the student. The market was said to empower students by making their choices drive the development of the higher education system.

The power that the market attributes to student is not any kind of power but a rather particular one. This can best be seen by comparing it to the demands for student power that were voiced in the 1960s student protests. Leaving aside the most radical calls for complete student power, the arguments for student representation as they were put forth by Jack Straw, for instance, were based on a relation of equivalence between students and academics. As both students and academics were part of a community, he argued, both should be involved in its government. The concept of student power that the market model is based on is a totally different one. The market does not establish a relation of equivalence between students and academics. Instead, a relation of difference is constructed between institutions of higher education, which are considered as service providers, and students, who are regarded as customers.

These two different models of higher education as community and as market correspond to two rather different forms of power: voice and choice. Whereas voice refers to participation, for instance, in political processes, choice is the power to choose between different offers and thus to influence provider behaviour (Greener 2008a: 255). While voice is the democratic and collective power of the citizen and is based on rights, choice is the individualistic power of the customer that derives from purchasing power (Pierre 1995: 72, Greener 2008b: 199).[6] The fight for student power in the 1960s and the power that students are provided in the market correspond to these two different forms of power. While the 1960s student protests demanded and used voice in order to change higher education, the market gives students choice – that is power in return for payments – but not any form of democratic power.

Quite interestingly, what was presented as student empowerment through choice was coupled with a degree of infantilisation. Though one may not agree with Benjamin R. Barber, who has claimed that consumer capitalism has led to infantilisation in general (2007),[7] there are a number of points with respect to the marketisation of higher education which clearly point in this direction. As has been shown above, the more the government put student choice at the centre, the more it tried to influence the choices students made. Students were not seen as independent agents, but they were considered as in need of guidance to make the 'right' choices. But even more strikingly, students were not the only ones who were supposed to make choices and thus needed information to guide them. Time and again, the White Paper 2011 emphasised that information should be presented in such a way as to "meet the needs of students, their parents, and careers advisers or teachers" (BIS 2011: 30). Even though it is not surprising that parents and teachers may influence prospective students in their choices, it is remarkable that these had not figured in the whole debate so far. Only when students were positioned as customers did parents become of relevance.

But parents were not only present as those who might influence students in their choice of a university or college. They also appeared as customers in their own right, for instance, when the White Paper 2011 stated that it was "reasonable for students and their parents to expect higher education institutions to make student welfare a priority" (BIS 2011: 35). Parents turned up as "co-consumers" here (Williams 2013: 124). While one may argue that this was a reaction to a further spread of what Frank Furedi has called 'paranoid parenting' (2001), the more crucial point is that the ideal of the independent customer-student was tainted exactly in the White Paper which most celebrated the customer and the market ideal. Precisely at the point when the student as an independent customer was supposed to become the champion of the system of higher education, parents turned up as the ones who needed to be satisfied as well. This is particularly paradoxical as it had been claimed in the White Paper 2003 that the move from up-front fees to graduate contribution schemes would make students independent of their parents (DfES 2003: 88).

The marketisation of higher education was not only said to enhance student power through choice, but supposedly it also gave students a greater 'voice' as evaluators of quality. While student choice was considered as the means to drive up quality, this choice was to be guided by information that was itself drawn from student views as captured, for instance, by the NSS (DfES 2003: 46). Students have therefore occupied a double role in the market as those who choose between different offers and those who evaluate the quality of what is on offer. Students have thus been given power as 'evaluators'. Though this is not the same as the power of choice of the customer, it has likewise put students and institutions of higher education in an oppositional relation as those who offer a service and those who evaluate it. Quite in contrast to the protests of the 1960s, the aim has not been to directly involve students, but to have them judge what they have been offered, which put the responsibility for change entirely upon the institution of higher education. Moreover, mechanisms like the NSS have even supported the marketisation of higher education. In contrast to internal student feedback, the NSS was designed to enable comparison and to enhance competition between institutions. In other words, students have provided the information that was necessary in order to drive marketisation forward. As league tables based on the NSS were created and as universities and colleges proudly put NSS results on prospectuses and websites, the 'student voice' became part of the marketing package.

The commodification of the student

The changes of higher education that have taken place since the Thatcher government are often said to have led to a commodification of higher education. Mike Molesworth, Elizabeth Nixon, and Richard Scullion have tried to capture this development with reference to Erich Fromm's distinction between 'having' and 'being'. According to them, marketisation has made higher education part of the consumer society – a society in which the possession of objects is of paramount significance for the constitution of an individual's identity (2009: 280). Hence, the marketisation of higher education is said to promote "a mode of existence where students seek to 'have a degree' rather than 'be learners'" (2009: 278). Instead of transforming the student's identity, higher education, so they argue, reinforces it and "recreates the subject to fit closely into existing consumer culture" (2009: 282). This diagnosis presents, however, only half the story. Marketisation not only turns students into customers and higher education into a commodity, it also turns students themselves into commodities.

As higher education institutions are supposed to bargain over students, students become goods in the marketplace. At the same time, students are part of performance measurement and are considered as something to which 'value' can be 'added'. From the perspective of the higher education institution, the student is thus both a commodity and a resource of funding. But within the market, students are not only commodified by the higher education institution, they are also supposed to commodify themselves. How that functions can best be seen by theoretically analysing higher education as a commodity that has a use value, that is what is being learned, and an exchange value, that is what higher education can be exchanged for in terms of money.[8]

Proponents of 'liberal' and social conceptions of higher education like Brian Simon or Walter Moberly were primarily concerned with the use value of higher education as they focused on the content of higher education, what it did to the individual, as well as the purpose and function of higher education in society.[9] Likewise, the manpower doctrine concentrated on the use value of higher education when it emphasised its importance for the national economy. In contrast to that, the neoliberal discourse of marketisation has emphasised graduate earnings and student fees and hence the exchange value of education. As Rajani Naidoo and Ian Jamieson argue, there has been a

> transformation of educational processes into a form that has an economic worth of its own and has an 'exchange', rather than an intrinsic 'use-value'. Clearly, in the past educational credentials have had an exchange-value but, arguably, this has been a by-product of the values, processes and ethos of universities.
>
> (2005: 271)

While it is not the case that there is no longer a use value of higher education as students still acquire skills and knowledge, the market discourse has shifted the focus onto the exchange value. This exchange value, however, is not necessarily linked to the actual use value of higher education. When the White Paper 2003, for instance, declared that "students choose the good-quality courses that will bring them respected and valuable *qualifications*" (DfES 2003: 47, emphasis added), and that "[g]raduates derive substantial *benefits from having gained a degree*" (DfES 2003: 83, emphasis added), the focus was not on the use value of education. Instead, it claimed that students derived a benefit from 'respected and valuable qualifications' in the form of degrees or certificates. Though these degrees and certificates may be understood as signifiers that supposedly indicate the use value of higher education, they are not simply representations of a use value, but rather constitute what Jean Baudrillard calls the sign value (1981: 65–7).[10]

The crucial difference between the use value and the sign value is that the use value, which refers to the utility of the object, is insofar intrinsic to the commodity as its possible uses depend on its specific properties. To use an example from outside of higher education, it is the specific mechanical properties of the car, and not the chair, that enable it to be used for driving. In contrast to the use value, the sign value, that is the social status that is ascribed to a certain commodity, is nothing but the product of differences and thus depends entirely on its relation to other sign values. This is exactly what was at stake when the White Paper 2003 spoke of "*respected and valuable* qualifications" (DfES 2003: 47, emphasis added). The value of the qualification depends on those who 'respect' it, i.e. those who assign it a certain status. In contrast to the use value of higher education in the sense of what the student has actually learned, degrees and certificates only have value in comparison to other 'qualifications'.

Though the sign value has so far been described as denoting the status of the commodity, its function eventually is to impart that status on the possessor of the commodity. The certificates and degrees that the student is awarded supposedly bestow upon him or her a certain status, to which the labour market attributes an exchange value. Of course, there has for long been competition and self-marketing on the labour market, but the framing of higher education as a commodity and the focus on employability have reinforced this and have turned graduates into commodities whose value is supposedly indicated by the certificates attached. This ties in with Zygmunt Bauman, who has argued that "[t]he most prominent feature of the society of consumers [...] is the transformation of consumers into commodities; or rather their dissolution into the sea of commodities" (2013: 12). Indeed, in the neoliberal higher education market, the student as customer is the student as commodity.

Notes

1 The term 'entrepreneurial university' became popular with Clark's *Creating Entrepreneurial Universities* (1998), in which he studied five European universities and how these

proactively transformed themselves in the 1980s and 1990s. According to Clark, the entrepreneurial university "stands on its own feet in order to adapt, on its own terms, to a highly complex and highly uncertain world" (2001: 10). Entrepreneurial universities rely on strong management and autonomy but are not necessarily "handmaidens of industry" or "all-purpose shopping malls" (2001: 10).

2 The phrase 'conduct of conducts' only appears in some translations of Foucault's "The Subject and Power" such as the one published in Rabinow and Rose (2003). In Dreyfus and Rabinow, it is instead translated as "guiding the possibility of conduct" (1983: 221).

3 See also Burchell (1993: 271), Lemke (2001: 200), Harris (2007: 18), Bröckling, Krasmann, and Lemke (2011: 15), and Marttila (2013: 18).

4 This aspect of compulsion has been highlighted by numerous critics such as Tight (1998a: 483–4, 1998b: 261–2), Bartlett (2003: 205), Coffield (1999: 488), or Simons and Masschelein (2006: 417).

5 In disciplinary societies, the individual moved from one enclosed space such as the school or the factory to another. In the societies of control, "the corporation replaces the factory, *perpetual training* tends to replace the *school*, and continuous control to replace the examination" (Deleuze 1992: 5). The enclosed spaces and institutions are thus replaced by more open systems that are "based on the control model of the network" (Peters 2001: 105).

6 The differentiation between voice and choice goes back to Albert O. Hirschman's *Exit, Voice and Loyalty: Responses to Decline in Firms, Organizations and States* (1970). If people are dissatisfied with a provider or organisation, they may thus choose to 'exit' (choice) or use 'voice', for instance through protest, in order to improve the situation (Greener 2008b: 197). In practice, the two different forms may often be combined, and there are often mechanisms which do not that easily fall within one category. Thus, complaint mechanisms in higher education, which New Labour, for instance, wanted to strengthen (DfES 2003: 49), can be seen as allowing for voice but without any direct control. Indeed, Greener describes complaints as a "bridging notion" between choice and voice as they may "give individuals the chance to make collective changes" (2008a: 263).

7 A short but sharp criticism of Barber is, for instance, brought forward in Ritzer (2008).

8 The distinction between use and exchange value roughly follows Karl Marx, who defined the two different forms of value in the following way: "The usefulness of a thing makes it a use-value. But this usefulness does not dangle in mid-air. It is conditioned by the physical properties of the commodity, and has no existence apart from the latter. [. . .] Use-values are only realized in use or in consumption. [. . .] Exchange-value appears first of all as the quantitative relation, the proportion, in which use-values of one kind exchange for use-values of another kind" (Marx 1976: 126). While the use value refers to the utility of a commodity and the satisfaction of human needs, the exchange value is only established when commodities are actually exchanged against each other (Morrison 2006: 84–7).

9 The Robbins Report, for instance, argued that the word 'wastage', as it was then commonly used for those students who dropped out, "is perhaps an unfortunate term, for it suggests that those who fail to complete their courses have gained nothing, which is rarely true" (Committee on Higher Education 1963: §575). Thus, higher education was considered as having a value in itself without necessarily leading to a degree.

10 Baudrillard extended Marx's differentiation between use value and exchange value by adding the further dimension of the sign value (1981: 65–7). Commodities are thus part of sign systems and derive their value through their differential relation to other commodities. The consumer society is then characterised by the sign value replacing both the use value and the exchange value in their importance. For a short overview of Baudrillard and his concept of the sign value as well as a critique of Baudrillard see Dunn (2008: 54–7) and Sassatelli (2007: 82–4).

Part IV

Beyond the customer and neoliberal higher education

Chapter 16

Looking forward to the past

As the government advanced on its course towards marketisation, not all academics just watched silently. Though Martin Trow might be right that the universities and their representative bodies showed relatively little resistance towards the reforms introduced under Thatcher (2006: 79–80),[1] numerous academics published articles and books that criticised the ongoing marketisation of higher education. In particular in response to the 2010 funding reforms, academics raised their voice, for instance, with the Campaign for the Public University or the publication of the Alternative White Paper *In Defence of Higher Education* (2011). However, even before then there had been lively discussions about the purpose, structure, values, and role of higher education. Indeed, the debate had never stopped.

The numerous articles and books that have appeared on the idea of higher education since the 1970s can be roughly divided into two different strands: on the one side, writings that have tried to formulate new visions of higher education, and on the other side, the abundance of publications that have primarily tried to defend higher education against the rise of neoliberalism. Of course, these two types of writings cannot be neatly divided as the argument has been frequently made that the future of higher education could be found in a partial return to the past.

While Chapter 18 turns to new ideas of higher education, the following chapter concentrates on predominantly defensive writings. As the number of such writings is simply too extensive to be covered in detail, the focus is on a few representative examples in order to identify how the issues that sparked criticism and the concept of the student have shifted.

Higher education in crisis

In order to see how the issues that sparked criticism have shifted over time, it is helpful to start with two publications of the 1970s: Kenneth Minogue's *The Concept of a University* (1973) and W.R. Niblett's *Universities between Two Worlds* (1974). Though published at nearly the same time, both offered two rather different accounts of the condition and future of the universities.

Minogue's *The Concept of the University* put forth a vehement critique of all those who wanted to instrumentalise the universities and turn them into "powerhouses of industrial society, institutions of 'social criticism', [or] promoters of the rate of industrial growth" (1973: 2). While he did not deny that social change and economic progress could all be "side-effects", Minogue insisted that none of these could be considered the primary function of the university (1973: 4–5). The only function that a university had, he argued, was to inquire into truth and to "sustain the academic world" (1973: 222–3). Hence, instead of fulfilling any demands from society or the economy, universities, he claimed, ought to be places detached from "the practical world" (1973: 100).

Such a detachment from society was no option for Niblett, who identified a crisis of a rather different kind. According to Niblett,

> [t]he problems facing higher education at the start of the 1970s are obviously very great and very many. But essentially they stem from the difficulty of educating young people brought up in a society so uncertain and confused as ours about its own objectives, at a time when an enormous increase in our technical accomplishment and control over nature and human nature has occurred. Any solution demands a moral insight and moral choices that are products of a profoundly humane temper, one very different from that likely to be produced by an education directed to the production of technical skills, however complex and demanding of intelligence.
>
> (1974: 61)

Similar to Minogue, Niblett thus argued that a university education should not only be concerned with the production of skills and manpower. But in contrast to Minogue, Niblett did not see the university's function to be exclusively intellectual. Instead, the university had the "job of civilising and sensitising [. . .] students both morally and aesthetically" (1974: 71).[2] According to Niblett, the universities should be socially responsible and help people "develop further and more sensitively their powers of enjoyment, their sense of purpose, their capacity for empathy and moral action" (1974: 160).

Minogue and Niblett thus provided two rather different accounts of the university's function and position in society. While Minogue saw the university as largely detached from wider society and considered its prime task to be the search for knowledge and the development of the student's intellectual capacities, Niblett claimed that the university had a guiding function in society and should focus on the student's moral development. These two opposing views to a certain extent mirrored two earlier writers. While Minogue's idea of the university in many ways overlapped with the ideas of Oakeshott, for whom the university was likewise defined through the nodal point 'the pursuit of learning', Niblett can be regarded as the successor of Moberly, who had also argued that the university should be a guiding force in society and help students form a philosophy of life. But what nevertheless united both Niblett and Minogue was that they considered the university as being threatened by a discourse that perceived education entirely in terms of manpower production.

In the 1980s, the notion of crisis became even more dominant with publications such as Peter Scott's *The Crisis of the University* (1984) and Marjorie Reeves's *The Crisis in Higher Education* (1988) – two books that, though similar in title, were rather different in approach and aim. While Scott primarily tried to entangle the pessimism of his age and the widespread feeling of crisis, Reeves was not only clear about the fact that there was indeed a crisis, but she also offered a normative ideal of higher education to counter the crisis. Similar to Niblett and Minogue, Reeves criticised an understanding of higher education that primarily focused on making students fit for the labour market. For Reeves, the main problem facing higher education was that the growing emphasis on the power to master skills and techniques and the acquisition of 'useful' knowledge had increasingly subdued "the feelings of delight and wonder at the intricacy, fascination or sheer beauty of what has been discovered" (1988: 1). Accordingly, it was the main task of higher education to set students "back on to the path of discovery which they have lost" (1988: 19). As Reeves suggested here, higher education had lost its path and had been in a better state in the past.

This notion of loss characterised numerous writings of the 1990s and 2000s. Ronald Barnett's *The Idea of Higher Education* (1990), for instance, diagnosed "a crisis to do with the way in which we understand higher education, the fundamental principles on which the idea of higher education has traditionally stood, and the way in which those principles are being undermined" (1990: 3). Though Barnett actually tried to formulate a new idea of liberal education based on "a culture of critical discourse" (1990: 175), the notion of loss was still prevailing, in particular as the central question for Barnett was whether and how "the idea of a liberal higher education [could] be *recovered*, and be implemented" (1990: x, emphasis added).

While Barnett's ideal of a critical and emancipatory higher education was still rather forward looking, there have been numerous publications that were much more defensive in tone. One of these was Duke Maskell and Ian Robinson's *The New Idea of a University* (2002), which complained that education had been confused with training, that standards had fallen, and that the ideal of a liberal education had been lost (2002: 184). In a similar vein, Gordon Graham's *The Institution of Intellectual Values* (2005) criticised the rising economic and utilitarian view of education – a development that could only be countered, he claimed, through a "recovering of the essential idea of a university" (2005: 169). Instead of being concerned with producing 'useful' knowledge and skills, the university, according to Graham, ought to be "a place in which the pursuit of truth and understanding are given special protection, not to the exclusion of useful or socially relevant subjects, but not principally in their service either" (2005: 165).

The number of publications that were primarily critical and defensive in tone did not diminish in the following years. In particular in response to the 2010 funding reforms, numerous publications appeared that tried to defend higher education against the growing hegemony of neoliberalism. Thomas Docherty's *For the University* (2011), for instance, provided a thorough critique of the economic view of education and marketisation and claimed that the university was not primarily a means of achieving economic growth but was "above all governed by actions of discovery" (2011: 4) and existed "in order to allow us to search for what is true, what is good and what is beautiful" (2011: 18). The Alternative White Paper *In Defence of Public Higher Education* (2011), a collective work of numerous campaigns that had been formed in 2010, was as defensive in outlook as its title indicates, and so was Stefan Collini's popular book *What Are Universities For?* (2012), which not only relentlessly criticised the new market model of higher education and its focus on the economic benefit of education but also wanted "to revitalize ways of understanding the nature and importance of universities that are in danger of being lost sight of in the present" (2012: 19).

As these few examples indicate, there is a strong tradition of writings that perceive higher education and in particular the university as being in crisis. Of course, this is also part of the genre as such because the search for the idea of higher education has often been a reaction to changes within society that resulted in new demands that were placed on higher education (Rothblatt 2009: 182). What is striking, though, is that some of the issues that have generated criticism and a feeling of crisis have been largely the same for decades. Thus, writers as diverse as Truscot, Leavis, Moberly, or Oakeshott criticised the utilitarian view of education as a means of manpower production in the 1940s and 1950s, and as the examples above show, this line of argument has been present ever since. Though by no means uniform with regard to the proposed ideas of higher education or the nodal points that have structured these, there clearly exists a relatively homogeneous tradition of writings that have tried to defend higher education against a discourse that emphasised the economic value of education. But as stable and uniform as this tradition might appear in its opposition to a discourse in which 'economic benefit' functioned as dominant nodal point,[3] the concept of the student within these writings has considerably shifted.

The value of community

As previous chapters have shown, the notion of community had been a particularly strong nodal point within the debate on the idea of higher education. For writers like Truscot, Moberly, Sloman, as well as the Robbins Report, the ideal had been that institutions of higher education should form communities and that students should consider themselves part of these communities. Hence, these writers focused strongly on means to create such communities, for instance, through the provision of social facilities and accommodation. This notion of the university as a community was still of importance in the early 1970 and central to Niblett's *Universities between Two Worlds* (1974).[4] Though Niblett recognised that students in the 1970s wanted more independence than had been the case in earlier decades, he emphasised the role of residence and social activities and stressed that institutions of higher education needed "to be communities, and communities in which both rigorous expression of thought and disciplined expression of feeling will find encouragement" (1974: 114).

This ideal, that institutions of higher education constitute social communities, has significantly lost in importance since the 1980s. Indeed, none of the examples from the 'crisis literature' listed above made the building of communities through a common way of life a central issue any longer. And yet, this does not mean that the nodal point 'community' has entirely lost in value. While the ideal of the community based on a common way of life drastically decreased in significance, the idea that institutions of higher education formed communities that were united by common values has had a longer life. Reeves, for instance, conceded that it had become increasingly difficult to speak of an 'academic community' (1988: 64), but then argued that there were still a number of values that academics shared such as "openness in the quest, persistence in following the clues and integrity in recording and communicating their findings" (1988: 47). The notion of community was also central to Barnett's *The Idea of Higher Education* (1990), which asserted that students ideally subscribed to the same values as academics (108).

In recent years, the concept of community has further lost in prominence. Even though the idea of the 'community of scholars' was still dominant in Graham's *The Institution of Intellectual Values* (2005), there have otherwise only been occasional references. Hence, Maskell and Robinson claimed that "students join in a community of scholars" (2002: 89), and the Alternative White Paper declared that universities were "diverse communities, made up of researchers, teachers, students, administrators and support staff who work together to provide an education" (*In Defence* 2011: §3.41). But in these cases the concept of community was no longer central to the idea of higher education that these texts put forth. The ideal of the community, which had been one of the most central concepts in the discourse of higher education for decades and had been valued by numerous writers, the UGC, the Robbins Report, and for long also the NUS, has thus greatly lost in appeal over the last decades and no longer functions as one of the organising nodal points of the higher education discourse.

Expansion and the 'new student' debate

The history of higher education since World War II is a history of expansion. With a few exceptions, the number of students has continuously risen since the 1940s. Hence, it is not surprising that expansion was also a central issue within the debate about higher education. Though expansion was favoured by many, there were also a number of critical voices, such as Oakeshott, Leavis, or the Black Papers, that called for stricter selection and wanted to limit access to higher education and in particular the university.

Criticism of expansion did not die out after the 1960s. Writing in the 1970s, Minogue, for instance, complained that the university had been opened to people who did "not see much point to it" and who "attributed this situation not to their own temperamental incomprehension but to senile incompetence on the part of the long-established custodians" of the university (1973: 75). Expansion, he claimed, posed a major problem for the university because "the mulish, the discontented and the untalented constitute an active weight upon its progress" (1973: 218). In contrast to Minogue, Niblett did not resist expansion but argued that it was precisely the expansion of higher education that required the university to get involved and no longer stand aside from the problems of society (1974: 15). But as much as Minogue and Niblett differed in their attitude towards expansion, the one thing they agreed on was that an increasing number of students had a rather instrumental outlook and primarily regarded education as a means to enter a career. Hence, Minogue complained that "[c]areerism and a flabby contentment with grasping such externals of a subject as are necessary to pass examinations are very frequent" (1973: 71), and likewise Niblett believed that

> [m]ost of the vast numbers of students entering higher education [. . .] in the next quarter of a century will be looking to their period in a college or university or polytechnic to fit them for a profession or to give them expertise to equip them to survive in the technological world they will live in.
>
> (1974: 71)

This view was also shared by Reeves in *The Crisis in Higher Education* (1988). While she did not argue against expansion, Reeves claimed that a utilitarian ethos and instrumentalist view of education was growing amongst students as more and more students primarily wanted the knowledge that would "furnish them with a paper qualification to open desirable career-doors" (1988: 2).[5] Similar to earlier variants of the 'new student' debate, writers like Minogue, Niblett, and Reeves shared the belief that the student intake was changing and that a growing number of students had an instrumental attitude towards education that ran counter to the purpose of higher education.

Over the years, expansion seemed to have lost in importance as a cause of major criticism. Though Maskell and Robinson, for instance, wanted to "reduce the numbers both of universities and of university students by more than three quarters" (2002: 186), such open elitism was not that widespread any longer. Indeed, in recent years, it was in particular the defenders of expansion who levelled criticism at government policies. As the 2010 funding reforms raised the fees level, concern was voiced that these reforms would deter further expansion and hamper widening participation – an issue that Chapter 18 will turn to in more detail.

But while criticism of expansion was less dominant in more recent debates on higher education, what did not fade was the belief that most students had an instrumentalist view of education and were primarily interested in gaining certificates in order to improve their career prospects. As Chapter 17 will show, such assumptions were also behind many of the attacks that have been waged against the notion of the student as customer.

Student power and the autonomy of the university

While the notion of community and the issue of expansion had already been central to the debate on higher education for decades, the 1960s saw another issue rise in prominence: student power. Students not only fought against the *in loco parentis* system, but they also demanded representation on the governing bodies of their institutions of higher education. Writing in the direct aftermath of the student troubles, these demands for increased student power were still of concern to writers like Minogue and Niblett.

For Minogue, the student protests presented a vicious attack on the university as in particular radical students were part of those forces that wanted to instrumentalise the university as a means of social change or even "destroy it altogether" (1973: 205). But Minogue was not only critical of the radical protesters. He also derided more moderate demands for increased student power because for him the ideal student was "a Socrates, whose wisdom consists in the fact that he knows he knows nothing" (1973: 69–70). In contrast to Minogue, Niblett was much more sympathetic towards the student protests. While he opposed some of the remedies that the radical students offered, he complimented the student protesters of the late 1960s for having raised the right questions "about objectives both in education and social life" (1974: 50) and even thought that students might be "the only likely source of initiative for some much needed changes in university outlook" (1974: 55). Hence, he approved that in many institutions students had been given seats on committees and sometimes even on the governing bodies (1974: 10).

While for both Niblett and Minogue the student protests were still relatively near, questions of student power lost in relevance in the following decades. Apart from Barnett, who claimed that it was vital that "the social relations between teacher and taught were made more equal" (1990: 140), the topic seemed to have been of no major concern in the 1980s and 1990s as neither Scott nor Reeves took particular issue with the position of the student in terms of power.

However, questions of power again moved to the forefront of the debate as the marketisation of higher education advanced. While the writers of the 1940s to 1960s could still assume that at least the universities were in a position in which they themselves could define what was worthwhile and what they ought to do, the situation radically altered from Thatcher onwards. As funding became more stratified and the government increased control in general, questions of power became a central concern, and many writers put forth defences of the autonomy of academic inquiry. Graham, for instance, claimed that the concept of autonomy lay at the heart of the idea of the university because "intellectual inquiry should be allowed to go where it will" (2005: 163), and likewise Collini argued that institutional autonomy with regard to its intellectual activities was one of the defining features of the university (2012: 7). With the further marketisation and the empowering of the student as customer, this criticism was also directed towards students. While Graham had still argued in favour of student fees in order to secure the autonomy of the university (2005: 166), the growing dependence on fees and the reconfiguration of students as customers raised widespread disapproval. Indeed, the criticism of the notion of the customer has become so widespread and central in the debate on higher education that it requires a chapter of its own.

Notes

1 Of course, there was the famous refusal of an honorary degree to Margaret Thatcher by the University of Oxford in 1985. But this was a mere symbolic act that did hardly have any political effect.
2 While Minogue was only concerned with the universities, Niblett, though speaking primarily of universities, had a much wider focus and actually wrote about higher education more generally.
3 The growing economic rationale that governed higher education policies from the 1980s onwards was also criticised within numerous fictional works such as Malcolm Bradbury's *Cuts* (1987), David Lodge's *Nice Work* (1988), or Andrew Davies's *A Very Peculiar Practice* (1986). (See, amongst others, Kühn (2002) for a detailed discussion of these texts.) One of the most striking examples of such criticism in fictional form is Frank Parkin's *The Mind and Body Shop* (1986) as it also problematises the economic concept of the student. Not only is student hardship a major topic, but the role of the student for and within the university is explicitly questioned, for instance, when the reader is informed about the vice-chancellor's attitude towards students. As a man who thinks that the main function of the university is "to give customer satisfaction", he sees no relevance in students as "the very concept of student had become outdated. Their fees made up only a small proportion of total revenue, so that the resources and personnel tied up in teaching them would be used far more constructively on contract research for foreign governments and the multi-nationals. Besides, the university would be a much better place without them; there would be fewer germs, fewer social diseases, more parking space" (Parkin 1986: 38–9). More than a decade later, Ralph Messenger, one of the protagonists in David Lodge's *Thinks . . .*, describes the attitude of university management in rather different terms when he explains that "[t]here's money in student numbers. Higher education is a market nowadays, you know" (Lodge 2002: 46).
4 Only a few years before the publication of Niblett's *Universities between two Worlds* (1974), Joan Brothers and Stephen Hatch had published their study *Residence and Student Life*, which Niblett actually referred to and which had concluded that residence was an important means to enable students to identify and participate in their institution of higher education (1971: 362).

5 Scott argued in a rather different direction at that time and asserted that a further widening of the student body might have a positive effect because "[w]orking-class students, after all, may retain some vestigial collectivist and even fraternal values which are in opposition to the highly individualistic and competitive values of the entrepreneurial middle class" (1984: 249–50).

Chapter 17

Contesting the customer

The marketisation of higher education was not welcomed by everyone. In particular the reconfiguration of students as customers sparked widespread criticism. Though many critics acknowledged that the customer model had led to a number of improvements, for instance, in the quality of the provided facilities and services or feedback procedure for students (McMillan and Cheney 1996: 3–5; Naidoo and Jamieson 2005: 272; Schwartzman 1995: 217), the idea that students were consumers or customers has often been met with disapproval – not only in Britain but also in other countries where neoliberal reforms of marketisation had been introduced.

One of the most common criticisms against the concept of the customer has been that it allegedly had a negative impact on the students' self-understanding and their idea of education. Students who identified as customers were said to "wait for the 'quick information fix'" and to "expect to receive an education rather than to claim one: to be 'acted upon' rather than to 'act' in the pursuit of their educational goal" (McMillan and Cheney 1996: 9). Supposedly, such students primarily wanted "certification and sufficiently good references to enable them to enter the job market at a relative advantage" (McCulloch 2009: 174) and assumed that they had "a right to a degree because they have purchased it" (Bailey 2000: 356). These assumptions, that students who saw themselves as customers were passive, only interested in gaining certificates, and thought that they were actually entitled to be given those without any major effort, have been shared by numerous critics.[1]

However, as Kevin Love has argued, the customer model as such is more open than these critics asserted as it all depended on what was considered as the 'product of education': "The customer, for instance, could well be in the market for a 'fully rounded educational experience'" (2008: 18). Similarly, Ronald Barnett has claimed that it was not necessarily the case that students who identified as customers were passive and felt entitled to a certificate. Indeed, the notion of the customer might actually lead to students taking a greater interest in their studies and being more engaged.

> The point turns on what it means for the student to become a customer. It means in the first place, as we saw earlier, that the student has a real stake in

their own learning. But what might that mean? If it means that the student adopts a 'commodified' view of his or her learning with an eye for the short term, then there is a problem.

(Barnett 2011b: 46)

What Barnett here indirectly points to is that the notion of the customer is not fixed in its meaning but needs to be articulated in a specific discourse. However, as has been shown above, the neoliberal discourse of higher education that has dominated government thinking since the 1980s has indeed conceived of higher education in purely instrumental terms as an investment in human capital, it has put the focus on certificates, and it has shifted responsibilities for learning success away from students towards teachers. It is these issues that the critics of the customer metaphor have actually attacked. This, however, means that the critics assumed that neoliberal governmentality would actually succeed and that students would fully internalise the neoliberal view of higher education.

Another issue that raised considerable criticism as far as the notion of the customer is concerned was the idea that student choice and satisfaction ought to be the main drivers of the higher education system. Elizabeth Staddon and Paul Standish, for instance, argued that the problem with making student choice and satisfaction the main steering mechanisms was that "[w]ith regard to determining the worth of what is studied, authority is now being ceded to the novice" (2012: 635). The same point was made by Stefan Collini, who asserted that

[c]hildren may be best placed to judge what they want to get from the sweetshop, but they are not best placed to judge what they should get from their schooling. University students are, of course, no longer children, but nor are they simply rational consumers in a perfect market.

(2012: 184)

Likewise, Laurie Lomas claimed that students might "not be clear of what they need because of their lack of experience of higher education" (2007: 35). According to Gordon Graham, the problem was that students were unable to identify what was worth studying and might choose not what was worthwhile but what they considered an easy option:

A student, reasonably, may find Kant tedious and difficult, and find Alain de Botton more to their liking. Nevertheless, it is in Kant that far greater intellectual worth lies, which is not a judgement they are in a position to make, but one which they need to be taught how to make.

(Graham 2005: 66)

Even more criticism has been levelled against the concept of 'customer satisfaction' as a means to evaluate the quality of education. Joanna Williams, for instance, stated that

> [t]he demand for satisfaction may be antithetical to education and the development of positive pedagogical relationships, as it implies that teaching should confirm what the student believes, rather than challenging students' assumptions in an intellectual process of transformation requiring sustained commitment.
>
> (2013: 100)

Similarly, W.A. Hart argued that it was not the teacher's job "to satisfy the student, in the sense of giving him what he wants, but to help him to form new wants and interests, new possibilities of satisfaction – and, of course, dissatisfaction" (1997: 301). Numerous other writers have likewise warned that education was not about satisfying wants but about creating them and that an overemphasis on satisfying students could lead to a diminishing of standards.[2]

Leaving aside the question to what extent these arguments against student choice and satisfaction were empirically true, the important thing is that all these criticisms worked with a particular image of the student. Students were said to have a distorted understanding of education, to be passive, and to prefer easy courses. Students supposedly did not know what they needed and thus made wrong choices, and they were unqualified to actually judge the quality of what they were being offered. It is striking how much these points of criticism mirrored some of the arguments that had been brought forward against student representation in the late 1960s, for instance, in the Black Papers. In both cases, students were portrayed not only as unqualified but as having a mistaken understanding of what education was good for. And in both cases, this image of the student was used in order to defend academic authority.

The criticisms levelled against the notion of the customer not only mirrored the arguments against student representation in the 1960s. There was also a considerable overlap with the neoliberal discourse of marketisation itself. When critics of marketisation claimed that student choice and satisfaction were inappropriate instruments to shape the provision of higher education because students were unable to know what was worth studying, the underlying concept of the student was not unlike the concept of the 'informed customer' that the market discourse proposed. The market model that New Labour and the following governments tried to establish did not simply make the student-customer king. It was only the customer who had been guided by especially designed information like KIS whose choices were supposed to govern the system of higher education. In other words, both the academics who defended traditional academic authority and the proponents of the market assumed that students were incapable of making the 'right' choices independently. But while the market model tried to shift power towards the economy as students were supposed to have their choices guided by economic considerations, the critics of the customer model asserted that power and authority should be with the academic as a professional instead. In both cases, however, the assumption was that students needed to be strongly guided.

Alternative metaphors

Instead of only criticising the customer metaphor, some critics have also put forth alternative metaphors. Jeffrey Bailey, for instance, proposed regarding students not as customers but rather as 'clients'. In contrast to customers, who expected that the service or goods they bought simply satisfied their wants, students who considered themselves as clients, he argued, "would ideally want to be challenged, guided, and engaged in the pursuit of learning" (2000: 356). Moreover, the client relationship would invoke "a professional service framework" and hence put students and academics in a different relationship than the customer model (2000: 355). As professionals such as lawyers, doctors, or consultants were marked by special competences and knowledge, clients supposedly placed "a high degree of confidence in the beliefs, decisions, and advice of the professional" (2000: 355). Similarly, Michael Armstrong claimed that, in contrast to customers, who relied "on their own judgment to evaluate a purchase", clients had to "rely on the professionals to tell them what they need" (2003: 372). The central issue that the client metaphor thus tackled was the power relationship that the customer analogy implied. As the customer model shifted power to the student, the client metaphor was put forth in order to defend the authority of the academic, who, given his or her expert status, ought to have the power to determine the student's needs. But while the client metaphor repositioned the academic in terms of power, it did not fundamentally question the differential relation that the customer model constructed between students and academics as far as their interests were concerned. Precisely this relation of difference was challenged by Alistair McCulloch, who suggested the metaphor of the 'co-producer' instead.[3]

According to McCulloch, the co-producer metaphor recognised "that both student and university bring resources to the educational process, and that both make demands and levy expectations on each other during that process" (2009: 177). In contrast to the notion of the customer, the co-producer metaphor was supposed to highlight that the student was actively engaged in the learning process (2009: 177). Moreover, instead of fostering individualism and competition, the co-producer metaphor, McCulloch argued, placed "an emphasis on community and the involvement of individuals in the process alongside other individuals" (2009: 181). Hence, instead of putting students and academics in the averse positions of customer and service provider, the co-production metaphor constructed a relation of equivalence between students and academics as both contributed to the production of knowledge and learning. But this was not the only the reason why McCulloch proposed the metaphor. As he claimed, the co-production metaphor supported "the devolution of authority and responsibility" and thus served "to reprofessionalise the academic role" (2009: 180). Just like the metaphor of the client, the co-producer metaphor was thus supposed to reclaim academic authority as it provided the academic with a mentoring role.

Another, but in many ways similar, concept of the student was proposed by NUS president Wes Streeting and Graeme Wise, Political Officer of the NUS. Based on the work of Frank Coffield, they suggested that

> the learning process is not seen as delivery or production, but as induction. It is the journey learners take on their way to becoming active participants and practitioners in a particular trade, profession, discipline or discourse.
>
> (Streeting and Wise 2009: 3)

Again, the focus was on equivalences between students and teachers as both were considered as part of the same 'community of practice' (Streeting and Wise 2009: 3). And again, a major issue was the power relations between students and academics. While in the market model power was cleaved between the customers who could choose and the providers who could determine how they responded to customer demands, the 'community of practice' model, they claimed, understood power as "relational, dynamic and ever-shifting" and emphasised that everybody had power that could "be exercised through their commitment and contribution to their community of practice" (Streeting and Wise 2009: 5).

Similar concerns have been central to the concept of the 'student as partner' as suggested by Mick Healey, Abbi Flint, and Kathy Harrington. In contrast to the discourse of marketisation, which assigned students power through choice and through surveys like the NSS, Healey, Flint, and Harrington argued that students should actively collaborate in the shaping of their learning experience and institution (2014: 16). Hence, students ought to be engaged as partners in learning, teaching, assessment, subject-based research and inquiry, as well as in curriculum design and pedagogic consultancy (2014: 24). Such an emphasis on active collaboration instead of mere feedback was also at the heart of the concept of the 'change agent' as it was suggested by Elisabeth Dunne and Roos Zandstra. What they proposed was to have "student led research [. . .] drive developments in teaching, learning and organisational change" (2011: 3). Instead of listening to the student voice in order to improve quality, the concept of the student as change agent thus emphasised that students ought to be active in the reshaping of the institution.

The concept of the 'student as partner' has also been endorsed by the NUS with its *A Manifesto for Partnership* published in 2012. The manifesto shared the typical criticism of marketisation, but its prime concern was the form of power that the market model attributed to students. According to the manifesto, students' power appeared great in the customer model but was "in fact limited to commenting only on what has been sold to them" (NUS 2012: 6). Instead of relying on evaluations and other forms of feedback that sit "neatly in a consumer model", the NUS demanded that students should be "enabled to contribute to educational and institutional change" and "to co-create, not just knowledge or learning, but the higher education institution itself" (NUS 2012:

8). The NUS thus rejected the customer model not because it gave students too much power but because it denied them democratic power within the institutions of higher education.

Yet another concept has been proposed by Mike Neary and his colleagues, who suggested understanding students as 'producers'. While McCulloch's concept of the co-producer already shifted the focus from education as consumption towards education as production, Neary went further and proposed that through research-engaged teaching students were to be engaged in real academic work and should thus "become part of the academic project of the university" (2012: 7). The idea was that students worked "in collaboration with academics to create work of social importance that is full of academic content and value, while at the same time reinvigorating the university beyond the logic of market economics" (Neary and Winn 2009: 130). In contrast to other alternative concepts of the student such as partner or co-producer, the concept of the student as producer was not only suggested in order to redefine the relation between students and academics or to improve the learning experience but to bring about wider social changes. Embedded in a Marxist perspective, 'student as producer' was supposed to realise an education of social and political impact for which the production of critical knowledge was central, for instance through the development of a curriculum that involved "a critique not simply of the politics of consumption but the politics of production" (Neary and Hagyard 2011: 219). As Andy Hagyard and Sue Watling argued, the 'student as producer' model was aimed at fostering a critical culture that would empower students "to be active within the public sphere, engaging with anti-oppressive practices and working towards social justice and change" (2012: 81). The goal was "to design an alternative model for the university, as a rehearsal for an alternative social world within which it might subsist" (Neary 2010: n.p.). In this respect, the 'student as producer' went beyond concepts like co-producer or partner as it linked the question what a student was to the idea of higher education and actually aimed not just at the transformation of the pedagogical relationship or adjustments within the institutions of higher education but the transformation of society.

Challenging marketisation?

The concept of the student as customer has raised widespread criticism from within academia. What is striking though is to what extent that criticism was primarily concerned with either the pedagogical situation or the power relations within the institution of higher education. Much of the criticism against the customer model as well as the alternative metaphors of the client or co-producer primarily tried to resurrect academic authority. In contrast to that, alternative metaphors like partner or change agent were not only aimed at regaining academic authority but also questioned the form of power that the notion of the customer implied as well as the students' role within the institutions of higher education. However, apart from Neary's concept of the student as producer, the alternative metaphors all had a rather limited focus and hardly questioned the neoliberal idea of education as an individualised investment or marketisation in general. Indeed, as metaphors like Healey, Flint, and Harrington's 'students as partners' and Dunne and Zandstra's 'students as change agents' stayed confined to the level of the individual institution of higher education and actually aimed at the improvement of the student experience that was provided by the institution, they fit rather well within the neoliberal discourse of marketisation.

This limited focus actually explains why the language of partnership, learning community, and engagement found entry even in those government papers that most spurred the marketisation of higher education. The White Paper *Higher Ambitions* (2009), for instance, presented the University of Exeter's 'students as change agents' scheme as a case study (BIS 2009: 76). The White Paper 2011 spoke of higher education as "a learning community" that ought to be based "on a partnership between staff and students" (BIS 2011: 33) and featured a subchapter on student engagement, which, however, focused on student surveys and other forms of feedback and not on making students partners in the sense of Healey, Flint, and Harrington. While these government papers only paid lip service to the concepts of the student as partner or change agent, HEFCE actually took up the concept of the student as partner and claimed that they helped "students and their associated representative bodies become partners in the student experience" (2015: n.p.). Students, it was said, ought to be given "an active role in the development, management and governance of their institution, its academic programmes and their own learning experience" (2015: n.p.). Moreover, student engagement was included in the *UK Quality Code for Higher Education*, which explicitly defined students as partners and suggested that "[b]y working together to a common agreed purpose, steps can be taken that lead to enhancements for all concerned" (QAA 2016: 5). Therefore, students ought to be engaged through questionnaires, student representative structures, research activities, consultation events, online discussion forums, or formal quality processes (QAA 2016: 9). The concept of the student as partner has thus been absorbed into the 'official' higher education discourse, and the extent to which institutions treat students as partners has itself become a sign of 'quality'.

Notes

1 See also Trout (1997: 50), Franz (1998: 64), Naidoo and Jamieson (2005: 270–3), Kaye, Bickel, and Birtwistle (2006: 86), Halbesleben and Wheeler (2009: 185–6), McArdle-Clinton (2008: 196–203), Maringe (2011: 147–150), and Tight (2013: 293).

2 See, for instance, Potts (2005: 63), Furedi (2011: 4–5), Smith (2012: 657), Baldwin (1994: 130), or Bay and Daniel (2001: 3).

3 Jonathon R.B. Halbesleben, Jennifer A.H. Becker, and M. Ronald Buckley have suggested a rather different concept of the student as 'labour contributor'. This concept has been modelled after businesses such as fast-food restaurants where customers have to do part of the work themselves as they, for instance, carry their food themselves and clear the tables (2003: 255).

Chapter 18

Towards the future

As Anthony Smith and Frank Webster observed in 1997, neoliberal policies of marketisation and entrepreneurialism caused widespread demoralisation and resignation amongst academics (1997a: 4). But it was not only government policies which many within academia felt damaging to higher education. The position of the university was also undermined from various other sides, it was thought. As knowledge was increasingly produced outside the university and had become more pluralistic and contested, the university could no longer claim authority as the main producer of knowledge.[1] As Zygmunt Bauman declared, the university's "last rampart of authority may be, perhaps, the exclusive entitlements of the credentials-certifying agency" (1997: 23). Moreover, as Smith and Webster asserted, the plurality of knowledges had brought an "an end to established and common purposes of the university" as there was "no identifiable unity and no possibility of agreement on goals or even methods of work" any longer (1997b: 104). But while Smith and Webster thought that, amongst all the resignation and condemnation of neoliberal policies, no alternative visions of higher education were in sight (1997a: 4), numerous writers have actually formulated alternative ideas of higher education.

The ruins of postmodernity

While for decades, if not centuries, concepts like 'knowledge', 'culture', 'truth', or 'criticism' had functioned as nodal points in the higher education discourse and had thus legitimised the work of academia, the legitimising power of these concepts apparently diminished as society entered what Jean-François Lyotard famously coined 'the postmodern condition' – a condition that was characterised by a rising "incredulity towards metanarratives" (1984: xxiv). According to Lyotard, knowledge production in modernity had been legitimised by two grand narratives: the speculative grand narrative, that is the belief that knowledge formed an ideal unity and which justified the inquiry into knowledge and the search for truth for their own sake, and the grand narrative of emancipation, in which knowledge drives the development of human liberty and helps improve the human condition (1984: 31–7). These grand narratives, he argued, could no longer legitimise the institutions of higher education and had been replaced instead by performativity, that is "the logic of maximum performance" (1984: xxiv). Though one may question Lyotard's account of the postmodern condition, in particular as neoliberalism has established itself as a kind of grand narrative (Peters 2001: vii, 2011: 156), his observation that traditional grand narratives had lost their legitimising power certainly posed a problem for higher education as it raised the question how to formulate an idea of education without recourse to any of its traditional foundations.

One such attempt to formulate a 'postmodern' idea of higher education was made by Bill Readings in *The University in Ruins* (1996). Tracing the evolution of the Western university, Readings suggested that both the 'university of reason' and the 'university of culture' had been superseded by the 'university of excellence', that is a university that like any corporation served "nothing other than itself" (1996: 43). Instead of being legitimised by 'culture' or 'truth', it appealed only to the "empty notion of excellence" and thereby signified that the idea of the university had "lost all content" (1996: 39). Following the postmodern claim that there was no longer any unifying ideal which could serve as a basis for the university and thus being unable to go back to the 'university of reason' or the 'university of culture' in order to counter the corporate 'university of excellence', Readings proposed that the future university could only be understood as a 'community of dissensus':

> We are left, then, with an obligation to explore our obligations without believing that we will come to the end of them. Such a community, the community of dissensus that presupposes nothing in common, would not be dedicated either to the project of a full self-understanding (autonomy) or to a communicational consensus as to the nature of its unity. Rather, it would seek to make its heteronomy, its differences, more complex.
>
> (1996: 190)

What exactly this could mean for the university was, however, left open. Indeed, as Gerard Delanty has claimed, Readings did "not offer anything of substance for those seeking an alternative institutional embodiment" (2001: 140).[2] But what appeared like a failure was indeed the postmodern argument carried to its conclusion. As there was no fundamental idea through which to legitimise higher education, all that Readings was left with was 'dissensus'.

The problem of postmodernity has also been central to the work of Ronald Barnett, who, however, offered a rather different reading of it than Readings. While in *The Idea of Higher Education* (1990) Barnett had still tried to find a way how "the idea of a liberal higher education [could] be recovered" (x) and claimed that 'criticism' could function as the nodal point of higher education (162),[3] he took a new departure with *Realizing the University in an Age of Supercomplexity* (2000). Accepting the postmodern diagnosis, Barnett acknowledged that for the idea of the university "any straightforward essentialist argument

[was] simply not a serious runner" (2000: 4). This, however, did not mean that there necessarily was no universal foundation of the university. Although Barnett agreed that there were no longer any universals, he argued that this claim itself was precisely the new universal: "That there are no universals is itself a universal." (2000: 73) As he explained elsewhere:

> The postmoderns are wrong: in a postmodern world, universals are not at an end. The new universal is precisely the capacity to cope, to prosper and to delight in a world in which there are no universals; and this is the new universal.
>
> (2005: 794)

Though Barnett thus took on the criticism and anti-essentialism of postmodern theory, he did not accept the conclusion that there could no longer be a universal idea of the university. Moreover, he did not follow Lyotard's diagnosis of an 'incredulity towards metanarratives', but what he identified instead was a situation of 'supercomplexity':

> We are in a situation of supercomplexity when our very frameworks for making the world intelligible are in dispute. The resulting fragility that confronts us is not that our frameworks are dissolving as such; rather, it is that for any one framework that appears to be promising, there are any number of rival frameworks which could contend against it and which could legitimately gain our allegiance.
>
> (2000: 75)

This situation of supercomplexity gave the university a particular function and task ahead. Instead of shying away from the situation in front of it, the university ought to actively engage with supercomplexity and take on

> the dual responsibility not only of compounding uncertainty but also of helping us live with the uncertainty; even to revel in it. This is the task in front of the university. In a world where everything is uncertain, there is no other task.
>
> (2000: 172).

According to Barnett, this new conception of the university also required a different understanding of the student and of the university's pedagogical task. As supercomplexity did not primarily present "challenges of knowing but of *being*" (2000: 157), the task was not just to transmit knowledge but to produce "forms of human being appropriate to conditions of supercomplexity" (2000: 164). Therefore, students needed to be given "the space to develop their own voice, their own sense of themselves and their own being" (2000: 160). For Barnett, it was thus precisely the condition of supercomplexity that not only provided a new founding idea of the university but which also demanded a greater focus on the student's being.[4]

In his latest writings, Barnett developed a new conception of the university. Though not abandoning either the notion of 'supercomplexity' or the focus on 'criticality', Barnett now argued for what he termed the 'ecological university'. According to Barnett, the university needed to consider itself as being part of multiple ecologies, "including knowledge ecologies, social institutional ecologies, ecologies of the person, economic ecologies and ecologies of the physical world" (2013: 136). Recognising that it was interconnected with the wider environment, which for Barnett comprised not only the natural environment but also "personal, social, cultural, institutional and technological environments and knowledge of those environments" (2011a: 143), the ecological university was aware of its "wider responsibility towards those interconnections" (2011a: 142). Instead of only serving the interests of society and providing knowledge and skills, the ecological university that Barnett argued for was concerned with personal and social well-being and care about and for the world (2011a: 141). What exactly the 'ecological university' would look like stayed, however, rather unclear in the books and articles, in which Barnett expounded the concept. But this was for a reason. The 'ecological university' was supposed to function as an "umbrella concept, overarching more specific ideas of the university" (2013: 144–5). Two of these were Nicholas Maxwell's 'university of wisdom' and Jon Nixon's 'virtuous university' – two ideas which explicitly made it the task of the university to improve society for the better.

Higher education for the good society

In *How Universities Can Help Create a Wiser World* (2014), Maxwell argued for no less than "an academic revolution" (2014: 138). According to Maxwell, instead of focussing solely on knowledge production, the university ought to engage in 'wisdom-inquiry' and should help create a wiser world – a topic that Maxwell had explored since the 1980s. Such a focus on wisdom-inquiry was necessary, he claimed, because, in a time when humanity faced numerous crises from threats of war to poverty to the ongoing destruction of the environment, it was vital to have "institutions of learning rationally designed and devoted to helping us learn how to solve our global problems, how to make progress towards a better world" (2014: 3). Therefore, it was necessary to "put tackling problems of living – global problems – at the heart of the academic enterprise" and to "transform the relationship between universities and the social world – universities becoming fundamentally concerned to promote public understanding of what needs to be done to create a better, wiser world" (2014: 138).[5]

To change the world for good has also been a central concern to Jon Nixon, who argued for a university founded on the virtues of truthfulness, respect, authenticity, and magnanimity (2008: 2). According to Nixon, universities should be "potentially civic spaces within which individuals can gain the resources necessary for civic leadership" (2008: 1) – the final aim being to "re-connect the university with the idea of the good society" (2008: 130). This notion of the good society was also paramount in Nixon's following writings such as *Higher Education and the Public Good* (2011). Therein, he argued that the primary purpose of higher education was not to accumulate knowledge "but to frame a debate within which fine judgements can be made as to what constitutes useful knowledge for particular groups and individuals" (2011a: 29). Higher education, he claimed, had not only the task to transmit knowledge but to enable individuals to "use that knowledge to make complex choices regarding the right uses and applications of that knowledge" (2011a: 26). Therefore, universities needed to become places where people could find a voice and discover "purposefulness" (2011a: 42). According to Nixon, higher education was thus supposed to help students develop agency while at the same time posing the question what this agency might aspire to and how it could contribute to the well-being of society (2011a: 81). This, he claimed, was the "point and purpose" of learning: "to combine one's achievements and one's potentiality and direct them towards the public good" (2011a: 81).

Such a concern with education as a means to develop agency and change society for good has also been at the heart of what is often referred to as 'critical pedagogy'. Based on the Critical Theory of the Frankfurt School, Marxism, and the work of Paulo Freire, critical pedagogy has developed in particular in North America with writers like Michael W. Apple, Henry Giroux, or Peter McLaren. While its focus was primarily on secondary education, recent years have not only seen a rising number of UK based works on critical pedagogy but also a growing concern with higher education. The basic assumption of critical pedagogy is that education is inherently political and that education should have an emancipatory function and aim for greater social justice (Amsler 2013: 199; Cowden and Singh 2015: 559; McLean 2006: 1). But apart from these common goals, 'critical pedagogy' is a field that is far from homogenous. While Monica McLean, for instance, has followed Jürgen Habermas and emphasised the development of "the students' intellectual and moral attributes (communicative reason) so that they are disposed to think creatively and act responsibly with others to ameliorate the problems of contemporary society" (2006: 128), others have shown stronger alliances with Marxism or postmodern theories including feminist and post-structuralist theory. There has been much controversy between these approaches, in particular as Marxist educators have criticised postmodernists for having "failed to provide an effective counterstrategy to the spread of neoliberal ideology" (McLaren and Farahmandpur 2002: 43, 46) – a criticism that is often levelled against postmodern theorists in general.[6] But besides these points of divergence, critical pedagogues have agreed that education should aim for political and social change by making students conscious of the power relations that structure everyday life and by raising political awareness and enabling students to take action.[7]

With these objectives, critical pedagogy mirrors writers like Brian Simon or the student protests of the late 1960s, in which students likewise appeared as agents of social and political change. But in contrast to these, many of the writings within the field of 'critical pedagogy' have been aimed at academics and their pedagogical practice and have not formulated a broader ideal concerning the role of the higher education system in society. However, there have also been a number of writers who have explicitly rejected that focus on pedagogy. Joice Canaan, Dave Hill, and Alpesh Maisuria, for instance, have argue that critical education was not just about democratic and participative forms of teaching but should also question the curriculum and aim at a democratisation of the governance of educational institutions (2013: 187–9). As they claimed, headway for such forms of critical education had in particular been made with alternative forms of higher education such as the Social Science Centre at Lincoln, the Free University of Liverpool, the Really Open University (ROU), or the London Free University, which developed outside of the universities in response to the coalition government's higher education policy (2013: 189–90). These alternative forms of education, often set up by academics and students together, not only tried to disband the hierarchy between teacher and student – an issue that has been at the heart of critical pedagogy in general – but they also attempted to break the boundary between institutions of higher education and the public and thus between student and non-student.

Higher education as a public good

In most recent years and in particular in response to the 2010 funding reforms, numerous articles, books and other publications have appeared bearing titles like *In Defence of Public Higher Education* (2011), *A Manifesto for the Public University* (ed. Holmwood, 2011a), *Higher Education as a Public Good* (eds. Filippakou and Williams 2015), or Nixon's already referred to *Higher Education and the Public Good* (2011), to name just a view. As this sample, which contains only books and not even articles, indicates, the term 'public' and more specifically the question whether higher education was a 'public good' has moved to the centre of the debate on higher education. This has been a direct response to the ongoing marketisation of higher education and in particular the funding reforms of 2010, which many considered an assault on one of the allegedly fundamental tenets of British higher education: that higher education was a public good and should thus, at least partially, be funded by the public purse. As Labour peer Lord Triesman claimed after the House of Commons had accepted the new fee structure and reduced the teaching grants: "This afternoon's decision will switch the concept of universities from being a public good, as they have always been in modern history [. . .], to, in essence, a private-sector market that is driven by personal-private investment." (2010: n.p.) The assumption was that higher education had once been a public good that was now being destroyed by the policies of marketisation.

Given this claim, it is striking that the phrases 'public good' and 'public higher education' are relatively new inventions within the debate on higher education and have not been of major significance before. However, this does not mean that higher education was not considered as being of value to the public. Though there were also voices like Oakeshott or Minogue, who refuted the idea that the university had any purpose other than fostering learning for its own sake, it was widely accepted that higher education had a function in and for society. The question rather was what exactly that function was. While from an economic perspective, as it was present, for instance, in the Barlow and Percy reports, the emphasis was on higher education's contribution to the creation of the nation's wealth and the standard of living, writers like Moberly or Leavis claimed that higher education ought to guide society morally and intellectually, and yet others stressed that education was a means to foster social equality – an idea that could, for instance, be found in the Robbins Report. As these few examples indicate, higher education's contribution to the well-being of society was understood rather differently. Higher education was variously seen as making an economic, cultural and intellectual, as well as social contribution to the public good.

In the recent debate, all of these three dimensions have been referred to in order to prove that higher education could best serve the public good if it was publicly funded and not subordinated to the market. Hence, the Alternative White Paper *In Defence of Public Higher Education* (2011), which was published as an alternative to the government's White Paper 2011, claimed that higher education contributed to economic growth "through technical innovation and the provision of a skilled work force" (*In Defence* 2011: §3.1), and David D. Dill underlined that graduates paid higher taxes, participated more in voluntary work, and, as they were less likely to end in poverty or have health problems, were less of a burden to the public purse (2015: 142). From this economic perspective, the public good has been interpreted as improving the economic situation of society as well as the finances of the state.

More widespread than the economic argument has been the claim that higher education contributed to the public good because it had a social function. The Alternative White Paper, for instance, claimed that a market system based on high and differentiated fees ignored that universities had "a social mission, contributing to the amelioration of social inequality" (*In Defence* 2011: §1.8). This argument was shared by numerous writers.[8] The public good was in this case equated with social equality and with offering equal opportunities to all of the public's members.

The third widely shared argument that was offered to defend the public funding of higher education referred to the intellectual and cultural function of higher education. The assumption in this case was that universities supplied the public with knowledge and fostered public debate – a function that, supposedly, could only be fulfilled if there existed an autonomous realm of knowledge production that was independent of research councils, businesses, or student choices.[9] Moreover, a university education was said to enable individuals to participate in the public and to be therefore essential for the constitution of the public. As the Campaign for the Public University asserted, the university was an "institution that facilitates the development of a public, through its role in education about associated life and in developing the capacity for full participation" (2010: n.p.). This constitutive role of education for the public was also stressed by Nixon, who highlighted that higher education played a vital role in a democracy as a democracy required "educated and informed publics that are both inclusive and questioning" (2015: 163). Higher education was said to be of public value because education supposedly enabled people to actively participate in society and form a public.

The public funding of higher education was thus defended on various grounds. Higher education was said to be of public value for economic, social, cultural and intellectual reasons, and to be vital for a functioning democracy. Hence, the notion of the 'public good' has functioned as an intersection of various discourses each with their respective nodal points such as 'wealth', 'equality', or 'citizenship'. While this means that the signifier 'public good' is rather multi-layered and open as far as its meaning is concerned, it also means that 'the public good' has the potential to function as a major nodal point that organises various specific ideas of higher education.

The future of higher education

There is no shortage of ideas concerning the future role and function of higher education in society. Numerous writers have formulated such visions, and indeed several other ideas of higher education could have been added to the ones that were discussed above, including, for instance, Stephen Rowland's 'enquiring university' (2006). What the selected examples nevertheless have shown is that there has been and still is a widely shared concern about higher education having more than a purely economic function. One particularly persisting theme has been that higher education had ethical and social obligations and ought to enable students to gain a voice, become agents in society, and actively contribute to the good of society.

But though many ideas of higher education have been proposed in recent years, one may wonder about their impact. As publications on the idea of higher education have become so numerous, it has become increasingly difficult for individual publications to stand out and spark off such a debate as Moberly's *The Crisis in the University* (1949) or Truscot's *Red Brick University* (1943) had done. But the difficulty to get heard is not just a result of the sheer amount of publications – itself a side effect of the marketisation of higher education and publish-or-perish policies. Higher education is no longer such a confined realm as it was 70 or 80 years ago. As the number of institutions of higher education as well as the number of students has grown, higher education has become much more of a public issue. Hence, it is necessary to speak to the public and to make issues relating to higher education issues of public concern – a task that in particular students embarked on when they took to the streets in order to protest against the further marketisation of higher education.

Notes

1 Often this is referred to as the shift from Mode 1 to Mode 2 knowledge – a concept that was introduced by Michael Gibbons et al. While in the past knowledge was disciplinary and hierarchical and problems were "set and solved in a context governed by the, largely academic, interests of a specific community" (Mode 1), it has supposedly become more heterarchical, transdisciplinary, heterogeneous, reflexive, and socially accountable (Mode 2) (Gibbons et al. 1994: 3).

2 Delanty himself argued for a communicative understanding of the university as "a space in which different discourses interconnect" (2001: 152). Hence, universities ought to "establish zones of interconnectivity between the opposing domains of technology and culture" (2001: 157).

3 Barnett further developed this argument in *Higher Education: A Critical Business* (1997), in which he claimed that the focus of higher education should not be on critical thinking alone but rather on "critical being, which embraces action and the self together with thought" (1997: 1).

4 This focus on the being of the student was further elaborated in *A Will to Learn* (2007), in which Barnett advanced the thesis that the student's being was more important than knowledge and understanding and that "a genuine higher education is none other than a transformation of being" (2007: 38–9).

5 According to Maxwell, such a call for wisdom-inquiry did not mean to impose values on the university. While the supposedly neutral knowledge-inquiry also made numerous value judgements, for instance, in what it prioritised in research but denied its "value and political assumptions", wisdom-inquiry subjected its values and assumption "to sustained, explicit imaginative and critical exploration" (2014: 115–16).

6 For some Marxists, postmodern theory was even "an obstacle to the formation of open and radical perspectives that challenge inequalities and the deepening rule of capital in all areas of social life" (Rikowski and McLaren 2002: 3). Similarly, Terry Eagleton argued that because of "its cultural relativism and moral conventionalism, its scepticism, pragmatism and localism, its distaste for ideas of solidarity and disciplined organization, its lack of any adequate theory of political agency [. . .], postmodernism is in the end part of the problem rather than of the solution" (1996: 134–5). See also Richard Taylor, Jean Barr, and Tom Steele, who claimed that postmodern theory not only provided "seriously misleading theorizations of contemporary society" but that it was "predominantly and dangerously reactionary and negative in its consequences" (2002: 13).

7 A different idea of how higher education ought to change the world has been provided by Michael A. Peters, Garett Gietzen, and David J. Ondercin. Instead of focussing on the function of pedagogy, they have emphasised that new information and communication technologies provided the means to radically alter access to education and the use of knowledge. As they argued, the whole knowledge 'economy' could actually change from 'knowledge capitalism', which focused on the maximisation of profit, to a 'knowledge socialism', in which "knowledge and its value are ultimately rooted in social relations" and that allowed for "a truly free exchange of ideas" (Peters, Gietzen, and Ondercin 2012: 199).

8 See, for example, Holmwood (2011b: 18), McKay and Rowlingson (2011: 97), Reay (2011: 122), Nixon (2011b: 63–5, 2015: 167).

9 See, for instance, *In Defence* (2011: §1.8), Miller and Sabapathy (2011), Moriarty (2011), King (2011).

Chapter 19

The 2010 student protests

Though there had been protests against the introduction of fees in 1998 and against their rise in 2004, it was in reaction to the Browne Review that Britain saw the re-emergence of large-scale student activism. On 10 November 2010, about 50,000 people followed the call of the NUS and the University and College Union (UCU) and took to the streets of London to protest against government plans to raise the fees cap, to cut higher education expenditure, and to abolish the Education Maintenance Allowance (EMA) (Bloom 2012: 59). This first mass demonstration, which was followed by further demonstrations and occupations throughout England, was overshadowed by the occupation of the Conservative Campaign Headquarters at 30 Millbank. Not only did media reports focus on the occupation, but it also had a major effect on the organisational structure of the protests. When Aaron Porter, president of the NUS, condemned the action at Millbank,[1] many students turned their backs on the NUS, and more radical bodies like the National Campaign Against Fees and Cuts (NCAFC) gained in importance.[2] Even though the protests could not prevent parliament from raising the fees cap, they at least achieved two things: they were the beginning of the more widespread anti-austerity protests of 2011, and they brought higher education back into public debate.

Of course, the large-scale protests of 2010 lend themselves to a comparison with the protests of the late 1960s and early 1970s – a comparison that also many protesters, activists, and journalists made. Patrick Kingsley, for instance, spoke of "a grassroots social movement the breadth of which some feel we have not seen since the late 1960s" (2010: 12). Michael Chessum, one of the leading figures of the protest, published an article in *The Guardian* entitled "Student Protests: Today is Our 1968 Moment" (2010: 38), and *Springtime*, a compendium of articles on various protests around the world including the UK, Italy, France, Greece, and Tunisia, contained so called 'Flashbacks' on the movement of the late 1960s (Solomon and Palmieri 2011). But though the comparison with the 1960s was often made, it actually has its flaws.

Apart from the fact that massive numbers of students were protesting, there were considerable differences between 2010 and 1968. As Anthony Barnett has pointed out, the student movement of the late 1960s was often confined to the universities and art schools and mainly consisted of middle-class students (2010: 12). In contrast to that, the protests of 2010 included lecturers and school students and marked the beginning of the larger anti-austerity protests including the 2011 March for the Alternative that attracted more than 250,000 people. The biggest difference, however, lay in the aims of the protesters. The 1968 movement was about various issues such as the war in Vietnam, authoritarian structures in universities, and the creation of a more open and just society. Compared to that, the protests of 2010 seem rather single-minded and narrow as they primarily focused on the impending cuts and the rise of tuition fees. However, this fight against the cuts was not just about questions of finance but also about the role of higher education in society.

Fighting the cuts

The NUS and UCU called for the first great mass demonstration on 10 November 2010 under the motto "Fund our Future: Stop Education Cuts" and appealed to students "to fight against the looming savage education cuts" (2010: n.p.). Similarly, UCL Occupation stated that they fought "against fees and devastating cuts to higher education" (2010: n.p.), and the NCAFC demanded prior to the publication of the Browne Review, "[a] halt to all education cuts, the abolition of all fees and a living grant for every student" (2010b: n.p.). Though student finance might not have been the only issue that sparked the protests, it was without doubt the most important one. This strong focus on financial issues not only lets the comparison with 1968 seem out of place, but it also suggests that students had increasingly identified as *homines economici* who were primarily interested in their own financial benefit. This interpretation, however, falls too short. Behind the focus on questions of finance, there were actually moral and ethical concerns.

One of the reasons for the protests was that the planned cuts and rise in fees were believed to have no democratic mandate. As many Liberal Democrats and in particular Nick Clegg had pledged, prior to the election, not to vote in favour of a rise in fees, their change of mind after the election was regarded as anti-democratic and as a betrayal of the electorate. Protesters at the University of Sussex, for instance, argued that Clegg had "openly manipulated student voters" (Defend Sussex 2010: n.p.). Likewise, occupiers of University College London (UCL) justified their occupation with the words: "Promises have been broken, the political process has failed and we have been left with no other option." (UCL Occupation 2010: n.p.) The protests were thus also directed against the government's understanding of politics and thereby relocated higher education within the political discourse of democracy.

Moreover, the protests were driven by a concern for fairness and justice. The NCAFC, for instance, stated on a leaflet that was issued even before the publication of the Browne Review that "[w]e should not accept that the majority have to pay for a crisis caused by a tiny minority" (2010a: n.p.). Likewise, occupiers at UCL claimed that the "government attempts to force society to pay for a crisis it didn't cause" (UCL Occupation 2010: n.p.). This feeling of injustice was even intensified as the state was largely bailing out banks, who were considered the source of the financial crisis (Meadway 2011: 19). Moreover, many protesters disagreed that the cuts were necessary as the state could have, for instance, tackled tax avoidance and tax evasion (Rees 2011: 45). Hence, students staged sit-ins, blockades, and occupations against tax-avoiders such as Top Shop, Vodafone, and British Home Stores. While these actions and arguments could still be regarded as showing that the student protests were driven by the individual economic motives of the protesters, the protests were not so much motivated by individual self-interest but by wider concerns about the aims and purposes of education.

As the increase in fees did not affect students already enrolled in higher education, the protests cannot be solely explained by individual economic motives. Instead, they were triggered by moral concerns about the role of higher education in society. As Joseph Ibrahim has argued, "the student protests were motivated by moral questions of entitlement to affordable higher education, not just for themselves, but for future generations" (2011: 420). Hence, the NUS and UCU called on students to join the protest in order to "secure accessible further and higher education for generations to come" (2010: n.p.). Protesters at Sussex issued a statement declaring that education was "a right, not a privilege" (Defend Sussex 2010: n.p.). And groups like the NCAFC claimed that they fought against fees in order to prevent higher education from becoming "a privilege for the wealthy" (2010b: n.p.). Such moral concerns were also voiced by numerous occupiers who emphasised that they did not fight for their own economic benefit but for the principle of publicly funded education (Ibrahim 2014; Rheingans and Hollands 2013; Salter and Kay 2011).

Some protesters even went further and took issue with the ideology of marketisation that was behind the government's policy. Thus, Chessum claimed in an article in *The Guardian* that the government was "fundamentally changing the purpose of education: not simply orientating it towards the logic of the market, but introducing the market directly into the system" (2010: n.p.). Similarly, the NCAFC in its Statement of Intent of February 2010 demanded that the focus of higher education should be on "[e]ducation not profit" (2010b: n.p.), and Defend Sussex claimed that the cuts would "destroy the prospect of free and critical academic enquiry, on which universities should be based" (2010: n.p.). Similar to the criticisms that had been voiced by numerous academics, these protesters considered the marketisation of higher education as an attack on the ideal of higher education as critical and independent enquiry.

Like most of the criticism from within academia, the student protests of 2010 as well as the many smaller ones that followed in the years thereafter were largely defensive in outlook. As several commentators and activists have pointed out, the main drive of the protests was rather conservative as students did not protest in the streets to demand change but rather to prevent change from taking place (Bechler 2011: 173; Johnson 2011: 169–70; Power 2012: 412). This is indeed the most central difference between 2010 and 1968. While in 1968 students were attacking conservative forces, students in 2010 presented themselves as the conservatives fighting against a neoliberal radicalism. Indeed, Chessum himself came up with this comparison and stated that "while in 1968 protesters fought for a new society and a new history, today we contest the supposed end of history – the idea that human progress is now and forever linked to free markets and corporate interests" (2010: n.p.).

Beyond the reactionary

While the protests in general were primarily concerned with defending higher education, some protesters explicitly demanded to move beyond the mere reactionary. Writing for the *Oxford Left Review*, Cailean Gallagher, for instance, argued that though the reactionism of the protests was understandable, it was necessary to develop "radical alternatives" that attacked not only the government "but the whole structure of society, with assertive ideological language" (2011: 41–2). Hence, he called upon students to "fight for the real benefits of free education: not just free to access but free from the limitations imposed by the academic system" (2011: 44). Occupiers of Radcliffe Camera, Oxford even went further and claimed that, as the university was "the location of the meticulous government of individuals" that were "divided, ranked, graded, homogenised and under surveillance", it was necessary not just to reform the university but "to destroy it" (Anonymous 2010: 7).

This desire to go beyond the mere defensive and establish new forms of higher education was also the basis for the various 'free universities' such as the University for Strategic Optimism, the Really Open University (ROU), or the Social Science Centre at Lincoln that were established often in collaboration between students and academics.[3] As André Pusey and Leon Sealey-Huggins have argued, all these projects attempted to "go beyond the existent, towards an affirmation of another form, or forms, of knowledge production and learning" (2013: 451). Hence the ROU, which was launched already in March 2010, adopted the slogan "We don't want to defend the university. We want to transform it!" and tried to create "a space where people share and develop their skills and knowledge not in the individual quest for jobs and profit but in a mutual attempt to create a more equitable and sustainable world" (ROU 2010: n.p.).

Such radical alternative ideas of higher education, however, stayed rather marginal as the mass protests focused not on the development of new forms of higher education but rather tried to preserve the principle that the state was at least in part responsible for the funding of higher education.

Protesting customers

While the neoliberal discourse of marketisation positioned students as self-interested *homines economici* who understood higher education primarily as an investment in their own human capital and as customers that made informed choices between institutions and courses, the student protests actually defied that neoliberal governmentality and relocated higher education within an ethical and political discourse. But beyond this level of the actual demands, the very act of protesting itself challenged the neoliberal market discourse.

One effect of the demonstrations and occupations was that they created a feeling of community between students and at times also staff. This was stated by protesters (Rheingans and Hollands 2013: 555), it was pointed out by commentators like Joanna Biggs, who reported about the occupation of the University College London (2010: 22), and it was also expressed in many tweets on Twitter accounts like UCL Occupation (Troschitz 2012: 183–4). Though such a feeling of community is nothing special and may be found in most protests, it has particular relevance in the context of neoliberalism. The creation of a community can be read as a rejection of the competitive individualism that the neoliberal discourse of marketisation proclaimed, and, the moment the protests included academics, also as an overcomming of the oppositional relationship between customers and service providers.[4]

The real challenge to the market discourse, however, lay in the type of agency that the protests claimed. When Chessum published an article in *The Guardian* entitled "Today is Our 1968 Moment" (2010: n.p.) and when the flyers for the protest march on 10 November 2010 appealed to students to "[m]ake history this November" and "to stand up as a student movement" (NUS and UCU 2010), they called upon students to regard themselves as collective agents of change.[5] This collective agency and the act of protesting actually contradicted the position and the type of power that students had been assigned in the neoliberal market. As Chessum proclaimed, while the proposed funding reforms tried to turn universities into businesses and students into consumers, the one thing that the protests had shown was that students were "nothing of the sort" (2010: n.p.). Though students did not necessarily reject the power of choice that they had been given in the market, they claimed a rather different form of power as they took collective action and started to protest. By taking to the streets and occupying university buildings, students did not act like customers or consumers. As Harry Kidd once remarked, "if consumers are dissatisfied, taking over the shop is not their usual remedy" (1969: 138). But precisely this is what the 2010 protests signify. Instead of being content with the market power of individualised choice, students claimed democratic power and formed a collective voice.

Notes

1 In contrast to Porter, who condemned the Millbank occupation, several student unions supported it and published the petition "Unity to Defend Education, No Victimisation!" (2010) in order to counter Porter.

2 The NCAFC, which had been formed in February 2010 following a conference at University College London (UCL), aimed at providing a more radical and severe opposition to the Browne Review than the NUS (Ibrahim 2011: 417).

3 Overviews of other initiatives like the University of Strategic Optimism or the Really Free School can be found in Pusey and Sealey-Huggins (2013) and Noterman and Pusey (2012).
4 In many cases, the dividing lines between students and academics were blurred by the protests. Hence, publications like *Fight Back!* (2011) edited by Dan Hancox or *The Assault on Universities* (2011) edited by Michael Bailey and Des Freedman contained both chapters by students and academics. In the introduction to the *The Assault on Universities*, Des Freedman explicitly spoke to those "who work in universities or who are prospective or current students" (2011: 10).
5 Several commentators have highlighted that the discovery of agency was one of the major effects of the protests. As Jeremy Gilbert has argued, "[t]he other, less tangible, gain [of the protests] was the rise in political awareness not just amongst school and university students who discovered a sense of their own agency after years of passivity and inertia" (2012: 33). This was also reported by Salter and Kay from their interviews with occupants of the University of the West of England (2011: 425). Likewise, Anthony Barnett claimed that the protests had led to an "experience of agency" (2011: 23).

Conclusion

Chapter 20

Conclusion

Higher education in Britain is rather different today from what it was in the 1940s. The number of universities and colleges has multiplied and so has the number of students. Higher education is no longer the privilege of a tiny élite as today nearly half of those aged between 17 and 30 partake in higher education in one form or another (BIS 2015b: 1). At the same time, the student body has significantly widened in terms of class, gender, ethnicity, and age. But expansion and widened participation are by no means the only changes that have taken place. New institutions of higher education such as the Open University and the polytechnics were founded, the latter of which were granted university status in 1992. Moreover, funding arrangements have become more competitive, and universities have increasingly had their performance measured through the REF, NSS, and TEF. Maintenance grants for students, which had been introduced universally in the 1960s, have been largely abolished, and since 1998 students have had to pay tuition fees, which have risen ever since.

These are only some of the most remarkable changes that have taken place within British higher education, but what they clearly show is how radically the position and function of higher education in British society has altered over the last 75 and more years. These changes have not come about swiftly, but they were the result of struggles between different ideas of higher education striving for hegemony within the higher education discourse.

The purpose of higher education

There is no single idea let alone purpose of higher education. Indeed, the history of higher education in the twentieth and twenty-first centuries has been a continuous debate over the question what higher education is good for and what its objectives are. Academics, politicians, and students have formulated numerous ideas of higher education in order to define the position and function of higher education in society. As diverse as these proposals have been, it is still possible to identify three dominant ideas of higher education that have shaped the debate on higher education:

1. The economic idea of higher education, in which case higher education is framed within a discourse structured by nodal points such as 'economy', 'prosperity ', or 'employability'. The main purpose of higher education is seen in supplying the economy with manpower and/ or in improving the career prospects of the individual.
2. The 'liberal' idea of higher education that is organised around concepts like 'truth', 'learning', 'tradition', 'criticality', 'culture', and 'moral growth'. Though this comprises rather diverse ideas of higher education, such as the pursuit of learning for its own sake or the formation of character, what unites these is their focus on the development of the individual as well as the claim that higher education has values of its own and is not only a service to society.
3. The social idea of higher education with nodal points such as 'equality', 'justice', and 'the people'. In this case, the focus is on the benefits of higher education to society, the role of education in social reproduction, and on education as a means for social change.

These three ideas have structured the debate on higher education. However, this does not mean that every writer or text can easily be put into one of these categories. Though this might be the case with writers like Michael Oakeshott and Kenneth Minogue or documents like the Percy Report (1945) or the White Paper *Technical Education* (1956), it immediately becomes more complicated with writers like Walter Moberly or F.R. Leavis, who stressed the moral and cultural education of the individual and considered such an education a means to change society for the better. In particular the social idea has often included the economic and 'liberal' idea but positioned these as subservient to the overarching goal of creating a more socially just society. Thus, Brian Simon, for example, claimed that higher education had a cultural, intellectual, and economic function but argued that these should all serve the people at large. And in other cases, such as the Robbins Report (1963) or the Dearing Report (1997), all three major ideas of higher education were referred to, albeit always with a different emphasis. The three ideas are thus not exclusive of each other, but they are in constant struggle for hegemony as they rival each other and try to dominate the discourse of higher education.

The economic idea of higher education as a means of manpower production was present throughout the debate. In the 1940s and 1950s it was promoted, for instance, by the Percy Report and the Barlow Report (1946) as well as the White Paper *Technical Education* (1956). But though these texts emphasised the economic relevance of higher education, this view was not dominant in the debate at that time. The economic function of higher education was also referred to in the Robbins Report, and it had been central to the proposals for the foundation of the Open University and even more so the polytechnics. Since the 1980s, however, it has dominated government thinking. Since then, the economic idea has not only gained in power but it has also undergone transformation. While the expansion of higher education was still primarily justified with the economic need for graduates and thus in terms similar to the manpower doctrine of the 1940s and 1950s, higher education policies were now increasingly reframed by a market discourse, and nodal points like 'quality' and 'competition' gained in power. Under New Labour and all following governments, this transformation continued. References to 'the economy' and 'the nation' were gradually substituted by a focus on the individual economic benefit of higher education and 'student choice' became a central nodal point. But even though higher education was reconfigured in terms of the market and the focus shifted towards the economic benefit of higher education for the individual, the underlying idea was still that higher education's main purpose was to provide the economy with manpower.

The 'liberal' idea of education dominated the debate on higher education, in particular the university, in the 1940s and 1950s. While only few writers such as Oakeshott claimed that the university had no purpose apart from fostering learning for its own sake, the idea that a university education was about more than manpower production and training for a job was widespread and also subscribed to by the UGC. Quite often this 'liberal' idea of higher education was especially set in opposition to the economic view of education, which was considered not only as a distortion of education but also as an attack on the autonomy of the universities. The 'liberal' ideal of higher education stayed strong well into the 1960s. It characterised the new campus universities, it was central to the Robbins Report, and it was also present in the arguments for the Open University. Though the 'liberal' idea was still referred to in the Dearing Report, it has clearly lost in power in the policy discourse, which has increasingly been governed by the economic view since the 1980s. Nevertheless, the 'liberal' idea of higher education has not totally disappeared from the debate. Numerous writers have defended 'liberal' values, and many new conceptions of higher education such as 'the university of wisdom', 'the virtuous university', or 'the ecological university' have been put forth in order to counter the view that higher education primarily served economic goals.

The social idea of higher education that is structured by nodal points such as 'justice' and 'equality' was promoted by writers like Brian Simon in the 1940s, and it gained in power as higher education increasingly became part of the welfare state. For both the Anderson Report (1960) and the Robbins Report one of the functions of higher education was to promote greater equality of opportunity. The social idea of higher education was central in the arguments for the foundation of the Open University; it was at the heart of Eric Robinson's *The New Polytechnics* (1968); and in a certain way it was also present in the student protests of the late 1960s, in particular amongst radicals who fought for an overthrow of capitalism. While this social view of education was not really prominent under the Thatcher and Major governments, it was revitalised under New Labour albeit in a highly neoliberal variation. Though the social idea of higher education increasingly lost in power in the policy discourse as the marketisation of higher education proceeded in the following years, it figured strongly in the student protests of 2010 and in the notion of higher education as a 'public good'.

As this short and necessarily simplifying overview shows, higher education has been the site of constant struggle between different ideas of higher education. Within this struggle, the concept of the student has considerably shifted. While the preceding chapters have analysed in detail how students were conceptualised within individual texts and which issues have dominated thinking about higher education at a certain time, there are two issues that clearly stand out and which thus warrant special attention: the expansion and widening of the student intake and the shifting position of the student in terms of power.

Expansion and the 'new student'

Probably the most remarkable change that has appeared in British higher education since the 1940s has been its continuous expansion. Apart from a few exceptions, the number of students has constantly increased and what was once the privilege of a few has turned into a mass system. This expansion has been argued for on various grounds. From the 'liberal' perspective, expansion could be justified as bringing culture and knowledge to the people, an idea that was present in the arguments for the establishment of the Open University and also in the Robbins Report, but which was never really dominant in the debate. From the economic point of view, expansion was seen as an answer to increasing manpower demands. This view prevailed in government reports of the 1940s, and it has become particularly dominant since the Thatcher years. From the social perspective, the expansion of higher education was considered a means to achieve greater equality. While this view was already promoted by the NUS in the 1940s, it is particularly linked to the Robbins Reports and the principle that higher education should be available to all those "qualified by ability and attainment" (Committee on Higher Education 1963: §31). This meritocratic principle, which opened access to students with sufficient A-levels, was widened by the polytechnics and the Open University, which also offered higher education to students without traditional qualifications. Though the social idea of education was still referred to in the Dearing Report's arguments for widening participation and also invoked by New Labour, the further expansion and opening of access were mainly driven forward by economic motives which have dominated government policies since the 1980s.

With the expansion of higher education, the concept of the student significantly altered. Being a student increasingly ceased to be a privilege of the few, and the student intake considerably widened in terms of age, ethnicity, class, gender, and nationality. Strikingly, not all of these changes were equally central in the debate on higher education. This is particularly noteworthy with regard to gender as today more than half of the students are female quite in contrast to the 1940s when women only made up about a quarter of all students (BIS

2015b: 9; Carpentier 2009: 239). Of course, gender did play a role in the policy discourse. The Robbins Report, for instance, argued that the number of women in higher education ought to rise in particular in the applied sciences, and it also suggested ways to bring more women into higher education who had not continued education because of family responsibilities (Committee on Higher Education 1963: §50, 378, 514). Gender was also attended to in the Dearing Report, which, however, recognised that women were well represented in higher education (NCIHE 1997: §7.6). Though questions of gender were thus an issue, the growing number of female students did not arouse major worries or cause considerable debate – quite in contrast to expansion in terms of class.

Although the most decisive changes in student intake took place with regard to gender and although the number of part-time students, mature students, and international students increased significantly, expansion was primarily problematised in terms of class.[1] Throughout the debate and in particular in the 1940s to 1960s, the alleged increase of students from a working-class background was considered a problem. The UGC in its report on residence of 1957 was worried about the widening gap between the home culture of the student and the culture of the university. The Robbins Report expressed similar concerns about the rising number of students "without a background of [. . .] culture" (Committee on Higher Education 1963: §570) as did writers as diverse as Oakeshott, Lord James, Sloman, Minogue, or several of the contributors to the Black Papers. Though the reactions varied from those who sought to integrate the 'new students' to those who called for their exclusion, the assumption that the number of student from a lower socio-economic background was rising and that this constituted a problem was widely shared. The 'new students' were said to be lacking in culture and to have a much too utilitarian understanding of education seeing it as nothing but a means to secure a job. Such an attitude towards the working-class student could even be found in Crosland's Woolwich speech, and it was also subscribed to by Walter Perry, the first Vice-Chancellor of the Open University. Though the problem of the 'new student' declined in importance in the 1980s and 1990s as other topics such as marketisation began to shape the debate, the idea that students from lower classes were primarily interested in higher education as a means to improve their employment prospects did not vanish completely and could, for instance, still be found in New Labour's proposals for the introduction of foundation degrees.

This continuous problematisation of the 'new student' in terms of class actually shows how dominant the ideal of the student as middle-class actually was and partly still is. This ideal was hardly ever expressed directly, but it came to the foreground through the 'new student' which functioned as the ideal student's Other. No matter whether the 'new students' were despised or whether the question was, as in the Robbins Report, how to ensure that the 'new students' could actually succeed, the ideal was a culturally homogeneous student body. Behind the debate on the 'new student' was, however, not only the dominance of middle-class culture. The 'new student' also raised questions of authority and power.

Student power and agency

To what extent students were agents and ought to be given power within the system of higher education, the individual colleges and universities, as well as the pedagogical situation has been an issue that has raised considerable debate. In the economic idea as it was present in various government papers of the 1940s and 1950s, power ultimately rested with the economy. It was the economy's need for graduates that determined expansion, and institutions of higher education were required to supply the demanded graduates. Within this perspective, students did not appear as agents at all. Instead, they were regarded as a resource to the nation's economy, and it was the task of the institutions of higher education to mould them into whatever the economy requested.

In contrast to this focus on manpower production, the 'liberal' idea of higher education concentrated much more on the individual and emphasised the emancipatory function of higher education. Power, in this case, derived from knowledge and culture, which legitimised the authority of the universities in society and towards the students, but which also meant that students would become agents through education. But otherwise, students were hardly recognised as agents – a point at which the 'liberal' idea actually mirrored the economic view. Even though some writers like Moberly emphasised the adult status of the student and wanted to give students more power, for instance, in choosing their courses, the general view was that power lay with the institutions of higher education and the academics who both functioned as representatives of knowledge and culture. This rationale was also present in some of the arguments against the demand for student power as it arose in particular in the late 1960s as well as in the arguments against the notion of the student as customer. Students, it was argued, could not be given much power, in particular with regard to academic matters, precisely because they were still learners.

When in the 'liberal' idea of higher education, the power of the academic and the institution of higher education was legitimised through their claim to knowledge and culture, their authority towards students ultimately depended on the students' recognition and appreciation of that very knowledge and culture for which higher education supposedly stood. Hence, writers like Truscot, Moberly, Sloman, or Niblett as well as the UGC and the Robbins Report emphasised that being a student meant to enter a community and to subscribe to its values. Such an integration into a community of values was considered particularly important for the 'new students'. As the 'new students' allegedly did not share the cultural background of the universities, it was regarded all the more vital that these students were socialised and enculturated, for instance, through living in a hall of residence. The institution of higher education was thus supposed to exercise power by socialising the student into a cultural norm. Though this enculturation was often believed necessary in order to ensure that the 'new students' could succeed, it was also a means to reproduce the values that legitimised the very authority of the institution of higher education and the academics. How much the problem of the 'new student' included questions of authority could also be seen in the 1960s when some writers identified the 'new students' no longer in terms of class but youth culture – a culture whose values were allegedly 'alien' to the university. Youth culture was perceived as a threat because it abolished the difference between academia and the outside world and instead emphasised the difference between the young and the old. Hence, youth culture, it was feared, dissolved the ideal of the academic community and thus one of the main foundations of academic authority.

In contrast to the 'liberal' idea, in which power lay with the academic, the discipline, and the institution as these represented knowledge and culture, the social conception of higher education emphasised that power derived from the people whom higher education should serve. As higher education was there for the people, it was the people who should have a say not only with regard to the amount of places available but also with regard to what was taught and how. While the NUS had already demanded in the 1940s that access to higher education should be opened and that demand from below should determine expansion, this view increasingly gained ground towards the 1960s. The Anderson Report emphasised that students should have freedom of choice between colleges and universities, and the Robbins Report placed student demand at the centre of expansion. However, student agency was restricted to the choice of colleges and universities and to the amount of places in higher education that should be provided. The idea that higher education might change in content and structure according to student demand was not yet on the agenda.

Questions of power increasingly came to forefront of the debate in the late 1960s. Not only did writers like Robinson argue that students and their wants ought to be much more at the centre of higher education, but students themselves now demanded a say in their institutions of higher education. Though the NUS had already argued in 1940 that students ought to be given a share in the government and administration of the universities, the position of the student in terms of power became the central issue in the student protests of the late 1960s when students not only protested against the *in loco parentis* system but demanded participation in the government of their institution of higher education. With such claims for power, students not only contested the 'liberal' idea of higher education and its underlying narrative of emancipation, but by emphasising the differential relation between academics and students in terms of power, they questioned the ideal of the community that united students and academics and proposed a common student consciousness instead.

Apart from the actual arguments for and against student power, the most interesting feature of the debate about student power in the late 1960s was the increasing use of analogies. Students referred to themselves as 'class' whereas proponents of the 'liberal' idea, who wanted to secure academic authority, suggested that students were similar to 'patients' or 'apprentices'. The use of such analogies was an attempt to fix the meaning of the term student, and what their increasing use in the late 1960s thus testified was how much the concept of the student had become unstable by that time. Strikingly, it was in this context that the discourse of the market found entrance into higher education as some protesters, in an attempt to justify increased student power, referred to students as 'consumers'.

Such a market discourse in which students appeared as consumers increasingly shaped the government's higher education policies from the 1980s onwards. While the performativity regime as it emerged following the Jarratt Report (1985) still regarded students as objects, the growing marketisation of higher education fundamentally shifted the position of the student. Student choice was now supposed to steer the development of higher education. Following a simple market logic, the universities and colleges' funding was increasingly made dependent on their ability to attract students, which, so it was argued, would force them to improve the quality of what they offered in accordance with what students wanted. This market model fundamentally challenged the 'liberal' ideal of higher education. While the ideal of the academic community emphasised a relation of equivalence between students and academics as both ought to share the same values and goals, the discourse of the market constructed an equivalence between higher education and the world of consumption and thus put students and the institutions of higher education in the differential relation of customers and service providers.

This reconfiguration of higher education in terms of the market was continuously presented as a major empowerment of the student. As students judged the quality of the higher education they received and the services they were offered, for instance through the NSS, and as their choices were supposed to shape the system of higher education, they were, as the White Paper 2011 claimed, "put in the driving seat" (BIS 2011: 2). This empowerment, however, went hand in hand with attempts to regulate students' behaviour and their self-understanding. Students were not meant to function as customers who chose as they like. Instruments like KIS or the NSS were set up to guide students' choices, and fees and loans were introduced in order to turn students into *homines economici* and make them see themselves as human capital and education as an investment. To stay with the metaphor used in the White Paper 2011: whilst students have been put in the driving seat, they have been given a navigation device on which 'employability' appears as the only possible destination.

Apart from the fact that students were supposed to exercise their choices in a certain direction, another salient feature of the market discourse has been that it assigned students a rather specific form of power. In the late 1960s, students increasingly demanded to be given a say within their institutions of higher education, for instance through representation on the governing bodies, and since then they have considerably gained in power within their universities or colleges. The market discourse, however, has promoted an entirely different model of power. Students were supposed to exercise power not through 'voice' but through 'choice'. Their choices and evaluations, for instance in form of the NSS, were expected to regulate the supply of higher education and hence force the institutions of higher education to respond to students' wants. Instead of having democratic powers as members of a community, students were positioned as customers who could choose between different providers. It is precisely in this context that the student protests, as they occurred on a mass scale in 2010 and continued on a smaller scale in the following years, were so noteworthy. Though they could not halt the rise in fees, they challenged the marketisation of higher education as students formed a collective voice and, instead of acting as customers, became political actors.

The end of the story?

Within relatively short time, Britain, and in particular England, has seen a radical transformation of its higher education system. While only a generation ago tuition was still free, today's students pay up to £9,000 per year, and plans have been made to further raise the fees cap. But though the market has certainly become the game in town, this does not mean that it must necessarily stay like that. As this book has shown, at the heart of the neoliberal transformation have been two concerns: first, to install means that require institutions of higher education to be more responsive to student demand; and second, to regulate students' self-understanding and make them consider themselves as human capital and higher education as an investment. But precisely this means that there is nothing natural about the market or about how it functions. It is a particular discursive formation that can change.

What the future of higher education beyond the market could look like has been hotly debated, and numerous ideas of higher education have been put forth. One notion that has become rather central in recent debates, in particular in response to the scrapping of the teaching grants in 2010, has been that of higher education as a 'public good'. In order to defend the public funding of higher education, the notion of the public good has brought the question of what the purpose of higher education is back on the table. Apart from the economic benefits that higher education produced for the wider society, two issues have been central here. First, it has been argued that higher education ought to promote social equality which links the public good directly to the question of access. Second, higher education has been said to play a fundamental role in constituting the public – a view which actually calls for a different understanding of students not as customers but as citizens who have a voice and whom higher education enables to actively participate in society. Though these two notions of the public are by no means the same – the first focussing on higher education being open to the public while the second highlights higher education's role in constituting the public – what unites them is that they attack the neoliberal claim that society is a marketplace of atomised individuals with only private interests. Instead, they emphasise that human beings are social beings with collective responsibilities.

Though the notion of the public good has figured prominently in recent debates on higher education, it is impossible to predict to what extent the idea of the public good, or any other idea for that matter, will come to shape higher education in the future. The only thing that is certain is that the struggle over higher education will continue and that the question of what a student is will be at the heart of it.

Note

1 How dominant the issue of class was in the debate on higher education can also be seen in numerous campus novels such as Philip Larkin's *Jill* (1946), Kingsley Amis's *Lucky Jim* (1954), Malcolm Bradbury's *Eating People Is Wrong* (1959), as well as numerous others (Carter 1990: 103–29). Quite in contrast to class, the changing student intake in terms of gender was hardly a central topic in these novels. Indeed, quite often gender was only an issue in so far as female students were repeatedly presented as sexual objects such as Lynne Shorthall in Howard Jacobson's *Coming from Behind* (1983), Felicity Phee in Malcolm Bradbury's *The History Man* (1975), or Melanie Byrd in David Lodge's *Changing Places* (1975). International students were even less problematised. While in the debate on higher education, the presence of international students was of concern when it came to student fees and subsidies, these students were no significant issue in the popular campus novels. Bradbury's *Eating People Is Wrong* (1959) is an exception here as it, though largely satirical in tone, nevertheless pays attention to the problems that students from a non-British background might experience.

Works cited

Adams, J.W.L. (1948). "Halls of Residence." *Universities Quarterly* 2(3): 239–46.

Adelstein, David (1967). "On Students." *New Left Review* 1(43): 88–90.

——— (1969). "Roots of the British Crisis." *Student Power: Problems, Diagnosis, Action*. Eds. Alexander Cockburn and Robin Blackburn. Harmondsworth: Penguin. 59–81.

Ainley, Patrick (1998). "The End of Expansion and the Consolidation of Differentiation in English Higher Education." *Teaching in Higher Education* 3(2): 143–56.

Alexander, F.K. (2000). "The Changing Face of Accountability: Monitoring and Assessing Institutional Performance in Higher Education." *The Journal of Higher Education* 71(4): 411–31.

Althusser, Louis (1971). *Lenin and Philosophy, and Other Essays*. London: New Left Books.

Amis, Kingsley (1960). "Lone Voices: Views of the 'Fifties'." *Encounter* 15(1): 6–11.

——— (1969). "Pernicious Participation." *Fight for Education: A Black Paper*. Eds. C.B. Cox and A.E. Dyson. London: Critical Quarterly Society. 9–10.

——— (1976). *Lucky Jim*. London: Penguin Books.

Amsler, Sarah (2013). "Sarah Amsler on Critical Pedagogy, Critical Theory and Critical Hope." *Acts of Knowing: Critical Pedagogy in, against and beyond the University*. Eds. Stephen Cowden, Gurnam Singh, Sarah Amsler, Joyce Canaan, and Sara C. Motta. New York: Bloomsbury. 193–207.

Andersen, Niels Å. (2003). *Discursive Analytical Strategies: Understanding Foucault, Koselleck, Laclau, Luhmann*. Bristol: Policy.

Anderson, Perry (1969). "Components of the National Culture." *Student Power: Problems, Diagnosis, Action*. Eds. Alexander Cockburn and Robin Blackburn. Harmondsworth: Penguin. 214–86.

Anderson, Robert D. (1995). *Universities and Elites in Britain since 1800*. Cambridge: Cambridge University Press.

——— (2006). *British Universities: Past and Present*. London: Hambledon Continuum.

Annan, Lord (1982). "British Higher Education, 1960–80: A Personal Retrospect." *Minerva* 20(1–2): 1–24.

Anonymous (2010). "Notes from the Occupation." *Oxford Left Review* (3): 6–7.

Arestis, Philip, and Malcolm Sawyer (2005). "Neoliberalism and the Third Way." *Neoliberalism: A Critical Reader*. Eds. Alfredo Saad-Filho and Deborah Johnston. London: Pluto. 177–83.

Armstrong, Michael J. (2003). "Students as Clients: A Professional Services Model for Business Education." *Academy of Management Learning & Education* 2(4): 371–4.

Armytage, W.H.G. (2009). "Community Service Stations: The Transformation of the Civic Universities, 1898–1930." *The History of Higher Education, Vol. III*. Ed. Roy Lowe. London: Routledge. 57–76.

Ashby, Eric (1951). "A Note on an Alternative to Halls of Residence." *Universities Quarterly* 5(2): 150–4.

——— (1958). *Technology and the Academics: An Essay on Universities and the Scientific Revolution*. London: Macmillan.

——— (1970). *Masters and Scholars: Reflections on the Rights and Responsibilities of Students*. London: Oxford University Press.

——— (1973). "The Structure of Higher Education: A World View." *Higher Education Quarterly* 2(2): 142–51.

Ashby, Eric, and Mary Anderson (1970). *The Rise of the Student Estate in Britain*. Cambridge, MA: Harvard University Press.

'B' (1969). "Decline and Fall of the University Idea." *Fight for Education: A Black Paper*. Eds. C.B. Cox and A.E. Dyson. London: Critical Quarterly Society. 60–2.

Bailey, Jeffrey J. (2000). "Students as Clients in a Professional/ Client Relationship." *Journal of Management Education* 24(3): 353–65.

Bailey, Michael, and Des Freedman, eds. (2011). *The Assault on Universities: A Manifesto for Resistance*. London: Pluto.

Baldwin, Gabrielle (1994). "The Student as Customer: The Discourse of 'Quality' in Higher Education." *Journal of Tertiary Education Administration* 16(1): 125–33.

Ball, Stephen J. (2003). "The Teacher's Soul and the Terrors of Performativity." *Journal of Education Policy* 18(2): 215–28.

——— (2006). *Education Policy and Social Class: The Selected Works of Stephen J. Ball*. London: Routledge.

Barber, Benjamin R. (2007). *Consumed: How Markets Corrupt Children, Infantilize Adults, and Swallow Citizens Whole*. New York: Norton.

Barnett, Anthony (2010). "Student Power: 1968 . . . 2010." *Oxford Left Review* (3): 11–14.

——— (2011). "Foreword: A Fight for the Future." *Fight Back! A Reader on the Winter of Protest*. Ed. Dan Hancox. London: Open Democracy. 14–30.

Barnett, Ronald (1990). *The Idea of Higher Education*. Milton Keynes: Open University Press.

——— (1997). *Higher Education: A Critical Business*. Buckingham: Open University Press.

——— (1999). "The Coming of the Global Village: A Tale of Two Inquiries." *Oxford Review of Education* 25(3): 293–306.

——— (2000). *Realizing the University in an Age of Supercomplexity*. Buckingham: Open University Press.

——— (2005). "Recapturing the Universal in the University." *Educational Philosophy and Theory* 37(6): 785–97.

——— (2007). *A Will to Learn: Being a Student in an Age of Uncertainty*. Maidenhead: Open University Press.

——— (2011a). *Being a University*. London: Routledge.

——— (2011b). "The Marketised University: Defending the Indefensible." *The Marketisation of Higher Education: The Student as Consumer*. Eds. Mike Molesworth, Elizabeth Nixon, and Richard Scullion. Abingdon: Routledge. 39–51.

——— (2013). *Imagining the University*. Milton Park: Routledge.

Barr, Nicholas (2005). "Funding Higher Education: Policies for Access and Quality." *Financing Higher Education: Answers from the UK*. Eds. Nicholas Barr and Iain Crawford. London: Routledge. 231–61.

Barr, Nicholas, and Iain Crawford (1998). "The Dearing Report and the Government's Response: A Critique." *Political Quarterly* 69(1): 72–84.

Bartlett, Steve (2003). "Education for Lifelong Learning." *Education Studies: Essential Issues*. Eds. Steve Bartlett and Diana Burton. London: SAGE. 190–211.

Bathmaker, Ann-Marie (2003). "The Expansion of Higher Education: A Consideration of Control, Funding and Quality." *Education Studies: Essential Issues.* Eds. Steve Bartlett and Diana Burton. London: SAGE. 169–89.

Baudrillard, Jean (1981). *For a Critique of the Political Economy of the Sign.* St. Louis: Telos.

Bauman, Zygmunt (1997). "Universities: Old, New and Different." *The Postmodern University? Contested Visions of Higher Education in Society.* Eds. Anthony Smith and Frank Webster. Buckingham: Open University Press. 17–26.

——— (2001). *Community: Seeking Safety in an Insecure World.* Cambridge: Polity.

——— (2013). *Consuming Life.* Hoboken: Wiley.

Bay, Darlene, and Harold Daniel (2001). "The Student Is Not the Customer: An Alternative Perspective." *Journal of Marketing for Higher Education* 11(1): 1–19.

Bechler, Rosemary (2011). "Universities Should Be More Inventive than the Profit Motive." *Fight Back! A Reader on the Winter of Protest.* Ed. Dan Hancox. London: Open Democracy. 170–3.

Beloff, Max (1975). "Can the Universities Survive?" *Black Paper 1975: The Fight for Education.* Eds. C.B. Cox and Rode Boyson. London: Dent. 45–50.

Beloff, Michael (1970). *The Plateglass Universities.* Cranbury: Associated University Press.

Benn, Roseanne, and Roger Fieldhouse (1993). "Government Policies on University Expansion and Wider Access: 1945–51 and 1985–91 Compared." *Studies in Higher Education* 18(3): 299–313.

Berger, Peter L., and Thomas Luckmann (1991). *The Social Construction of Reality.* London: Penguin.

Bevir, Mark (2005). *New Labour: A Critique.* London: Routledge.

Bibby, Cyril (1953). "Residence in Redbrick." *Universities Quarterly* 7(2): 184–91.

Biggs, Joanna (2010). "At the Occupation." *London Review of Books* 32(24): 22.

Birks, Tony, and Michael Holford (1972). *Building the New Universities.* Newton Abbot: David and Charles.

Blackburn, Robin (1969). "A Brief Guide to Bourgeois Ideology." *Student Power: Problems, Diagnosis, Action.* Eds. Alexander Cockburn and Robin Blackburn. Harmondsworth: Penguin. 163–213.

Blackett, P.M.S. (1950). "The Education of the Scientist in the University of Today." *Universities Quarterly* 4(3): 226–36.

Blackshaw, Tony (2010). *Key Concepts in Community Studies.* Los Angeles: SAGE.

Blackstone, Tessa (2001). "Why Learn? Higher Education in a Learning Society." *Higher Education Quarterly* 55(2): 175–84.

Blair, Tony. "Speech on Public Services Delivered at Guys and St Thomas' Hospital London, on 23 June 2004." *BBC.* (23 June 2004) 27 June 2016. <http://news.bbc.co.uk/2/hi/uk_news/politics/3833345.stm>

Bloom, Clive (2012). *Riot City: Protest and Rebellion in the Capital.* Basingstoke: Palgrave Macmillan.

Blunkett, David (2000). "Modernizing Higher Education: Facing the Global Challenge." *University of Greenwich.* (6 June 2000) 13 Dec 2013. <http://cms1.gre.ac.uk/dfee/#speech>

Bochel, Hugh, Bochel, Catherine, Page, Robert, and Robert Syke (2005). *Social Policy: Issues and Developments.* Harlow: Pearson.

Bocock, Jean, and Richard Taylor (2003). "The Labour Party and Higher Education: 1945–51." *Higher Education Quarterly* 57(3): 249–65.

Bourdieu, Pierre, and Jean-Claude Passeron (1990). *Reproduction in Education, Society and Culture.* London: SAGE.

Bradbury, Malcolm (1978). *Eating People Is Wrong*. London: Arrow.
——— (2012). *The History Man*. London: Picador.
Bradney, Anthony (2001). "The Quality Assurance Agency and the Politics of Audit." *Journal of Law and Society* 28(3): 430–42.
Bravenboer, Darryll W. (2009). *Commodification and the Official Discourse of Higher Education* (PhD Thesis). Institute of Education, University of London. (18 Aug 2010) 5 May 2014. <http://eprints.mdx.ac.uk/6406>
Brennan, John, and Ulrich Teichler (2008). "The Future of Higher Education and of Higher Education Research." *Higher Education Management and Policy* 56(3): 259–64.
Brew-Riverson, Irene (2012). "Widening Participation and Social Class – The Mystery of Unchanging Levels of Engagement: A Critique of the 5th Chapter of the Future of Higher Education White Paper (2003)." *Policy, Discourse and Rhetoric: How New Labour Challenged Social Justice and Democracy*. Ed. Marie Lall. Dordrecht: Springer. 79–97.
Brewis, Georgina (2014). *A Social History of Student Volunteering: Britain and Beyond, 1880–1980*. New York: Palgrave Macmillan.
Brewster, Ben (1967). "Reply to Martin Shaw." *New Left Review* 1(44): 90–2.
Brewster, Ben, and Alexander Cockburn (1967). "Revolt at the LSE." *New Left Review* 1(43): 11–25.
Briggs, Asa (1961). "The Welfare State in Historical Perspective." *European Journal of Sociology* 2(2): 221–58.
——— (1964). "Drawing a New Map of Learning." *The Idea of a New University: An Experiment in Sussex*. Ed. David Daiches. London: Deutsch. 60–80.
Bröckling, Ulrich, Krasmann, Susanne, and Thomas Lemke (2011). "From Foucault's Lectures at the Collège de France to Studies of Governmentality: An Introduction." *Governmentality: Current Issues and Future Challenges*. Eds. Ulrich Bröckling, Susanne Krasmann, and Thomas Lemke. New York: Routledge. 1–33.
Brockliss, L.W.B. (2016). *The University of Oxford: A History*. Oxford: Oxford University Press.
Brothers, Joan, and Stephen Hatch (1971). "Conclusions." *Residence and Student Life: A Sociological Inquiry into Residence in Higher Education*. Eds. Joan Brothers and Stephen Hatch. London: Tavistock. 349–64.
Brown, Roger. "Reflections on the Green Paper: The Teaching Excellence Framework." *Council for the Defence of British Universities*. (22 Nov 2015) 26 Jan 2016 <http://cdbu.org.uk/reflections-on-the-green-paper-tef/>
Brown, Roger, and Helen Carasso (2013). *Everything for Sale? The Marketisation of UK Higher Education*. Abingdon: Routledge.
Bruce, Tony (2016). "Scotland and the Higher Education Market." *Dimensions of Marketisation in Higher Education*. Eds. Peter John and Joëlle Fanghanel. Abingdon: Routledge. 57–65.
Burchell, Graham (1993). "Liberal Government and Techniques of the Self." *Economy and Society* 22(3): 267–82.
Burke, Joseph (2011). "Institution." *The Concise Encyclopedia of Sociology*. Eds. George Ritzer and J.M. Ryan. Chichester: Blackwell. 321–2.
Callender, Claire (2012). "The 2012/13 Reforms of Higher Education in England: Changing Student Finances and Funding." *Analysis and Debate in Social Policy: 2012*. Eds. Majella Kilkey, Gaby Ramia, and Kevin Fransworth. Bristol: Policy. 77–96.
Campaign for the Public University (2010). "Manifesto for the Public University." *Campaign for the Public University*. (6 Dec 2010) 4 May 2014. <http://publicuniversity.org.uk/manifesto/>

Canaan, Joyce, Dave Hill, and Alpesh Maisuria (2013). "Resistance in England." *Immiseration Capitalism and Education: Austerity, Resistance and Revolt*. Ed. Dave Hill. Brighton: Institute for Education Policy Studies. 155–81.

Carpentier, Vincent (2009). "Funding in Higher Education and Economic Growth in France and the United Kingdom, 1921–2003." *The History of Higher Education, Vol. III*. Ed. Roy Lowe. London: Routledge. 228–49.

Carswell, John (1988). "What Robbins Took for Granted." *Oxford Review of Education* 14(1): 21–32.

Carter, Ian (1990). *Ancient Cultures of Conceit: British University Fiction in the Post-War Years*. London: Routledge.

Chafe, Wallace (2003). "Discourse: Overview." *International Encyclopedia of Linguistics, Vol. 1*. Ed. William Frawley. Oxford: Oxford University Press. 439–42.

Chessum, Michael (2010). "Student Protests: Today Is Our 1968 Moment." *The Guardian*. (9 Dec 2010) 10 Dec 2010. <http://www.theguardian.com/commentisfree/2010/dec/09/student-protest-tuition-fees-vote>

Clark, Burton R. (1998). *Creating Entrepreneurial Universities: Organizational Pathways of Transformation*. Oxford: Pergamon.

——— (2001). "The Entrepreneurial University: New Foundations for Collegiality, Autonomy, and Achievement." *Higher Education Management and Policy* 13(2): 9–24.

Clark, Burton R., and Guy R. Neave (1992). *The Encyclopedia of Higher Education*. Oxford: Pergamon.

Clarke, John, Newman, Janet, and Louise Westmarland (2008). "The Antagonisms of Choice: New Labour and the Reform of Public Services." *Social Policy and Society* 7(2): 245–53.

Clarke, Simon (2005). "The Neoliberal Theory of Society." *Neoliberalism: A Critical Reader*. Eds. Alfredo Saad-Filho and Deborah Johnston. London: Pluto. 50–9.

Clegg, Stewart (2009). "Power and Hegemony." *The SAGE Handbook of Power*. Eds. Stewart Clegg and Mark Haugaard. London: SAGE. 239–55.

Clegg, Stewart, David Courpasson, and Nelson Phillips (2006). *Power and Organizations*. Thousand Oaks: SAGE.

Cobban, Alan (1999). *English University Life in the Middle Ages*. London: UCL Press.

Cockburn, Alexander (1969). "Introduction." *Student Power: Problems, Diagnosis, Action*. Eds. Alexander Cockburn and Robin Blackburn. Harmondsworth: Penguin. 7–24.

Coffield, Frank (1999). "Breaking the Consensus: Lifelong Learning as Social Control." *British Educational Research Journal* 25(4): 479–99.

Collini, Stefan (2012). *What Are Universities for?* London: Penguin Books.

Colville, Derek (1975). "The American University: The Anatomy of Current Peace." *Black Paper 1975: The Fight for Education*. Eds. C.B. Cox and Rode Boyson. London: Dent. 50–2.

Committee of Vice-Chancellors and Principals (CVCP) (1985). *Report of the Steering Committee for Efficiency Studies in Universities*. London: CVCP.

Committee of Vice-Chancellors and Principals and the National Union of Students (CVCP and NUS) (1968). "Students and Universities in Great Britain II: Joint Statement." *Minerva* 7(1–2): 67–72.

Committee on Higher Education (1963). *Higher Education: Report of the Committee appointed by the Prime Minister under the Chairmanship of Lord Robbins, 1961–63* (Robbins Report). London: HMSO.

Conquest, Robert (1969). "Undotheboys Hall." *Fight for Education: A Black Paper*. Eds. C.B. Cox and A.E Dyson. London: Critical Quarterly Society. 17–20.

Corbett, J.P. (1964). "Opening the Mind." *The Idea of a New University: An Experiment in Sussex*. Ed. David Daiches. London: Deutsch. 22–39.
Cowden, Stephen, and Gurnam Singh (2015). "Critical Pedagogy: Critical Thinking as a Social Practice." *The Palgrave Handbook of Critical Thinking in Higher Education*. Eds. Martin Davies and Ronald Barnett. New York: Palgrave Macmillan. 559–72.
Cox, C.B., and A.E. Dyson (1969). "Letter to Members of Parliament." *Fight for Education: A Black Paper*. Eds. C.B. Cox and A.E. Dyson. London: Critical Quarterly Society. 1–6.
Crick, Bernard (1979). "Education and the Polity." *Higher Education for All?* Eds. Gordon W. Roderick and Michael D. Stephens. Lewes: Falmer. 55–72.
Crosland, Anthony (1962). *The Conservative Enemy: A Programme of Radical Reform for the 1960s*. London: Jonathan Cape.
——— (1974a). "Lancaster Speech." *Polytechnics: A Report*. Eds. John Pratt and Tyrrell Burgess. London: Pitman. 208–13.
——— (1974b). "Woolwich Speech." *Polytechnics: A Report*. Eds. John Pratt and Tyrrell Burgess. London: Pitman. 203–7.
Cross, Malcolm, and R.G. Jobling (1969). "The English New Universities: A Preliminary Enquiry." *Universities Quarterly* 23(2): 172–81.
Crouch, Colin (1970). *The Student Revolt*. London: Bodley Head.
Cunningham, Shirley (1984). "Women's Access to Higher Education in Scotland." *World Yearbook of Education 1984: Women and Education*. Eds. Sandra Acker, Jacquetta Megarry, Stanley Nisbet, and Eric Hoyle. London: Kogan Page. 173–87.
Cutler, Antony, and Barbara Waine (1997). *Managing the Welfare State: Text and Sourcebook*. Oxford: Berg.
Czarniawska, Barbara (2003). "Social Constructionism and Organization Studies." *Debating Organization: Point-Counterpoint in Organization Studies*. Eds. Robert I. Westwood and Stewart Clegg. Malden, MA: Blackwell. 128–39.
Davies, Jonathan S. (2005). "The Social Exclusion Debate." *Policy Studies* 26(1): 3–27.
Davis, Madeleine (2008). "The Origins of the British New Left." *1968 in Europe: A History of Protest and Activism, 1956–77*. Eds. Martin Klimke and Joachim Scharloth. Basingstoke: Palgrave Macmillan. 45–56.
Davis, Miriam E. (2012). "Changing Policy Discourses on Equity and Diversity in UK Higher Education: What Is the Evidence?" *Widening Participation in Higher Education: Casting the Net Wide?* Ed. Tamsin Hinton-Smith. Basingstoke: Palgrave Macmillan. 22–36.
Deem, Rosemary, Hillyard, Sam, and Mike Reed (2007). *Knowledge, Higher Education, and the New Managerialism: The Changing Management of UK Universities*. Oxford: Oxford University Press.
Deephouse, David L., and Mark Suchman (2008). "Legitimacy in Organizational Institutionalism." *The SAGE Handbook of Organizational Institutionalism*. Eds. Royston Greenwood, Christine Oliver, Kerstin Sahlin, and Roy Suddaby. London: SAGE. 49–77.
Defend Sussex (2010). "Statement from the Occupation." *Defend Sussex*. (15 Nov 2010) 23 Nov 2010. <http://defendsussex.wordpress.com/2010/11/15/statement-from-the-occupation/>
DeGroot, Gerard (2013). *The Sixties Unplugged*. London: Pan Macmillan.
Delanty, Gerard (2001). *Challenging Knowledge: The University in the Knowledge Society*. Buckingham: Open University Press.
——— (2010). *Community*. London: Routledge.
Deleuze, Gilles (1992). "Postscript on the Societies of Control." *October* 59: 3–7.

Department for Business, Innovation and Skills (BIS) (2009). *Higher Ambitions: The Future of Universities in a Knowledge Economy*. London: BIS.

——— (2011). *Higher Education: Students at the Heart of the System*. London: HMSO.

——— (2015a). *Fulfilling Our Potential: Teaching Excellence, Social Mobility and Student Choice*. London: HMSO.

——— (2015b). *Participation Rates in Higher Education: Academic Years 2006 and 2007 to 2013 and 2014 (provisional)*. (2 Sep 2015) 16 Nov 2015. <https://www.gov.uk/government/uploads/system/uploads/attachment_data/file/458034/HEIPR_PUBLICATION_2013-14.pdf>

——— (2015c). *Widening Participation in Higher Education*. (15 July 2015) 16 Nov 2015. <https://www.gov.uk/government/uploads/system/uploads/attachment_data/file/443986/Widen-Partic-HE-2015s.pdf>

——— (2016). *Success as a Knowledge Economy: Teaching Excellence, Social Mobility and Student Choice*. London: HMSO.

Department for Education (DfE) (1993). *Higher Quality and Choice: The Charter for Higher Education*. London: Department for Education.

Department for Education and Employment (DfEE) (1998). *The Learning Age: A Renaissance for a New Britain*. London: HMSO.

Department for Education and Skills (DfES) (2003). *The Future of Higher Education*. London: HMSO.

Department of Education and Science (DES) (1966a). *A Plan for Polytechnics and Other Colleges: Higher Education in the Further Education System*. London: HMSO.

——— (1966b). *A University of the Air*. London: HMSO.

——— (1978). *Higher Education into the 1990s: A Discussion Document*. London: HMSO.

——— (1985). *The Development of Higher Education into the 1990s*. London: HMSO.

——— (1987). *Higher Education: Meeting the Challenge*. London: HMSO.

——— (1988). *Top-Up Loans for Students*. London: HMSO.

——— (1991). *Higher Education: A New Framework*. London: HMSO.

Derrida, Jacques (1982). *Margins of Philosophy*. Chicago: Chicago University Press.

Dill, David D. (2015). "Assuring the Public Good in Higher Education: Essential Framework Conditions and Academic Values." *Higher Education as a Public Good: Critical Perspectives on Theory, Policy and Practice*. Eds. Ourania Filippakou and Gareth Williams. New York: Lang. 141–62.

Docherty, Thomas (2011). *For the University: Democracy and the Future of the Institution*. London: Bloomsbury.

Dormer, Peter, and Stefan Muthesius (2001). *Concrete and Open Skies: Architecture at the University of East Anglia, 1962–2000*. London: Unicorn.

Doyle, Mike (2003). "Discourses of Employability and Empowerment: Foundation Degrees and 'Third Way' Discursive Repertoires." *Discourse: Studies in the Cultural Politics of Education* 24(3): 275–88.

Dudley, Janice (1999). "Higher Education Policy and the Learning Citizen." *Poststructuralism, Citizenship, and Social Policy*. Eds. Alan Petersen, Ian Barns, Janice Dudley, and Patricia Harris. London: Routledge. 65–113.

Duke, Chris (1999). "Lifelong Learning: Implication for the University of the 21st Century." *Higher Education Management and Policy* 11(1): 19–35.

Dunn, Robert G. (2008). *Identifying Consumption: Subjects and Objects in Consumer Society*. Philadelphia: Temple University Press.

Dunne, Elisabeth, and Roos Zandstra (2011). *Students as Change Agents: New Ways of Engaging with Learning and Teaching in Higher Education*. (n.d.) 23 Feb 2016. <http://escalate.ac.uk/downloads/8247.pdf>

Dyhouse, Carol (2002). "Going to University in England between the Wars: Access and Funding." *History of Education* 31(1): 1–14.

——— (2006). *Students: A Gendered History*. Abingdon: Routledge.

Eagleton, Terry (1994). "Ideology and Its Vicissitudes in Western Marxism." *Mapping Ideology*. Ed. Slavoj Žižek. London: Verso. 179–226.

——— (1996). *The Illusions of Postmodernism*. Malden, MA: Blackwell.

Edwards, Derek, Ashmore, Malcolm, and Jonathan Potter (1995). "Death and Furniture: The Rhetoric, Politics and Theology of Bottom Line Arguments against Relativism." *History of the Human Sciences* 8(2): 25–49.

Elvin, Lionel (1949). "The Universities & Social Change." *Universities Quarterly* 4(1): 24–36.

Fairclough, Norman, and Ruth Wodak (1997). "Critical Discourse Analysis." *Discourse as Social Interaction*. Ed. Teun A. van Dijk. London: SAGE. 258–84.

Farnes, Nicholas (1976). "An Educational Technologist Looks at Student-Centred Learning." *British Journal of Educational Technology* 7(1): 61–5.

Faure, Edgar, Herrera, Felipe, Kaddoura, Abdul-Razzak, Lopes, Henri, Petrovsky, Arthur V., Rahnema, Majid, and Frederick Champion Ward (1972). *Learning to Be: The World of Education Today and Tomorrow*. Paris: UNESCO.

Fawthrop, Tom (1968). "Hull." *New Left Review* 1(50): 59–64.

——— (1969). "Education or Examination?" *Student Power: Problems, Diagnosis, Action*. Eds. Alexander Cockburn and Robin Blackburn. Harmondsworth: Penguin. 99–102.

Ferlie, Ewan, Musselin, Christine, and Gianluca Andresani (2008). "The Steering of Higher Education Systems: A Public Management Perspective." *Higher Education Quarterly* 56(3): 325–48.

Fernbach, David (1969). "Strategy and Struggle." *New Left Review* 1(53): 37–42.

Filippakou, Ourania, and Gareth Williams, eds. (2015). *Higher Education as a Public Good: Critical Perspectives on Theory, Policy and Practice*. New York: Lang.

Foucault, Michel (1971). "Orders of Discourse." *Social Science Information* 10(2): 7–30.

——— (1983). "The Subject and Power." *Michel Foucault: Beyond Structuralism and Hermeneutics*. Eds. Hubert L. Dreyfus and Paul Rabinow. Chicago: University of Chicago Press. 208–28.

——— (1991). "Politics and the Study of Discourse." *The Foucault Effect: Studies in Governmentality*. Eds. Graham Burchell, Colin Gordon, and Peter Miller. Chicago: Chicago University Press. 53–72.

——— (2002). *The Archaeology of Knowledge*. London: Routledge.

——— (2003). "The Subject and Power." *The Essential Foucault: Selections from Essential Works of Foucault, 1954–1984*. Eds. Paul Rabinow and Nikolas S. Rose. New York: New Press. 126–44.

Fowler, Gerald T. (1972). "The Binary Policy in England and Wales." *Universities Facing the Future*. Eds. Brian Holmes, Robert F. Butts, and W.R. Niblett. San Francisco: Jossey-Bass. 268–80.

Fowler, Roger, Hodge, Bob, Kress, Gunther, and Tony Trew, eds. (1979). *Language and Control*. London: Routledge.

Franz, Randal S. (1998). "Whatever You Do, Don't Treat Your Students Like Customers!" *Journal of Management Education* 22(1): 63–9.

Fraser, Ronald (1988). *1968: A Student Generation in Revolt*. London: Chatto & Windus.

Freedman, Des (2011). "An Introduction to Education Reform and Resistance." *The Assault on Universities: A Manifesto for Resistance*. Eds. Michael Bailey and Des Freedman. London: Pluto. 1–11.

Frijhoff, Willem (2003). "Patterns." *A History of the University in Europe: Vol. 2, Universities in Early Modern Europe (1500–1800)*. Ed. Hilde de Ridder-Symoens. Cambridge: Cambridge University Press. 43–110.

Frow, John (2005). "Discourse." *New Keywords: A Revised Vocabulary of Culture and Society*. Eds. Tony Bennett, Lawrence Grossberg, and Meaghan Morris. Malden, MA: Blackwell. 91–2.

Fulton, John S. (1962). "The Shape of the Universities." *The Expanding University: A Report*. Ed. W.R. Niblett. London: Faber and Faber. 46–63.

——— (1964). "New Universities in Perspective." *The Idea of a New University: An Experiment in Sussex*. Ed. David Daiches. London: Deutsch. 9–21.

Furedi, Frank (2001). *Paranoid Parenting: Abandon Your Anxieties and Be a Good Parent*. London: Allen Lane.

——— (2011). "Introduction to the Marketisation of Higher Education and the Student as Consumer." *The Marketisation of Higher Education: The Student as Consumer*. Eds. Mike Molesworth, Elizabeth Nixon, and Richard Scullion. Abingdon: Routledge. 1–7.

Gallagher, Cailean (2011). "From the Reactive to the Creative." *Fight Back! A Reader on the Winter of Protest*. Ed. Dan Hancox. London: Open Democracy. 41–5.

Gergen, Kenneth J. (2009). *An Invitation to Social Construction*. London: SAGE.

Gevers, Lieve, and Louis Vos (2004). "Student Movements." *A History of the University in Europe, Vol. 3: Universities in the Nineteenth and Early Twentieth Centuries (1800–1945)*. Ed. Walter Rüegg. Cambridge: Cambridge University Press. 269–362.

Gibbons, Michael, Limoges, Camille, Nowotny, Helga, Schwartzman, Simon, Scott, Peter, and Martin Trow (1994). *The New Production of Knowledge: The Dynamics of Science and Research in Contemporary Societies*. London: SAGE.

Gilbert, Jeremy (2012). "Reflecting on the Student Movement: A Dialogue between Guy Aitchison and Jeremy Gilbert." *Soundings* 50: 32–44.

Glennerster, Howard (1999). *British Social Policy since 1945*. Oxford: Blackwell.

Godwin, C.D. (1998). "The Origin of the Binary System." *History of Education* 27(2): 171–91.

Göhler, Gerhard (2009). "'Power To' and 'Power Over'." *The SAGE Handbook of Power*. Eds. Stewart Clegg and Mark Haugaard. London: SAGE. 27–39.

Graham, Gordon (2005). *The Institution of Intellectual Values: Realism and Idealism in Higher Education*. Exeter: Imprint Academic.

Greenbank, Paul (2006). "The Evolution of Government Policy on Widening Participation." *Higher Education Quarterly* 60(2): 141–66.

Greener, Ian (2008a). "Choice and Voice: A Review." *Social Policy and Society* 7(2): 255–65.

——— (2008b). "Choice or Voice? Introduction to the Themed Section." *Social Policy and Society* 7(2): 197–200.

Gross, John (1969). "University Unrest." *Fight for Education: A Black Paper*. Eds. C.B. Cox and A.E. Dyson. London: Critical Quarterly Society. 63–4.

Hagyard, Andy, and Sue Watling (2012). "The Student as Scholar: Research and the Undergraduate Student." *Towards Teaching in Public: Reshaping the Modern University*. Eds. Mike Neary, Howard Stevenson, and Les Bell. London: Continuum. 68–82.

Halbesleben, Jonathon R.B., and Anthony R. Wheeler (2009). "Student Identification with Business Education Models: Measurement and Relationship to Educational Outcomes." *Journal of Management Education* 33(2): 166–95.

Halbesleben, Jonathon R.B., Becker, Jennifer A., and M.R. Buckley (2003). "Considering the Labor Contributions of Students: An Alternative to the Student-as-Customer Metaphor." *Journal of Education for Business* 78(5): 255–7.
Hale, Sarah (2006). "Widening Participation, Equalising Opportunity? Higher Education's Mission Impossible." *Politics* 26(2): 93–100.
Hall, Stuart (1961). "The New Student." *Universities Quarterly* 15(2): 152–63.
——— (1996). "The West and the Rest: Discourse and Power." *Modernity: An Introduction to Modern Societies*. Eds. Stuart Hall, David Held, Don Hubert, and Kenneth Thompson. Malden, MA.: Blackwell. 184–228.
Halsey, A.H. (1973). "Expansion and Equality." *Equal Opportunity in Education*. Ed. Harold Silver. London: Methuen & Co. 205–8.
——— (1992). *Decline of Donnish Dominion: The British Academic Professions in the Twentieth Century*. Oxford: Clarendon.
Halsey, A.H., and M.A. Trow (2009). "The Evolution of the British Universities." *The History of Higher Education, Vol. V*. Ed. Roy Lowe. London: Routledge. 77–99.
Hampson, Keith (1979). "A Conservative View." *Higher Education for All?* Eds. Gordon W. Roderick and Michael D. Stephens. Lewes: Falmer. 131–52.
Hancox, Dan, ed. (2011). *Fight Back! A Reader on the Winter of Protest*. London: Open Democracy.
Hanna, Esmee (2008). "The English Student Movement: An Evaluation of the Literature." *Sociology Compass* 2(5): 1539–52.
Harris, David (1976). "Educational Technology at the Open University: A Short History of Achievement and Cancellation." *British Journal of Educational Technology* 7(1): 43–53.
Harris, Suzy (2007). *The Governance of Education: How Neo-Liberalism Is Transforming Policy and Practice*. London: Continuum.
Hart, W.A. (1997). "The Qualitymongers." *Journal of Philosophy of Education* 31(2): 295–308.
Haselgrove, Susanne, ed. (1994). *The Student Experience*. Buckingham: Open University Press.
Haugaard, Mark (2006). "Power and Hegemony in Social Theory." *Hegemony and Power: Consensus and Coercion in Contemporary Politics*. Eds. Mark Haugaard and Howard H. Lentner. Lanham: Lexington. 45–64.
Healey, Mick, Flint, Abbi and Kathy Harrington (2014). *Engagement through Partnership: Students as Partners in Learning and Teaching in Higher Education*. (n.d.). 23 Feb. 2016. <https://www.heacademy.ac.uk/system/files/resources/engagement_through_partnership.pdf>
Henkel, Mary (2001). "The UK: The Home of the Lifelong Learning University?" *European Journal of Education* 36(3): 277–89.
Higher Education Funding Council for England (HEFCE) (2001). *Strategies for Widening Participation in Higher Education: A Guide to Good Practice*. (n.d.) 02 Oct 2016. <http://webarchive.nationalarchives.gov.uk/20100202100434/http://www.hefce.ac.uk/pubs/hefce/2001/01_36/01_36.pdf>
——— (2015). "Student Engagement". *Higher Education Funding Council for England*. (n.d.) 24 Feb 2016. <http://www.hefce.ac.uk/reg/forstudents/sp/se/>
Higher Education Statistics Agency (2015). "Higher Education Student Enrolments and Qualifications Obtained at Higher Education Providers in the United Kingdom 2013/14." *Higher Education Statistics Agency*. (15 Jan 2015) 16 Nov 2015. <https://www.hesa.ac.uk/news/15-01-2015/sfr210-enrolments-and-qualifications>
Hillman, Nicholas (2013). "From Grants for All to Loans for All: Undergraduate Finance from the Implementation of the Anderson Report (1962) to the Implementation of the Browne Report (2012)." *Contemporary British History* 27(3): 249–70.

Hindess, Barry (1996). *Discourses of Power: From Hobbes to Foucault*. Oxford: Blackwell.

Hoefferle, Caroline (2013). *British Student Activism in the Long Sixties*. New York: Routledge.

Hoggart, Richard (1979). "1968–1978: The Student Movement and Its Effect in the Universities." *Political Quarterly* 50(2): 172–81.

——— (2009). *The Uses of Literacy: Aspects of Working-Class Life*. London: Penguin.

Holmwood, John, ed. (2011a). *A Manifesto for the Public University*. London: Bloomsbury Academic.

——— (2011b). "The Idea of a Public University." *A Manifesto for the Public University*. Ed. John Holmwood. London: Bloomsbury Academic. 12–26.

Howarth, David. (2000). *Discourse*. Buckingham: Open University Press.

——— (2009). "Power, Discourse, and Policy: Articulating a Hegemony Approach to Critical Policy Studies." *Critical Policy Studies* 3(3–4): 309–35.

——— (2013). *Poststructuralism and After: Structure, Subjectivity, and Power*. Basingstoke: Palgrave Macmillan.

Howarth, David, and Steven Griggs (2012). "Poststructuralist Policy Analysis: Discourse, Hegemony and Critical Explanation." *The Argumentative Turn Revisited: Public Policy as Communicative Practice*. Eds. Frank Fischer and Herbert Gottweis. Durham: Duke UP. 305–42.

Hund, John (1998). "Review Symposium on Searle II: Searle's *The Construction of Social Reality*." *Philosophy of the Social Sciences* 28(1): 122–31.

Hutt, Maurice (1964). "Undergraduates and their Problems." *The Idea of a New University: An Experiment in Sussex*. Ed. David Daiches. London: Deutsch. 40–59.

Ibrahim, Joseph (2011). "The New Toll on Higher Education and the UK Student Revolts of 2010–2011." *Social Movement Studies* 10(4): 415–21.

——— (2014). "The Moral Economy of the UK Student Protest Movement 2010–2011." *Contemporary Social Science* 9(1): 79–91.

In Defence of Public Higher Education (Alternative White Paper) (2011). *The Guardian*. (27 Sep 2011) 29 Jan 2013. <http://www.theguardian.com/education/interactive/2011/sep/27/higher-education-alternative-white-paper?guni=Article:in%20body%20link>

Independent Review of Higher Education Funding and Student Finance (2010). *Securing a Sustainable Future for Higher Education* (Browne Review). (12 Oct 2010) 12 Feb 2014. <https://www.gov.uk/government/publications/the-browne-report-higher-education-funding-and-student-finance>

Jacobson, Howard (1983). *Coming from Behind*. London: Chatto & Windus.

Jäger, Siegfried, and Florentine Maier (2009). "Theoretical and Methodological Aspects of Foucauldian Critical Discourse Analysis and Dispositive Analysis." *Methods of Critical Discourse Analysis*. Eds. Ruth Wodak and Michael Meyer. London: SAGE. 34–61.

Jenkins, Richard (2002). *Pierre Bourdieu*. London: Routledge.

——— (2008). *Social Identity*. London: Routledge.

Johnson, Cathryn, Dowd, Timothy J., and Cecilia L. Ridgeway (2006). "Legitimacy as a Social Process." *Annual Review of Sociology* 32: 53–78.

Johnson, Peter (2011). "Where Are the Conservatives, as the True History of Education Goes Undefended?" *Fight Back! A Reader on the Winter of Protest*. Ed. Dan Hancox. London: Open Democracy. 168–71.

Johnston, Ron (2013). "England's New Scheme for Funding Higher Education through Student Fees: 'Fair and Progressive'?" *The Political Quarterly* 84(2): 200–10.

Jones, Bryn (2010). "All Along the Watershed: Sixties Values as Defence of Community Life-worlds in Britain 1968–2008." *Sixties Radicalism and Social Movement Activism: Retreat or Resurgence?* Eds. Bryn Jones and Mike O'Donnell. London: Anthem. 3–22.

Jones, Gareth Stedman (1969). "The Meaning of the Student Revolt." *Student Power: Problems, Diagnosis, Action*. Eds. Alexander Cockburn and Robin Blackburn. Harmondsworth: Penguin. 25–58.

Jones, Gareth Stedman, Barnett, Anthony, and Tom Wengraf (1967). "Student Power: What Is to Be Done?" *New Left Review* 1(43): 3–9.

Jones, Margaret, and Rodney Lowe (2002). *From Beveridge to Blair: The First Fifty Years of Britain's Welfare State 1948–98*. Manchester: Manchester University Press.

Jørgensen, Marianne, and Louise Phillips (2002). *Discourse Analysis as Theory and Method*. London: SAGE.

Kaye, Tim, Bickel, Robert R., and Tim Birtwistle (2006). "Criticizing the Image of the Student as Consumer: Examining Legal Trends and Administrative Responses in the US and UK." *Education and the Law* 18(2–3): 85–129.

Kidd, Harry (1969). *The Trouble at LSE: 1966–1967*. London: Oxford University Press.

King, Desmond (2011). "The Politics of Publicly-funded Social Research." *A Manifesto for the Public University*. Ed. John Holmwood. London: Bloomsbury Academic. 74–89.

King, Desmond, and Victoria Nash (2001). "Continuity of Ideas and the Politics of Higher Education Expansion in Britain from Robbins to Dearing." *Twentieth Century British History* 12(2): 185–207.

Kingsley, Patrick (2010). "The New Age of Student Protest." *The Guardian*. (29 Nov 2010) 7 Feb 2016. <http://www.theguardian.com/education/2010/nov/29/new-age-of-student-protest>

Kogan, Maurice (2000). "Lifelong Learning in the UK." *European Journal of Education* 35(3): 343–59.

Kogan, Maurice, and Stephen Hanney (2000). *Reforming Higher Education*. London: Kingsley.

Kress, Gunther R., and Bob Hodge (1979). *Language as Ideology*. London: Routledge.

Kühn, Thomas (2002). *Two Cultures, Universities and Intellectuals: Der Englische Universitätsroman der 70er und 80er Jahre im Kontext des Hochschuldiskurses*. Tübingen: Narr.

Kundnani, Hans (2009). "Great Britain: 'No Place for Street Fighting Man'." *1968: Memories and Legacies of a Global Revolt*. Eds. Philipp Gassert and Martin Klimke. Washington, DC: German Historical Institute. 205–8.

Labour Party (2002). "General Election Manifesto 1966: Time for Decision." *Labour Party General Election Manifestos: 1900–1997*. Ed. Iain Dale. London: Routledge. 129–52.

Laclau, Ernesto (1990). *New Reflections on the Revolution of Our Time*. London: Verso.

Laclau, Ernesto, and Chantal Mouffe (1987). "Post-Marxism Without Apologies." *New Left Review* 1(166): 79–106.

——— (2001). *Hegemony and Socialist Strategy: Towards a Radical Democratic Politics*. London: Verso.

Lakatos, Imre (1969). "A Letter to the Director of the London School of Economics." *Fight for Education: A Black Paper*. Eds. C.B. Cox and A.E. Dyson. London: Critical Quarterly Society. 27–31.

Larkin, Philip (1946). *Jill*. London: Fortune Press.

Lawson, John, and Harold Silver (1973). *A Social History of Education in England*. London: Methuen.

Lawton, Denis (2005). *Education and Labour Party Ideologies: 1900–2001 and Beyond*. London: RoutledgeFalmer.

Leathwood, Carole, and Barbara Read (2009). *Gender and the Changing Face of Higher Education: A Feminized Future?* Maidenhead: Open University Press.

Leathwood, Carole, and Paul O'Connell (2003). "'It's a Struggle': The Construction of the 'New Student' in Higher Education." *Journal of Education Policy* 18(6): 597–615.

Leavis, F.R. (1933). *For Continuity*. Cambridge: Minority.

——— (1962). *Two Cultures? The Significance of C.P. Snow*. London: Chatto & Windus.

——— (1979a). *Education and the University: A Sketch for an 'English School'*. Cambridge: Cambridge University Press.

——— (1979b). *English Literature in Our Time and the University*. London: Cambridge University Press.

Leavis, F.R., and Denys Thompson (1950). *Culture and Environment: The Training of Critical Awareness*. London: Chatto & Windus.

Lemke, Thomas (2001). "'The Birth of Bio-Politics': Michel Foucault's Lecture at the Collège de France on Neo-Liberal Governmentality." *Economy and Society* 30(2): 190–207.

Lewis, Ben (2002). "Widening Participation in Higher Education: The HEFCE Perspective on Policy and Progress." *Higher Education Quarterly* 56(2): 204–19.

Lodge, David (1975). *Changing Places: A Tale of Two Campuses*. London: Secker & Warburg.

——— (2002). *Thinks...* London: Penguin.

Lomas, Laurie (2007). "Are Students Customers? Perceptions of Academic Staff." *Quality in Higher Education* 13(1): 31–44.

Love, Kevin (2008). "Higher Education, Pedagogy and the Customerisation of Teaching and Learning." *Journal of Philosophy of Education* 42(1): 15–34.

Lowe, Rodney (1993). *The Welfare State in Britain since 1945*. Basingstoke: Macmillan.

Lowe, Roy (1988). *Education in the Post-War Years: A Social History*. London: Routledge.

Luhmann, Niklas (1992). *Universität als Milieu*. Ed. André Kieserling. Bielefeld: Haux.

Lukes, Steven (1995). *Power: A Radical View*. London: Macmillan.

Lunt, Ingrid (2008). "Beyond Tuition Fees? The Legacy of Blair's Government to Higher Education." *Oxford Review of Education* 34(6): 741–52.

Lyotard, Jean-François (1984). *The Postmodern Condition: A Report on Knowledge*. Minneapolis: University of Minnesota Press.

MacArthur, Brian (1974). "An Interim History of the Open University." *The Open University Opens*. Ed. Jeremy Tunstall. London: Routledge. 3–17.

Mann, Sarah (2005). "Alienation in the Learning Environment: A Failure of Community?" *Studies in Higher Education* 30(1): 43–55.

Marcucci, Pamela (2013). "The Politics of Student Funding Policies from a Comparative Perspective." *Student Financing of Higher Education: A Comparative Perspective*. Eds. Donald E. Heller and Claire Callender. Abingdon: Routledge. 9–31.

Maringe, Felix (2011). "The Student as Consumer: Affordances and Constraints in a Transforming Higher Education Environment." *The Marketisation of Higher Education: The Student as Consumer*. Eds. Mike Molesworth, Elizabeth Nixon, and Richard Scullion. Abingdon: Routledge. 142–54.

Marris, Peter (1964). *The Experience of Higher Education*. London: Routledge & Kegan Paul.

Marttila, Tomas (2013). *Culture of Enterprise in Neoliberalism: Specters of Entrepreneurship*. London: Routledge.

Marx, Karl (1976). *Capital, Vol. 1: Critique of Political Economy*. Harmondsworth: Penguin.

Maskell, Duke, and Ian Robinson (2002). *The New Idea of a University*. Charlottesville: Imprint Academic.

Masschelein, Jan, and Maarten Simons (2012). "The University: A Public Issue." *The Future University: Ideas and Possibilities*. Ed. Ronald Barnett. New York: Routledge. 165–77.

Maton, Karl (2005). "A Question of Autonomy: Bourdieu's Field Approach and Higher Education Policy." *Journal of Education Policy* 20(6): 687–704.

Maude, Angus (1969). "The Egalitarian Threat." *Fight for Education: A Black Paper*. Eds. C.B. Cox and A.E. Dyson. London: Critical Quarterly Society. 7–9.

Maxwell, Nicholas (2014). *How Universities Can Help Create a Wiser World: The Urgent Need for an Academic Revolution*. Exeter: Imprint Academic.

McArdle-Clinton, Deirdre (2008). *The Consumer Experience of Higher Education: The Rise of Capsule Education*. London: Continuum.

McCulloch, Alistair (2009). "The Student as Co-Producer: Learning from Public Administration about the Student-University Relationship." *Studies in Higher Education* 34(2): 171–83.

McCulloch, Gary, and William Richardson (2000). *Historical Research in Educational Settings*. Buckingham: Open University Press.

McHoul, Alec, and Wendy Grace (1993). *A Foucault Primer: Discourse, Power and the Subject*. Carlton: Melbourne University Press.

McIntosh, Naomi (1974). "The OU Student." *The Open University Opens*. Ed. Jeremy Tunstall. London: Routledge. 54–65.

McKay, Stephen, and Karen Rowlingson (2011). "The Religion of Inequality." *A Manifesto for the Public University*. Ed. John Holmwood. London: Bloomsbury Academic. 90–111.

McLaren, Peter, and Ramin Farahmandpur (2002). "Breaking Signifying Chains: A Marxist Position on Postmodernism." *Marxism Against Postmodernism in Educational Theory*. Eds. Dave Hill, Peter McLaren, Mike Cole, and Glenn Rikowski. Lanham: Lexington Books. 35–66.

McLean, Monica (2006). *Pedagogy and the University: Critical Theory and Practice*. London: Continuum.

McMillan, Jill J., and George Cheney (1996). "The Student as Consumer: The Implications and Limitations of a Metaphor." *Communication Education* 45(1): 1–15.

Meadway, James (2011). "The Rebellion in Context." *Springtime: The New Student Rebellions*. Eds. Clare Solomon and Tania Palmieri. London: Verso. 17–20.

Meyer, John W., Ramirez, Francisco, Frank, David John, and Evan Schofer (2007). "Higher Education as an Institution." *Sociology of Higher Education: Contributions and their Contexts*. Ed. Patricia J. Gumport. Baltimore: Johns Hopkins University Press. 187–221.

Minogue, Kenneth R. (1973). *The Concept of the University*. London: Weidenfeld and Nicolson.

Miller, Brian (2010). "The Price of Higher Education: How Rational Is British Tuition Fee Policy?" *Journal of Higher Education Policy and Management* 32(1): 85–95.

Miller, Nicola, and John Sabapathy (2011). "Open Universities: A Vision for the Public University in the Twenty-first Century." *A Manifesto for the Public University*. Ed. John Holmwood. London: Bloomsbury Academic. 42–55.

Mills, Sara (2003). *Michel Foucault*. London: Routledge.

——— (2004). *Discourse*. London: Routledge.

Ministry of Education (1945). *Higher Technological Education: Report of a Special Committee* (Percy Report). London: HMSO.

——— (1956). *Technical Education: White Paper*. London: HMSO.

——— (1960). *Grants to Students: Report of the Committee appointed by the Minister of Education and the Secretary of State for Scotland in June 1958* (Anderson Report). London: HMSO.

Moberly, Walter (1949). *The Crisis in the University*. London: SCM Press.

Molesworth, Mike, Nixon, Elizabeth, and Richard Scullion (2009). "Having, Being and Higher Education: The Marketisation of the University and the Transformation of the Student into Consumer." *Teaching in Higher Education* 14(3): 277–87.

Moodie, Graeme C., and Rowland Eustace (1974). *Power and Authority in British Universities*. London: Allen & Unwin.

Moran, Joe (2002). "F.R. Leavis, English and the University." *English* 51(199): 1–13.

Moriarty, Philip (2011). "Science as a Public Good." *A Manifesto for the Public University*. Ed. John Holmwood. London: Bloomsbury Academic. 56–73.

Morrison, Ken (2006). *Marx, Durkheim, Weber: Formations of Modern Social Thought*. London: SAGE.

Mountford, J.F. (1948). "The Selection of Students." *Universities Quarterly* 2(4): 367–75.

Mowat, C.L. (1969). "A Community of Scholars." *Fight for Education: A Black Paper*. Eds. C.B. Cox and A.E. Dyson. London: Critical Quarterly Society. 11–13.

Murray, John (1949). "Halls of Residence in Universities." *Universities Quarterly* 3(2): 563–70.

Naidoo, Rajani (2000). "The 'Third Way' to Widening Participation and Maintaining Quality in Higher Education: Lessons from the United Kingdom." *Journal of Educational Enquiry* 1(2): 24–38.

Naidoo, Rajani, and Ian Jamieson (2005). "Empowering Participants or Corroding Learning? Towards a Research Agenda on the Impact of Student Consumerism in Higher Education." *Journal of Education Policy* 20(3): 267–81.

National Audit Office (2008). *Widening Participation in Higher Education*. London: Stationery Office.

National Campaign Against Fees and Cuts (NCAFC) (2010a). "Now Is the Time to Fight Back." *NCAFC*. (11 Oct 2010) 23 Jan 2014. <http://anticuts.com/2010/10/11/ncafc-statement-on-browne-review-as-a-downloadable-leaflet/>

——— (2010b). "Statement of Intent." *NCAFC*. (12 Feb 2010) 23 Jan 2014. <http://anticuts.com/2010/02/12/statement-of-intent>

National Committee of Inquiry into Higher Education (NCIHE) (1997). *Higher Education in the Learning Society* (Dearing Report). London: HMSO.

National Union of Students (NUS) (2012). *A Manifesto for Partnership*. (n.d.) 28 Feb 2016. <http://www.nusconnect.org.uk/resources/a-manifesto-for-partnership>

National Union of Students and University and College Union (NUS and UCU) (2010). 'We Will March." *Demo 2010*. (5 Sep 2010) 12 Dec 2010. <http://www.demo2010.org/wp-content/uploads/2010/09/NUS-DEMO-A5-flyer.pdf>

Neary, Mike (2010). "Student as Producer: A Pedagogy for the Avant-Garde, or, How Do Revolutionary Teachers Teach?" *University of Lincoln*. (n.d.) 27 Feb 2016. <http://eprints.lincoln.ac.uk/4186/1/15-72-1-pb-1.pdf>

——— (2012). *Student as Producer: An Institution of the Common? [Or How to Recover Communist/Revolutionary Science]*. (n.d.) 29 Feb 2016. <https://www.heacademy.ac.uk/system/files/eliss0403a_guest_paper.pdf>

Neary, Mike, and Andy Hagyard (2011). "Pedagogy of Excess: An Alternative Political Economy of Student Life." *The Marketisation of Higher Education: The Student as Consumer*. Eds. Mike Molesworth, Elizabeth Nixon, and Richard Scullion. Abingdon: Routledge. 209–23.

Neary, Mike, and Joss Winn (2009). "Student as Producer: Reinventing the Student Experience in Higher Education." *The Future of Higher Education: Policy, Pedagogy and the Student Experience*. Eds. Les Bell, Mike Neary, and Howard Stevenson. London: Continuum. 126–38.

Nehring, Holger (2008). "Great Britain." *1968 in Europe: A History of Protest and Activism, 1956–77*. Eds. Martin Klimke and Joachim Scharloth. Basingstoke: Palgrave Macmillan. 125–36.

Newman, John H. (1996). *The Idea of a University*. Ed. by Frank M. Turner. New Haven: Yale University Press.

Niblett, W.R. (1962). "Universities in the Sixties." *The Expanding University: A Report*. Ed. W.R. Niblett. London: Faber and Faber. 11–7.

——— (1974). *Universities between Two Worlds.* London: University of London Press.

——— (1981). "Robbins Revisited." *Studies in Higher Education* 6(1): 1–12.

Nicholson, J.H. (1951). "Selection for University: III." *Universities Quarterly* 6(1): 27–30.

Nixon, Jon (2008). *Towards the Virtuous University: The Moral Bases of Academic Practice.* New York: Routledge.

——— (2011a). *Higher Education and the Public Good: Imagining the University.* London: Continuum.

——— (2011b). "Re-Imagining the Public Good." *The Assault on Universities: A Manifesto for Resistance.* Eds. Michael Bailey and Des Freedman. London and New York: Pluto Press. 59–70.

——— (2015). "Inequality and the Erosion of the Public Good." *Higher Education as a Public Good: Critical Perspectives on Theory, Policy and Practice.* Eds. Ourania Filippakou and Gareth Williams. New York: Lang. 163–77.

Noterman, Elsa, and Andre Pusey (2012). "Inside, Outside, and on the Edge of the Academy: Experiments in Radical Pedagogies." *Anarchist Pedagogies: Collective Actions, Theories, and Critical Reflections on Education.* Ed. Robert H. Haworth. Oakland: PM Press. 175–99.

"Notes." (1949). *Universities Quarterly* 4(1): 11–4.

Oakeshott, Michael (2001). *The Voice of Liberal Learning.* Indianapolis: Liberty Fund.

Ogilvie, R.M. (1962). "The Role of the Teacher." *The Expanding University: A Report.* Ed. W.R. Niblett. London: Faber and Faber. 85–102.

Oliphant, M.L. (1949). "University or Institute of Technology?" *Universities Quarterly* 4(1): 19–23.

Olssen, Mark, and Michael A. Peters (2005). "Neoliberalism, Higher Education and the Knowledge Economy: From the Free Market to Knowledge Capitalism." *Journal of Education Policy* 20(3): 313–45.

Owen, Tom (1980). "The University Grants Committee." *Oxford Review of Education* 6(3): 255–78.

Page, Sam (2004). "Searle's Realism Deconstructed." *Philosophical Forum* 35(3): 249–74.

Palfreyman, David, and Ted Tapper, eds. (2009). *Structuring Mass Higher Education: The Role of Elite Institutions.* London: Routledge.

——— (2014). *Reshaping the University: The Rise of the Regulated Market in Higher Education.* Oxford: Oxford University Press.

Panizza, Francisco, and Romina Miorelli (2013). "Taking Discourse Seriously: Discursive Institutionalism and Post-structuralist Discourse Theory." *Political Studies* 61(2): 301–18.

Parkin, Frank (1986). *The Mind and Body Shop.* London: Collins.

Parry, Gareth (2005). "British Higher Education and the Prism of Devolution." *Understanding Mass Higher Education: Comparative Perspectives on Access.* Eds. Ted Tapper and David Palfreyman. London: RoutledgeFalmer. 160–89.

Pearce, Malcolm, and Geoffrey Stewart (2002). *British Political History, 1867–2001: Democracy and Decline.* London: Routledge.

Perkin, Harold (2006). "History of Universities." *International Handbook of Higher Education: Global Themes and Contemporary Challenges.* Eds. James J.F. Forest and Philip G. Altbach. Dordrecht: Springer. 159–205.

——— (2009). "The Pattern of Social Transformation in England." *The History of Higher Education, Vol. V.* Ed. Roy Lowe. London: Routledge. 63–75.

Perry, Walter (1974). *Higher Education for Adults: Where More Means Better.* Cambridge: Cambridge University Press.

——— (1977). *The Open University*. San Francisco: Jossey-Bass.

Peters, Michael (2001). *Poststructuralism, Marxism, and Neoliberalism: Between Theory and Politics*. Lanham: Rowman & Littlefield.

——— (2010). "Education, Power and Freedom: Third Way Governmentality, Citizen-Consumers and the Social Market." *Contemporary Readings in Law and Social Justice* 2(1): 15–35.

——— (2011). *Neoliberalism and After? Education, Social Policy, and the Crisis of Western Capitalism*. New York: Lang.

Peters, Michael A., Gietzen, Garett, and David J. Ondercin (2012). "Knowledge Socialism: Intellectual Commons and Openness in the University." *The Future University: Ideas and Possibilities*. Ed. Ronald Barnett. New York: Routledge. 187–200.

Phillips, Nelson (2003). "Discourse or Institution? Institutional Theory and the Challenge of Critical Discourse Analysis." *Debating Organization: Point-Counterpoint in Organization Studies*. Eds. Robert I. Westwood and Stewart Clegg. Malden, MA: Blackwell. 220–31.

Phillips, Nelson, Lawrence, Thomas B., and Cynthia Hardy (2004). "Discourse and Institutions." *Academy of Management Review* 29(4): 635–52.

Pierre, Jon (1995). "The Marketisation of the State: Citizens, Consumers, and the Emergence of the Public Market." *Governance in a Changing Environment*. Eds. B.G. Peters and Donald J. Savoie. Montreal: McGill-Queen's University Press. 55–81.

Potts, Michael (2005). "The Consumerist Subversion of Education." *Academic Questions* 13(3): 54–64.

Power, Nina (2012). "Dangerous Subjects: UK Students and the Criminalization of Protest." *South Atlantic Quarterly* 111(2): 412–20.

Pratt, John (1970). "Gone to Lunch: A Critical Look at the Open University." *Education and Training* 12(10): 374–5.

——— (1997). *The Polytechnic Experiment: 1965–1992*. Buckingham: Open University Press.

——— (1999). "Policy and Policymaking in the Unification of Higher Education." *Journal of Education Policy* 14(3): 257–69.

——— (2001). "Higher Education in England and Wales: Unification, Stratification or Diversification?" *Tertium Comparationis* 7(1): 19–27.

Pratt, John, and Tyrrell Burgess (1974). *Polytechnics: A Report*. London: Pitman.

Pring, Richard (1993). "Liberal Education and Vocational Preparation." *Beyond Liberal Education: Essays in Honour of Paul H. Hirst*. Eds. Robin Barrow, and Patricia White. London: Routledge. 49–78.

Pritchard, Rosalind (1994). "Government Power in British Higher Education." *Studies in Higher Education* 19(3): 253–65.

Pusey, Andre, and Leon Sealey-Huggins (2013). "Transforming the University: Beyond Students and Cuts." *ACME* 12(3): 443–58.

Quality Assurance Agency for Higher Education (QAA) (2016). *UK Quality Code for Higher Education: Chapter B5*. (n.d.). 28 Feb. 2016. <http://www.qaa.ac.uk/assuring-standards-and-quality/the-quality-code/quality-code-part-b>

Readings, Bill (1996). *The University in Ruins*. Cambridge, MA: Harvard University Press.

Really Open University (2010). "What Is the ROU?" *Really Open University*. (19 Nov 2010) 23 Jan 2014. <http://reallyopenuniversity.wordpress.com/what-is-the-rou>

Reay, Diane (2011). "Universities and the Reproduction of Inequality." *A Manifesto for the Public University*. Ed. John Holmwood. London: Bloomsbury Academic. 112–26.

Rees, John (2011). "Who Can Pay for the Deficit?" *Springtime: The New Student Rebellions*. Eds. Clare Solomon and Tania Palmieri. London: Verso. 43–8.

Reeves, Marjorie (1988). *The Crisis in Higher Education: Competence, Delight, and the Common Good*. Milton Keynes: Open University Press.

Report of the Committee on the Age of Majority (Latey Report). (1967). London: HMSO.

Revolutionary Socialist Students' Federation (RSSF) (1969). "Manifesto." *New Left Review* 1(53): 21–2.

Rheingans, Rowan, and Robert Hollands (2013). "'There Is no Alternative?' Challenging Dominant Understandings of Youth Politics in Late Modernity through a Case Study of the 2010 UK Student Occupation movement." *Journal of Youth Studies* 16(4): 546–64.

Rich, Tony (2001). "The 1960s Universities." *The State of UK Higher Education: Managing Change and Diversity*. Eds. David Warner and David Palfreyman. Buckingham: Open University Press. 49–56.

Richards, E.J. (1975). *Adult Education: A Challenge to All*. Cardiff: University College.

Ridder-Symoens, Hilde de (2003). "Mobility." *A History of the University in Europe: Vol. 2, Universities in Early Modern Europe (1500–1800)*. Ed. Hilde de Ridder-Symoens. Cambridge: Cambridge University Press, 416–48.

Rikowski, Glenn, and Peter McLaren (2002). "Postmodernism in Educational Theory." *Marxism Against Postmodernism in Educational Theory*. Eds. Dave Hill, Peter McLaren, Mike Cole, and Glenn Rikowski. Lanham: Lexington Books. 3–13.

Ritzer, George (2008). "Review Essay: Not Consumed Enough: Benjamin R. Barber, *Consumed: How Markets Corrupt Children, Infantilize Adults, and Swallow Citizens Whole*." *Journal of Consumer Culture* 8(1): 147–51.

Robinson, Eric (1968). *The New Polytechnics*. Harmondsworth: Penguin.

——— (1969). "Comprehensive Tertiary." *Education+Training* 11(6): 230–6.

Ross, Alistair (2003a). "Access to Higher Education: Inclusion for the Masses?" *Higher Education and Social Class: Issues of Exclusion and Inclusion*. Eds. Louise Archer, Merryn Hutchings, and Alistair Ross. London: RoutledgeFalmer. 45–74.

——— (2003b). "Higher Education and Social Access." *Higher Education and Social Class: Issues of Exclusion and Inclusion*. Eds. Louise Archer, Merryn Hutchings, and Alistair Ross. London: RoutledgeFalmer. 21–44.

Rothblatt, Sheldon (2009). "The Idea of the Idea of a University and Its Antithesis." *The History of Higher Education, Vol. II*. Ed. Roy Lowe. London: Routledge. 178–221.

Rowland, Stephen (2006). *The Enquiring University: Compliance and Contestation in Higher Education*. Maidenhead: Open University Press.

Rowold, Katharina (2010). *The Educated Woman: Minds, Bodies, and Women's Higher Education in Britain, Germany, and Spain, 1865–1914*. New York: Routledge.

Rust, Joshua (2006). *John Searle and The Construction of Social Reality*. London: Continuum.

Rustin, Michael (1986). "The Idea of the Popular University." *A Degree of Choice: Education After Eighteen*. Eds. Janet Finch and Michael Rustin. Harmondsworth: Penguin. 17–66.

Ryan, Alan (2005). "New Labour and Higher Education." *Oxford Review of Education* 31(1): 87–100.

Ryan, Kevin (2006). "Hegemony and the Power to Act." *Hegemony and Power: Consensus and Coercion in Contemporary Politics*. Eds. Mark Haugaard and Howard H. Lentner. Lanham: Lexington. 191–210.

Sabri, Duna (2011). "What's Wrong with 'The Student Experience'?" *Discourse: Studies in the Cultural Politics of Education* 32(5): 657–67.

Salter, Brian, and Ted Tapper (1994). *The State and Higher Education*. Ilford: Woburn.

——— (2000). "The Politics of Governance in Higher Education: The Case of Quality Assurance." *Political Studies* 48(1): 66–87.

Salter, Lee, and Jilly B. Kay (2011). "The UWE Student Occupation." *Social Movement Studies* 10(4): 423–9.

Saltzman, Rachelle H. (1994). "Folklore as Politics in Great Britain: Working-Class Critiques of Upper-Class Strike Breakers in the 1926 General Strike." *Anthropological Quarterly* 67(3): 105–21.

Sanderson, Michael (1998). "Education and Social Mobility." *Twentieth-Century Britain: Economic, Social, and Cultural Change*. Ed. Paul Johnson. London: Longman. 374–91.

——— (1999). *Education and Economic Decline in Britain: 1870 to the 1990s*. Cambridge: Cambridge University Press.

——— (2002). *The History of the University of East Anglia, Norwich*. London: Hambledon and London.

Sassatelli, Roberta (2007). *Consumer Culture: History, Theory and Politics*. Los Angeles: SAGE.

Schmidt, Vivien A. (2008). "Discursive Institutionalism: The Explanatory Power of Ideas and Discourse." *Annual Review of Political Science* 11(1): 303–26.

Schüth, Matthias (2001). *Englands Politische Universitätsjugend, 1931–1940: Ein Beitrag zur Erforschung Politischer Kollektivmentalitäten im Europa der Dreißiger Jahre*. Münster: LIT.

Schwartzman, Roy (1995). "Are Students Customers? The Metaphoric Mismatch between Management and Education." *Education+Training* 116(2): 215–22.

Scientific Manpower: Report of a Committee Appointed by the Lord President of the Council (Barlow Report). (1946) London: HMSO.

Scott, Peter (1984). *The Crisis of the University*. London: Croom Helm.

——— (2007). "The Nationalisation' of UK Universities 1963-2007." *Towards a Cartography of Higher Education Policy Change: A Festschrift in Honour of Guy Neave*. Eds. Jurgen Enders and Frans van Vught. Enschede: Center for Higher Education Policy Studies. 59–66.

——— (2014). "Robbins, the Binary Policy and Mass Higher Education." *Higher Education Quarterly* 68(2): 14–63.

Scott, W.R. (2013). *Institutions and Organizations: Ideas, Interests, and Identities*. Thousand Oaks, CA: SAGE.

Searle, John R. (1995). *The Construction of Social Reality*. New York: Free Press.

——— (2005). "What Is an Institution?" *Journal of Institutional Economics* 1(1): 1–22.

Shattock, Michael (1994). *The UGC and the Management of British Universities*. Buckingham: Open University Press.

——— (1999). "The Impact of the Dearing Report on UK Higher Education." *Higher Education Management and Policy* 11(1): 7–17.

——— (2006). "Policy Drivers in UK Higher Education in Historical Perspective: 'Inside Out', 'Outside In' and the Contribution of Research." *Higher Education Quarterly* 60(2): 130–40.

——— (2008). "The Change from Private to Public Governance of British Higher Education: Its Consequences for Higher Education Policy Making 1980–2006." *Higher Education Quarterly* 62(3): 181–203.

——— (2012). *Making Policy in British Higher Education: 1945–2011*. Maidenhead: Open University Press.

——— (2013). "Public Expenditure and Tuition Fees: The Search for Alternative Ways to Pay for Higher Education." *Browne and Beyond: Modernizing English Higher Education*. Eds. Claire Callender and Peter Scott. London: Institute of Education Press. 15–31.

Shaw, Martin (1967). "On Students." *New Left Review* 1(44): 87–8.
Silver, Harold (1965). "Salaries for Students?" *Universities Quarterly* 19(4): 409–13.
——— (2003). *Higher Education and Opinion Making in Twentieth-Century England*. London: Woburn.
Silver, Harold, and Pamela Silver (1997). *Students: Changing Roles, Changing Lives*. Buckingham: Open University Press.
Simon, Brian (1943). *A Student's View of the Universities*. London: Longmans, Green & Co.
——— (1987). "The Student Movement in England and Wales during the 1930s." *History of Education* 16(3): 189–203.
Simon, Lord of Wythenshawe (1949). "University Crisis? A Consumer's View." *Universities Quarterly* 4(1): 73–81.
Simons, Maarten, and Jan Masschelein (2006). "The Learning Society and Governmentality: An Introduction." *Educational Philosophy and Theory* 38(4): 417–30.
Sloman, Albert (1964). *A University in the Making*. London: BBC.
——— (1970). "British Universities and their Students." *Universities: Boundaries of Change*. London: Panther. 29–46.
Smith, Anthony, and Frank Webster (1997a). "Changing Ideas of the University." *The Postmodern University? Contested Visions of Higher Education in Society*. Eds. Anthony Smith and Frank Webster. Buckingham: Open University Press. 1–14.
——— (1997b). "Conclusion: An Affirming Flame." *The Postmodern University? Contested Visions of Higher Education in Society*. Eds. Anthony Smith and Frank Webster. Buckingham: Open University Press. 99–113.
Smith, Richard (2012). "University Futures." *Journal of Philosophy of Education* 46(4): 649–62.
Solomon, Clare, and Tania Palmieri, eds. (2011). *Springtime: The New Student Rebellions*. London: Verso.
Stabler, Ernest (1987). *Founders: Inventors in Education, 1830–1980*. Edmonton: University of Alberta Press.
Staddon, Elizabeth, and Paul Standish (2012). "Improving the Student Experience." *Journal of Philosophy of Education* 46(4): 631–48.
Stanistreet, Paul (2009). "A University of the Air." *Adults Learning* 20(7): 8–11.
Stephens, John D. (2012). "The Social Rights of Citizenship." *The Oxford Handbook of the Welfare State*. Eds. Francis G. Castles, Stephan Leibfried, Jane Lewis, Herbert Obinger, and Christopher Pierson. Oxford: Oxford University Press. 511–25.
Stewart, W.A.C. (1989). *Higher Education in Postwar Britain*. Basingstoke: Macmillan.
Storey, John (2015). *Cultural Theory and Popular Culture: An Introduction*. Abingdon: Routledge.
Straw, Jack (1970). "Student Participation in Higher Education: Education for Democracy and Technology." *Universities: Boundaries of Change*. London: Panther. 7–27.
Streeting, Wes, and Graeme Wise (2009). *Rethinking the Values of Higher Education: Consumption, Partnership, Community?* (n.d.) 27 Feb 2016. <http://www.sparqs.ac.uk/ch/F2%20Rethinking%20the%20Values%20of%20Higher%20Education.pdf>
Suchman, Mark C. (1995). "Managing Legitimacy: Strategic and Institutional Approaches." *Academy of Management Review* 20(3): 571–610.
Sutherland, John (2008). "Higher Education, the Graduate and the Labour Market: From Robbins to Dearing." *Education+Training* 50(1): 47–51.
Swann, Michael (1969). "Student Problems in Edinburgh and Beyond." *Black Paper Two: The Crisis in Education*. Eds. C.B. Cox and A.E. Dyson. London: Critical Quarterly Society. 147–9.

Tapper, Ted (2005). "Access to Higher Education in England: Who Is in Control?" *Understanding Mass Higher Education: Comparative Perspectives on Access*. Eds. Ted Tapper and David Palfreyman. London: RoutledgeFalmer. 190–210.

——— (2007). *The Governance of British Higher Education: The Struggle for Policy Control*. Dordrecht: Springer.

Tapper, Ted, and Brian Salter (1992). *Oxford, Cambridge, and the Changing Idea of the University: The Challenge to Donnish Domination*. Buckingham: Open University Press.

Tapper, Ted, and David Palfreyman (2011). *Oxford, the Collegiate University: Conflict, Consensus and Continuity*. Dordrecht: Springer.

Taylor, Richard (2005). "Lifelong Learning and the Labour Governments: 1997–2004." *Oxford Review of Education* 31(1): 101–18.

Taylor, Richard, Barr, Jean, and Tom Steele (2002). *For a Radical Higher Education: After Postmodernism*. Buckingham: Open University Press.

Taylor, Richard, and Tom Steele (2011). *British Labour and Higher Education, 1945 to 2000: Ideologies, Policies and Practice*. London: Continuum.

Teale, A.E. (1949). "An Examination of Intellectualism." *Universities Quarterly* 4(1): 44–9.

Thoday, Doris (1957). "Halls of Residence." *Universities Quarterly* 12(1): 45–56.

Thomas, Nick (2002). "Challenging Myths of the 1960s: The Case of Student Protest in Britain." *Twentieth Century British History* 13(3): 277–97.

Thompson, David W. (2012). "Widening Participation from an Historical Perspective: Increasing our Understanding of Higher Education and Social Justice." *Social Inclusion and Higher Education*. Eds. Tehmina Basit and Sally Tomlinson. Bristol: Policy. 41–64.

Thompson, John, and Bahram Bekhradnia (2010). "The Government's Proposals for Higher Education Funding and Student Finance: An Analysis." *Higher Education Policy Institute*. (11 Nov 2010) 3 Jan 2013. <http://www.hepi.ac.uk/2010/11/11/the-governments-proposals-for-higher-education-funding-and-student-finance-an-analysis>

Tight, Malcolm (1998a). "Education, Education, Education! The Vision of Lifelong Learning in the Kennedy, Dearing and Fryer Reports." *Oxford Review of Education* 24(4): 473–85.

——— (1998b). "Lifelong Learning: Opportunity or Compulsion?" *British Journal of Educational Studies* 46(3): 251–63.

——— (2009). *The Development of Higher Education in the United Kingdom since 1945*. Milton Keynes: Open University Press.

——— (2012). *Researching Higher Education*. Maidenhead: Open University Press.

——— (2013). "Students: Customers, Clients or Pawns?" *Higher Education Policy* 26(3): 291–307.

Times Higher Education (THE) (2016). "World University Rankings 2015–2016." *Times Higher Education*. (n.d.) 2 Aug 2016. <https://www.timeshighereducation.com/world-university-rankings>

Tinkham, Linda (1969). "Learning One's Lesson." *Student Power: Problems, Diagnosis, Action*. Eds. Alexander Cockburn and Robin Blackburn. Harmondsworth: Penguin. 82–98.

Tomlinson, Sally (2005). *Education in a Post-Welfare Society*. Maidenhead: Open University Press.

Torfing, Jacob (1999). *New Theories of Discourse: Laclau, Mouffe and Z?iz?ek*. Oxford: Blackwell.

——— (2009). "Power and Discourse: Towards and Anti-Foundationalist Concept of Power." *The SAGE Handbook of Power*. Eds. Stewart Clegg and Mark Haugaard. London: SAGE. 108–24.

Trevelyan, G.M. (1948). "The Mission of the Universities." *Universities Quarterly* 3(1): 480–5.

Triesman, David (1969). "The Impermanent Stronghold." *New Left Review* 1(53): 33–5.

Triesman, Lord (2010). "Amendment to the Motion." *Hansard*. (14 Dec 2010) 23 Jan 2014. <http://www.publications.parliament.uk/pa/ld201011/ldhansrd/text/101214-0001.htm>

Troschitz, Robert (2012). "No Ifs, No Buts, No Education Cuts! Die Englischen Studentenproteste 2010." *Jahrbuch für Europäische Ethnologie: Großbritannien*. Eds. Heidrun Alzheimer, Sabine Doering-Manteuffel, Daniel Drascek, and Angela Treiber. Paderborn: Schöningh. 169–92.

Trout, Paul A. (1997). "Disengaged Students and the Decline of Academic Standards." *Academic Questions* 10(2): 46–56.

Trow, Martin (1996). "Academic Standards in Mass Higher Education." *The Creation of a University System*. Ed. Michael Shattock. Oxford: Blackwell. 202–24.

——— (2006). "Decline of Diversity, Autonomy, and Trust in British Education." *Society* 43(6): 77–86.

Trowler, Paul (2003). *Education Policy*. London: Routledge.

Truscot, Bruce (1951). *Red Brick University*. Harmondsworth: Penguin.

——— (1964). *First Year at the University*. London: Faber and Faber.

Tunstall, Jeremy (1974a). "Introduction." *The Open University Opens*. Ed. Jeremy Tunstall. London: Routledge. vii–xx.

———, ed. (1974b). *The Open University Opens*. London: Routledge.

"UCL Occupation." (2010). *ipetitions*. (n.d.) 20 Nov 2010. <http://www.ipetitions.com/petition/ucloccupation/>

UK Council for International Student Affairs (UKCISA) (2016). "International Student Statistics: UK Higher Education." *UKCISA*. (30 March 2016) 23 Oct 2016. <http://institutions.ukcisa.org.uk//Info-for-universities-colleges–schools/policy-research–statistics/research–statistics/international-students-in-UK-he/>

UNESCO Institute for Statistics (UIS) (2016). "Global Flow of Tertiary-Level Students." *UNESCO Institute for Statistics*. (3 Feb 2016) 23 Oct 2016. <http://www.uis.unesco.org/Education/Pages/international-student-flow-viz.aspx>

"Unity to Defend Education, No Victimisation!" (2010). *Petition Online*. (n.d.) 23 Jan 2014. <http://www.petitiononline.com/petitions/st53231/signatures?page=1>

Universities and Colleges Admissions Service (UCAS) (2016). "Undergraduate Tuition Fees and Student Loans." *UCAS*. (n.d.) 21 Sep 2026. <https://www.ucas.com/ucas/undergraduate/finance-and-support/undergraduate-tuition-fees-and-student-loans>

University Grants Committee (UGC) (1948). *University Development from 1935 to 1947*. London: HMSO.

——— (1957). *Report of the Sub-Committee on Halls of Residence* (Niblett Report). London: HMSO.

——— (1984). *A Strategy for Higher Education into the 1990s*. London: HMSO.

University of Sussex Socialist Cub (2008). "Students and the Class Struggle." *Socialism Today* (24 Apr 2008) 23 Feb 2013. <http://www.socialismtoday.org/118/students.html>

Vaizey, John (2012). *The Costs of Education*. London: Routledge.

van der Eyken, Willem (1974). "The Seeds of Radical Change." *The Open University Opens*. Ed. Jeremy Tunstall. London: Routledge. 28–33.

Vernon, Keith (2001). "Calling the Tune: British Universities and the State, 1880–1914." *History of Education* 20(3): 251–71.

——— (2004). *Universities and the State in England, 1850–1939*. Abingdon: Routledge Falmer.

Vincent, Andrew (2011). "Ideology and the University." *The Political Quarterly* 82(3): 332–340.

Wagner, Leslie (1974). "The Economic Implications." *The Open University Opens*. Ed. Jeremy Tunstall. London: Routledge. 21–7.

——— (1998). "Dearing Is Dead – Blunkett Is Born? The Future Funding of Higher Education." *Higher Education Quarterly* 52(1): 64–76.

Walsh, Lynn (2008). "RSSF Conference, November 1968." *Socialism Today*. (24 Apr 2008) 23 Feb 2013. <http://www.socialismtoday.org/118/conference.html>

Walsh, William (1969). "Dialogue and the Idea." *Fight for Education: A Black Paper*. Eds. C.B. Cox and A.E. Dyson. London: Critical Quarterly Society. 67–9.

Walters, William (2012). *Governmentality: Critical Encounters*. London: Routledge.

Watson, David, and Rachel Bowden (1999). "Why Did They Do It? The Conservatives and Mass Higher Education, 1979–97." *Journal of Education Policy* 14(3): 243–56.

Watson, David, and Richard Taylor (1998). *Lifelong Learning and the University: A Post-Dearing Agenda*. London: Falmer.

Watt, D.C. (1969a). "Expansion at the L.S.E." *Fight for Education: A Black Paper*. Eds. C.B. Cox and A.E. Dyson. London: Critical Quarterly Society. 3–35.

——— (1969b). "The Freedom of the Universities: Illusion and Reality, 1962–69." *Black Paper Two: The Crisis in Education*. Eds. C.B. Cox and A.E. Dyson. London: Critical Quarterly Society. 119–25.

Weber, Max (1978). *Economy and Society*. Berkeley: University of California Press.

White, Stuart (2012). "Ethics." *The Oxford Handbook of the Welfare State*. Eds. Francis G. Castles, Stephan Leibfried, Jane Lewis, Herbert Obinger, and Christopher Pierson. Oxford: Oxford University Press. 19–31.

Whyte, William (2015). *Redbrick: A Social and Architectural History of Britain's Civic Universities*. Oxford: Oxford University Press.

——— (2016). "Halls of Residence at Britain's Civic Universities, 1870–1970." *Residential Institutions in Britain, 1725–1970: Inmates and Environments*. Eds. Jane Hamlett, Lesley Hoskins, and Rebecca Preston. London: Routledge, 155–66.

Widgery, David (1969). "NUS: The Student's Muffler." *Student Power: Problems, Diagnosis, Action*. Eds. Alexander Cockburn and Robin Blackburn. Harmondsworth: Penguin. 119–40.

Willetts, David (2011). "Universities UK Spring Conference 2011." *GOV.UK*. (25 Feb 2011) 12 Jan 2013. <https://www.gov.uk/government/speeches/universities-uk-spring-conference-2011>

Williams, Gareth (2004). "The Higher Education Market in the United Kingdom." *Markets in Higher Education: Rhetoric or Reality?* Eds. Pedro Teixeira, Ben B. Jongbloed, David D. Dill, and Alberto Amaral. Dordrecht: Kluwer. 241–70.

——— (2011). "Some Thoughts on Higher Education, Browne and Coalition Policy." *London Review of Education* 9(1): 1–4.

Williams, Joanna (2011). "Constructing Consumption: What Media Representations Reveal about Today's Students." *The Marketisation of Higher Education: The Student as Consumer*. Eds. Mike Molesworth, Elizabeth Nixon, and Richard Scullion. Abingdon: Routledge. 170–82.

——— (2013). *Consuming Higher Education: Why Learning Can't Be Bought*. London: Bloomsbury.

Willmott, Hugh (2003). "Commercialising Higher Education in the UK: The State, Industry and Peer Review." *Studies in Higher Education* 28(2): 129–41.

Wilson, Bryan (1969). "Youth Culture, the Universities and Student Unrest." *Fight for Education: A Black Paper*. Eds. C.B Cox and A.E Dyson. London: Critical Quarterly Society. 70–8.

Wilson, Harold (1963). *Labour's Plan for Science*. London:Victoria House.

Wolf, Alison (1998). "Politicians and Economic Panic." *History of Education* 27(3): 219–34.

Wolfenden, J.F. (1951). "Selection for Universities." *Universities Quarterly* 6(1): 16–21.

Wood, Geoffrey (1985). "Does Distance Lend Enchantment? The Politics of Knowledge at the Open University." *Universities Quarterly* 39(2): 127–48.

Wyatt, John F. (1977). "The Idea of 'Community' in Institutions of Higher Education." *Studies in Higher Education* 2(2): 125–35.

Young, Michael (1958). *The Rise of the Meritocracy, 1870–2033: An Essay on Education and Society*. London: Thames and Hudson.

Zelditch, Morris (2001). "Theories of Legitimacy." *The Psychology of Legitimacy: Emerging Perspectives on Ideology, Justice, and Intergroup Relations*. Eds. John T. Jost and Brenda Major. New York: Cambridge University Press. 33–53.

Zweig, Ferdynand (1963). *The Student in an Age of Anxiety: A Survey of Oxford and Manchester Students*. London: Heidemann.

Index